Critical Concepts™ Series . . .

Catfish
Presentation

River Strategies

Critical Concepts™ Series . . .

Catfish
Presentation

River Strategies

Expert Advice from North America's
Foremost Authority on Freshwater Fishing

THE IN-FISHERMAN STAFF

In-Fisherman

Critical Concepts™ Series . . .
Catfish Presentation—River Strategies

Publisher *Steve Hoffman*
Editor In Chief *Doug Stange*
Managing Editor *Dr. Rob Neumann*
Project Editor *Dr. Rob Neumann*
Editors *Steve Quinn, Jeff Simpson*
Copy Editor *Kathy Callaway*
Layout *Jan Schneider*
Art Director *Jim Pfaff*
Editorial Assistant *Claudette Kitzman*
Cover *Nic Brenden*

Acknowledgments

Dan Anderson, "Prepared Baits," pp. 89-95; "Dipworm Dilemma," pp. 95-98; "One Man's Creek," p. 128; "Creek Catfish," p. 134; "About River Access," pp. 135-140; "Lock-and-Dam Pools," pp. 156-157.

Bill Dance, photo, p. 185.

Ed Grabowski, "Distance Casting," pp. 21-24.

Ned Kehde, "Reels for Catfishing," pp. 14-18; "Spinning Gear for Catfishing," pp. 18-20; "Crawlers for Cats," p. 75; "Chum Doctors," pp. 100-106; "Bloodmen of the High Plains," pp. 106-110; "Trolling Tactics," p. 119; "Kansas Fluffing," p. 154; "Spring," pp. 176-177; "Spawn Period," pp. 178-180; "Winter into Summer on the Mississippi," pp. 180-183; "Winter on the Ohio," p. 181; "Riprap Flatheads," pp. 198-199; "Barging in on Flatheads," p. 200; "Bass on the Cape Fear," pp. 246-251.

Peter Kohlsaat, illustrations, pp. 102-104.

Keith Lambert, "European Surface Rigging," pp. 59-64.

Bill Lindner, photos, p. 75.

Kirk McKay, "Colorado River Catfish Rig," p. 69; "Mack Attack," pp. 80-82.

Chester Moore, "Brackish Water Blue Cats," pp. 252-253.

Cory Schmidt, "Rods by Situation," pp. 7-12; "Circle Hook Scenarios," pp. 30-33; "A Line on Catfish," pp. 33-36; "Key Knots for Cats," pp. 36-40; "Floats that Don't," pp. 55-59; "Catfish Float Primer," pp. 56-58; "Livebait Care," pp. 83-88; "Softbait Surprise," pp. 118-123.

Larry Tople, illustrations, pp. 155, 158.

Dirk Wassink, "Summer Flatheads—Guaranteed Patterns in Big Rivers," pp. 210-215.

David West, "Catch More from Shore," pp. 231-238.

Don Wirth, "Cats on the Fly," pp. 123-126; "Means to Mighty Blues," pp. 167-171; "Moyer's Cumberland River Calendar," pp. 171-173; "Driftin' and Trollin' Below the Dam," pp. 238-242.

Catfish Presentation—River Strategies

For information write Editor In Chief, In-Fisherman, 7819 Highland Scenic Rd., Baxter, MN 56425-8011.
First Edition

Library of Congress Cataloging-in-Publication Data
ISBN 10: 1-934622-86-9

Dedication

To those who've lost a boot in the mud, a rod in the drink, a prop on a stump, or a good night's sleep following their passion to learn more about catfish and become better anglers.

Contents

Foreword

A Small Step Away from Success

A Word from In-Fisherman Editor In Chief Doug Stange

I had the opportunity several years ago to spend an afternoon fishing a stretch of river that I fished when I was growing up—almost 50 years gone by. The Little Rock River in Northwest Iowa is just about small enough to jump across in many areas during late summer, a small stream several rivers removed from a major river like the Missouri. In this case, the Little Rock flows into the Big Rock, which flows into the Big Sioux, which eventually enters the Missouri—all told, perhaps 150 river miles removed.

I waded wet in jeans and tennis shoes just as I used to, but now with a 10-foot ultralight spinning rod and reel loaded with 10-pound line, to plunk pieces of freshly cut chub and sucker into likely areas. There aren't many trees along this section of river, which flows in a continuous series of shallow riffles, followed by holes that often are no more than 2 or 3 feet deep. The weight of the cutbait on the hook was all that was required to get the bait down.

I walked about a mile and caught 12 fish ranging up to 2 pounds, and I didn't see another angler all afternoon. Wow! I thought to myself. The fishing is actually better than when I used to fish it in the old days.

Maybe. Fantastic fishing is available in these tiny rivers across the country. But I'm actually not sure the fish population is any different than when I fished it in the old days. Back then it would have been unusual for me to walk a mile to fish. I typically fished only a couple of spots in an afternoon, and I was always somewhat perplexed about just what bait to use during different yearly periods, although we did use freshly killed minnows, at times.

Today, anglers are catching more fish than ever before, be it in rivers, reservoirs, or lakes, because they know more. I didn't get it yet, back then, that rivers ran in a continuous series of riffles, holes, and runs, and that some riffle-hole complexes were far superior to others. I didn't understand that it was necessary to keep moving, never stopping or fishing the same spots for long. Thinking back, the difference between the modest fishing that I enjoyed as a youth, and the fantastic fishing I found that recent afternoon, may have been no more than a matter of a simple and short step forward in understanding.

That's one of the biggest changes in catfishing in the last two decades: We know so much more now, with the help of magazines like *In-Fisherman* and *Catfish In-Sider Guide*, and books like this one, where you can learn how to be a much more successful angler once you put the information to use in the field. For any of us today, with a little help we're only a small step away from improved fishing.

Introduction

From The Editors— A Word About This Book

If you've picked up this book, you're probably one of the almost 7 million anglers who fish for catfish in the U.S. today. You could be a beginner, a casual weekend angler, or a hardcore catfisherman with decades of experience. No matter, we all share a common goal—the pursuit of some of America's favorite fish species. Yet beyond the rewards at the end of the line, catfish anglers also have much more in common. For one, everybody starts at the beginning—tying that first rig, cutting that first bait, and taking the first cast.

We also know there's no secret formula, magic bait, shortcut, or single best way to go about the business of catching catfish, just a common thread of knowledge that all anglers move along to become more successful. In this book are lessons learned at In-Fisherman, along with input from some of the greatest catfish anglers ever, to help you move along this thread.

We're convinced there's something for everyone in this book. It starts with a foundation at your fingertips, covering rods and reels, tackle, riggings, knots, baits, and more—the nitty-gritty need-to-know stuff to be prepared and move forward with presentation, and to look back to now and again, whether you fish in rivers, small streams, lakes, or reservoirs. The second half of the book covers details of presentation strategies for catching catfish in rivers—channel cats, blues, and flatheads—it's all there, with advanced topics on some of the most unique environments and situations catfish anglers face.

This is the third book in the In-Fisherman *Critical Concepts Series* for catfish. Volume One, *Catfish Fundamentals,* focuses on learning about the nature of catfish, classifying waters, the seasonal period of catfish response, catfish management, and much more. Volume Two, *Catfish Location,* covers how to find catfish on various waterbody types, and when and where catfish move, including summaries of tracking studies. This volume builds upon the first two, with a focus on presentation strategies in rivers. Volume Four, to follow, will cover presentation tactics in lakes and reservoirs.

Whichever volume you read—and we hope you enjoy and use them all—you've chosen what we believe to be the best way to becoming a better catfish angler, as long as you take it to the water where the real schooling happens. And don't forget what catfish have given us: Be a champion for their conservation.

Chapter 1

Tackle Topics

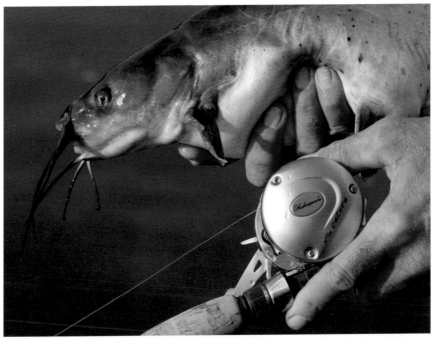

Selecting Rods and Reels

TOOLS OF THE TRADE

For years *In-Fisherman* editors have been telling you about the advantages of fine-quality equipment, namely rods and reels—not necessarily the priciest and most cutting-edge, but durable and functional equipment built to withstand the rigors of tackling some of the toughest fish swimming in freshwater.

We stand behind these statements. Time-tested reels like the Abu Garcia 7000-C3, for example, still rank among the top options for trophy flatheads and blue cats. Many reels are lighter, offer more line capacity, or are less expensive, but few are so dependable as the classic 7000-C3. The same is true of similar models from other top manufacturers.

As *In-Fisherman* Editor In Chief Doug Stange says, "Price is a factor in selecting rods and reels, but often it's not the most important consideration. The more experience you gain, the more you appreciate the exquisite feel of a fine rod-and-reel combination. Good equipment helps make you a better fisherman, and with proper care, a few well-selected purchases can provide a lifetime of enjoyment."

That's the reason we often use higher-end rods like those from St. Croix when we're chasing cats. The blank on an inexpensive rod may be just as functional and durable as some blanks costing three times as much, but the other components usually aren't. So, an angler on a budget can use a $30 rod to catch hundreds of fish before something fails and the rod must be replaced or repaired. The angler with a $200 rod, meanwhile, may pass it on to his grandchildren after a lifetime of use.

Catfish anglers have helped make Shakespeare's Ugly Stik the top-selling rod series of all time. While not designed specifically for catfishing, the original Ugly Stiks offer enough tip action to cast softbaits without tearing them off the hook and enough backbone to land most cats, even in moderate current.

Other models in the Ugly Stik Tiger and Big Water series feature the same durable blank construction as the original rods, in lengths and power ratings appropriate for larger cats and bigger waters. These rods also feature high-grade components, resulting in a more durable rod at a fraction of what some premium models cost.

From a marketing perspective, this middle-of-the-road position seems to work. Berkley has discontinued the once popular E-Cat series and now offers the Glow-Stik. Bass Pro Shops and Cabela's offer moderately priced and durable rods, and Shakespeare has introduced catfish-specific models in the Ugly Stik line, while the popularity of their Tiger rods and other options continues to radiate from Santee-Cooper to rivers and reservoirs across the country.

THE BEST CATFISH RODS SOMETIMES HAVE A SOFTER SIDE

The topic here is rod action rather than price. The two happen to be linked in this case, because the category of rods that we discuss—tip rods—is more commonly found in inexpensive rod series. While we might like the action of a South Bend Catfish Special, the rod would perform better if equipped with a better reel seat and a few additional guides.

What we're calling tip rods aren't anything new. Shakespeare's been selling Ugly Stiks for more than a quarter century, and this type of action almost certainly predates their popular offering. What we're not talking about are the slow-action noodle rods that bend almost uniformly from tip to butt, which have little place in most catfishing situations. They're just too light.

The tip rod we're talking about has a fast- or moderate-fast-action blank. This means that most of the flex occurs in the upper third or at least the upper half of the rod. What differentiates a tip rod from a standard moderate-action rod is that the tip section flexes more easily. Rods designed for lure presentations usually feature a faster-loading tip to allow better casting distance and accuracy.

As far as we know, there's no measurement system to describe or compare tip action. It's difficult enough for rod manufacturers to standardize power ratings

Categorizing Rod Options

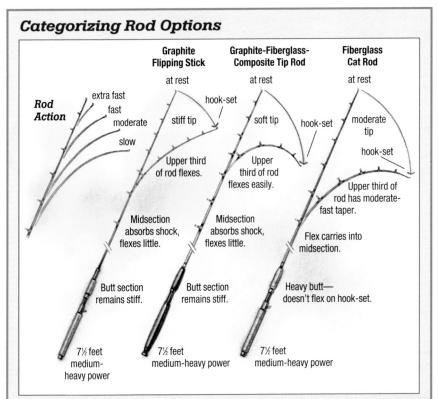

Action is the bend of the rod; power, the strength of the rod. They're related, but not the same. Most rods designed for lure presentations have fast tips, while those designed for natural bait have slower actions. Many traditional catfishing presentations call for rods with moderate tips and sufficient power to land heavy fish. Other situations—tightlining, drifting, and circle hooks, to name a few—are better met with moderate- to fast-action rods with a light tip.

for their rods, without adding tip flex to the equation. A system similar to the one used by hook manufacturers to describe shank length and diameter probably would work—hooks designated as "2X short" or "2X strong," for example, are the same length as a hook two sizes smaller, or as thick as a hook two sizes larger.

Many tip rods probably could be rated as "2X soft," meaning that the tip section is similar to one found on a rod that's two power ratings lighter. In other words, a moderate-action medium-heavy-power tip rod would have a tip section as soft as a standard medium-light- or light-power rod. This sounds more complex than it is; more simply, the lighter, more flexible tip section doesn't necessarily change the rod's action or power.

THE SOFT TIP ADVANTAGE

Tip rods aren't a good choice for all catfishing applications, but they do offer advantages. When casting soft natural baits, for example, the softer tip absorbs some of the energy to prevent the bait from flying off the hook. This is important when using fragile baits such as liver or chunks of congealed blood, but it's also an advantage for live baitfish, especially those hooked lightly through the base of the tail.

A softer tip also allows better casting accuracy with heavy rigs. A stiffer tip allows better control with lighter baits at moderate range, but a softer tip loads more quickly when lob-casting an 8-inch bullhead and three-ounce sinker 40 feet behind an anchored boat. A stiffer tip obviously is needed for casting longer distances from shore, but long-range work usually demands specialized equipment.

Tip rods also are a good choice for fishing downlines in rivers and reservoirs. One of the top flathead tactics at Santee-Cooper is suspending small white perch or other lively baitfish a foot or so off the bottom, near creek channels and other structure. A soft tip prompts the lightly anchored bait to swim and struggle against the rod pressure. When a stiffer rod is used in the same situation, the bait often tires quickly and dangles from the end of the leader.

Drifting also is more effective with tip rods than with stiffer sticks. Especially when baits are drifted a short to moderate distance behind a boat (say, 40 to 120 feet), a soft tip bobs slowly up and down as the sinker is dragged across uneven terrain, or through light cover such as sparse weeds or brush. A standard tip may bend on occasion, but usually recovers too quickly to reveal any meaningful information about the bottom composition.

Some reservoir guides also use tip rods coupled with superlines to drift baits more than 100 yards behind the boat. In this case, the no-stretch line is used to telegraph strikes and bottom composition, while the soft tip absorbs the shock of a snag or fast-running fish. Tip rods, in fact, are a good choice in many situations that call for braided lines, as the tip compensates for the lack of stretch.

TIP RODS FOR CIRCLES

Perhaps the best application for tip rods is tightlining—particularly with circle hooks. When we first began using circle hooks, we used them in much the same way as standard J-hooks. That is, once we cast a bait, we placed the rod in a holder and engaged the freespool bait clicker to control line tension. A fish picked up the bait, the clicker sounded, and we engaged the reel drive and slowly lifted the rod tip, or began a slow retrieve to allow the hook to begin to penetrate the corner of the fish's mouth.

After experimenting with several rod designs, we discovered that circle hooks were even more effective when used with tip rods. In this situation, the bait is cast and the rod placed into a sturdy holder as before, but the reel isn't in freespool. Instead, the drive is left engaged and the fish sets the hook on its own against the steadily building pressure of the rod tip. It's as close as you can get to a no-brainer hook-set, and the hook almost always ends up in the corner of the fish's mouth.

The amount of tip action needed depends largely on the size and activity level of the fish, and where and how you're fishing. A slightly stiffer tip often is beneficial for large blues and channel cats, especially when they're aggressively taking baits; the added tip pressure helps drive the hook point through the soft tissue in the corner of the fish's mouth. When pursuing smaller or more tentative cats, a lighter tip allows the fish to engulf the bait so the hook slides into the proper position.

A stiffer tip also is needed for still-fishing in heavy current or when dragging heavy rigs behind a drifting boat. In either situation, a lighter tip may be fully loaded by the pressure of the current against the line or the friction of the sinker dragging across bottom. A heavier tip keeps a bit of tip flex in reserve when a fish takes the bait. Likewise, a softer tip is a better choice for drifting with smaller baits or still-fishing in slacker water.

BEYOND CIRCLE HOOKS

Some anglers use the same type of tightline presentation with J-hooks, though they usually set the hook as soon as the fish begins to move with the bait. Tennessee catfish guide Jim Moyer, who has made numerous contributions to the wealth of cat-fishing information we share in the pages of *In-Fisherman* and the *Catfish In-Sider Guide*, rarely uses a bait clicker for big blue cats. When the current's slack and the fish are tentative, Moyer often uses a rod with a lighter tip, allowing fish to move with the bait without feeling too much tension.

We often use tip rods for flathead fishing in rivers, too, particularly when using large, lively baitfish near heavy cover. Instead of leaving the reel drive engaged as Moyer does, though, we use the freespool bait clicker to allow the fish to engulf the bait with minimal resistance. With a stiffer tip, larger baitfish like bull-heads, chubs, and carp may be strong enough to strip a few feet of line from the reel. Left unchecked, the bait eventually finds its way into the cover and is impossible to retrieve.

A softer tip usually absorbs the energy from these sudden surges, keeping the bait anchored a safe

In-Fisherman Editor In Chief Doug Stange plays a flathead with the aid of a St. Croix Classic Cat rod, the powerful CC80H, rigged with 50-pound line on an Abu Garcia 7000 reel.

distance from cover. The tip flexes lightly as the bait swims this way and that, looking for a holding area safe from potential predators. Tip rods also telegraph the frantic swimming of a startled bait when a predator draws near, then folds sharply when that predator engulfs the bait.

The thing about big cats, whether blues, flatheads, or channel cats, is that often as not you really don't dare give much quarter once you've stuck a fish. Battles near snags are no-give, all-take contests, with a cat using every muscle to turn away from pressure so it can take line into cover. Every time you give much ground, chances increase that you'll lose the fish. Tip rods for big cats must have sufficient power in the butt and midsection to drag fish away from cover.

Many rod manufacturers—Shakespeare, Berkley, South Bend, Bass Pro Shops, Cabela's, and others—offer a range of tip rods that work fine for a member of catfishing applications. Inexpensive saltwater boat rods with powerful butt sections and moderately soft tips also are available from a number of companies and work fine for larger cats in rivers and reservoirs.

RODS BY SITUATION

There's no such thing as a single perfect catfish rod, and there's no other family of freshwater fish that demands specialization from rod builders more than catfish. From shallow to deep water, stillwater to whitewater; from a quarter ounce of weight to 8 ounces; float-rigging to longcasting; and from 2 pounds of fish to over 100—no other fish requires such a diverse range of rod characteristics.

Building an ideal catfish rod means finding the right compromise between action and power; tip cushion and midsection muscle; and between measured give and solid leverage. It might be a moderate-action blank that flexes easily in its upper third, yielding soft casts with delicate baits but also offering a relatively stiff, powerful butt section to control hulking catfish. Obviously, though, not all catfishing situations involve 30-pound fish or heavy currents, so cat anglers continue to dip into other rod classes to tame catfish in their waters.

FROM SHORE IN RESERVOIRS AND TAILRACES

All across America, many catfish fanatics pursue their fish from shore. Almost no one knows shore duty in reservoirs better than Texas anglers Jason Holbrook and former world record-holder for blue cats, Cody Mullennix. Most weekends the duo's standing guard over an armada of 12- to 14-foot surf-action spinning rods spread up and down the beach. Most of their rods, including several 12-foot Ugly Stik Custom Graphite Surf Rods (USCSSP 1112-2M), offer power in the base for longcasting heavy sinkers and muscling big blues at long range. The same rods "give" throughout the upper third of the blank (moderately slow action) to softly roll a circle hook into the cat's jaw.

For rocket-long casts, 12 feet may be the ideal length, especially given that the Ugly Stik customs are of fine graphite construction. A 10 works great, too, and a 14 throws a real screamer, although this length begins approaching the limits of what most anglers can handle. Casts fly radically far by swinging the bait behind and slightly to the side—to nearly 3 o'clock—then whipping the rod forward fast, leaning in and following through. Grip the rod butt with the left hand while holding the reel seat with the other, catapulting the bait, in part, by using your hands to work the lever.

Once the bait submerges and anchors itself to bottom, reel up tight, engage the bail, and set it in a sandspike-type rod holder planted firmly into the ground. The rod tip should be up at about a 45-degree angle, holding extra line off the water. The steep rod angle aids circle-hook sets, which penetrate flesh as a catfish plays against a gradually flexing rod.

Hooking and battling catfish with such a rod at this distance is an exhilarating experience, with the catfish in brief bursts of retreat, giving shoulder-jarring headshakes, both softly absorbed within the rod's extended arc. That Mullennix beached his now-famous 121.5-pound blue with mere 20-pound monofilament says it all about the beauty of super-long surf rods for shore duty.

BIG RIVER BLUES

While mono lines aid some situations, experienced cat anglers have learned that low-stretch, ultrafine braided lines best match big fish in fast current. These lines don't absorb water like monofilament, and they minimize line drag on rigs. "E-glass," a rod material touted for its toughness, is well suited to couple with superlines. It loads more slowly than traditional fiberglass, or

Selected Catfish Rods, Reels and Lines

SITUATION	TARGET SPECIES	OTHER SPECIES	ROD OPTIONS
Longcasting from Shore in Reservoirs and Tailraces	■ Blues	■ Channels ■ Flatheads	■ 10-foot Shakespeare Ugly Stik Big Water (BWS 1100) ■ 12-foot Ugly Stik Custom Graphite Surf (USCSSP 1112-2M) ■ 11½-foot St. Croix Premier Surf (PSRS116MH2l) ■ 12-foot Cabela's Whuppin' Stick Magnum (WSM12H-2)
Classic Set-rigging in Ponds, Small Lakes & Reservoirs	■ Channels	■ Blues ■ Flatheads	■ 8-foot Shakespeare Ugly Stik (UCSP 1102) ■ 8-foot Bass Pro Cat Maxx (CTX80MHS) ■ 8½-foot Cabela's Fish Eagle II Steelhead Spinning (GS864)
Floatfishing Streams & Ponds	■ Channels	■ Flatheads ■ Blues	■ 11-foot Cabela's European Predator Spinning ■ 9-foot Shakespeare Ugly Stik (SPL 1100) ■ 8½-foot Cabela's Fish Eagle II Steel-head Spinning (GS864)
Drifting Reservoirs with Circle Hook Rigs	■ Blues	■ Channels ■ Flatheads	■ 7-foot Shakespeare Ugly Stik (CAL 1100) ■ 7-foot Berkley GlowStik (GSC702M) ■ 8-foot South Bend Catfish Special (CF-176)
Drifting Reservoirs with Traditional J-hook Rigs	■ Blues	■ Channels ■ Flatheads	■ 7½-foot Cabela's King Kat Pro (CKPC76HF) ■ 7-foot Shakespeare Ugly Stik Lite (CA 1170-1MH)
Big Rivers with Heavy Current	■ Blues	■ Flatheads	■ 7½-foot Quantum Big Cat (BCC76H) ■ 7-foot Cabela's King Kat Pro (CKPC70HM) ■ 7½-foot Bass Pro Cat Maxx (CTX76HT)
Set-rigging in Rivers near Dense Cover	■ Flatheads		■ 6'9" St. Croix Premier Musky (PM69HF) ■ 7½-foot Quantum Big Cat (BCC76MH) ■ 7-foot Cabela's King Kat Pro (CKPC70HM)
Classic Set-rigging in Rivers and Streams	■ Channels		■ 8-foot Berkley GlowStik (GSC802MH) ■ 6½-foot Cabela's King Kat (CKKS662-M)

by Situation

LINE OPTIONS	REEL OPTIONS
■ 14- to 20-pound Berkley Big Game ■ Ande Premium	■ Shakespeare Alpha Bigwater Spinning A180 ■ Penn 7500SS ■ Daiwa Emcast Plus ECP5500
■ 12- to 17-pound Berkley Big Game ■ Shakespeare Supreme Super Tough	■ Daiwa Black Gold 30 ■ Shimano Baitrunner BTR4500B
■ 14- to 25-pound Berkley Big Game ■ Berkley IronSilk	■ Abu Garcia Cardinal C774 ■ Shimano Sedona SE600FB ■ Daiwa Black Gold 60
■ 12- to 30-pound Berkley Big Game ■ Shakespeare Supreme Super Tough	■ Quantum Iron 410CX ■ Abu Garcia 5500C3 ■ Penn International 955
■ 15- to 30-pound PowerPro ■ Berkley FireLine ■ Stren Super Braid	■ Quantum Iron 410CX ■ Abu Garcia 5500C3 ■ Penn International 955
■ 50- to 60-pound PowerPro ■ Berkley FireLine ■ Stren Super Braid	■ Abu Garcia 7000C3 ■ Abu Garcia 6500C3 ■ Shimano Calcutta CT400 ■ Shakespeare Tidewater 20
■ 30- to 80-pound Berkley Trilene Big Cat ■ PowerPro ■ Berkley FireLine	■ Abu Garcia 7000C3 ■ Abu Garcia 6500C3 ■ Quantum Iron IR430 ■ Shakespeare Tidewater 20
■ 17- to 25-pound Berkley FireLine ■ Stren Super Braid	■ Abu Garcia 5500C3 ■ Quantum 1420 MG

S-glass, cushioning hook-sets and absorbing shock. E-glass is sturdy enough to wrench big cats through boiling current. For each specific rod, it's about finding the right compromise between action and power.

Catmen in years past who might have been forced to accept something unsuited to the situation (like a bass flippin' stick) now have rods available that tackle big rivers with power, durability, and give. Seven- to 10-foot moderately slow-action, medium-heavy to heavy power rods remain core offerings from catfish rod makers. Shakespeare, South Bend, and Cabela's all offer glass cat rods. Price varies by quality of reel seats, guides, and handles. Components by AFTCO and Fuji, including graphite reel seats reinforced by stainless steel, silicone carbide, or Hardloy guides, and cork handles, offer greater durability. Better-quality rods, though pricier, hold up to the stress of big cats and their waters perhaps for a lifetime, and ultimately mean more fish and more comfortable fishing.

One big-river rod you can trust is Quantum's Big Cat BCC76MH. The Big Cat is a 7½-foot moderately slow-action rod powerful enough in the lower half of the blank to easily heave 5 ounces of lead. The soft tip also lets you give just a bit of rod to a light-biting cat without too much negative resistance.

Relative to leverage over large fish, and with power and action being equal, longer rods mean increased torque on the angler. Shorter rods help the angler get more leverage on the fish. Sometimes it's tough for anglers to believe this, but they need only spend a day in saltwater cranking heavy fish from the depths to realize that shorter, solid-glass "boat rods" in the 5½- to 6-foot range whip saltwater bulls faster, while demanding less effort from the angler. Similarly, wise cat anglers faced with intense current and mega-heavy blues often look to shorter, stouter poles, as well. In this case, 7 feet of heavy-power E-glass does the trick.

CHANNEL CATS ON FLOATS

Longer, slower-action rods are great for float-fishing. Using a float to suspend and drift bait through promising river stretches, or across the surface of a pond or reservoir flat, is an amazingly efficient channel-cat presentation. If you're wrestling larger cats 20 pounds and up while tickling around lots of cover, casting tackle is best. Conversely, a spinning combo offers good float control in current. Many cat anglers use longer 9- to 11-foot rods, which help mend line in waves and current, steer the float's drift, and rapidly sweep up excess line on a hook-set.

For years, Cabela's has offered European-style long rods like the 11-foot European Predator spinning rod, a nice option in small to medium channel-cat rivers. The rod easily handles 14- to 17-pound mono loaded on a reel such as a Daiwa Black Gold 60. A slower-action alternative for delicate baits—such as blood or live baitfish—is Shakespeare's 9-foot Ugly Stick SPL 1100. For finesse-drifting smaller baits in smaller streams, 8½- to 9-foot steelhead spinning rods, such as Cabela's Fish Eagle II GS864, offer excellent alternative actions, particularly while wading. Bass flippin' sticks (7.5 feet) are nice compromise rods in most situations.

DRIFTING RESERVOIRS FOR BLUES AND CHANNELS

Downline-drifting multiple baits over large reservoir flats often yields some of the hottest fishing imaginable for 2- to 8-pound blue and channel cats, including shots at brutes. This presentation excels when coupled with circle hooks, which don't require immediate attention when a strike occurs—ideal for multiple rod sets.

For circle hooks to perform properly, rod length isn't so critical as action in the upper third of the blank. Seven to 9 feet remains a good standard length range, but you want a tip section that flexes deeply without much strain. The lower 2/3 of the rod should transition into a faster action that flexes little. Placed in solid rod-holders, these rods play perfectly against a biting cat—moving, rotating, then planting the circle hook. Functional circle-hook rods are the 7-foot Ugly Stik CAL 1100 or Berkley's GlowStik GSC702M. Couple either rod with a reliable casting reel such as an Abu Garcia 5500 or 6500, spooled with a modestly stretchy 17- to 30-pound monofilament like Berkley Trilene Big Game.

When faced with light-biting cats—a situation for traditional J-hooks—a rod like Cabela's King Kat Pro is a good choice. Try professional angler Phil King's 7- and 7½-foot graphite King Kats for light-biting channel cats.

FLATHEADS NEAR COVER

Many cat anglers opt for a Quantum Big Cat BCC76M or an Ugly Stik Tiger BWC 2202, both slower-action E-glass rods. The tips on the E-glass models bounce nicely, allowing wild baitfish to play against the hook without ripping free. And the slower action also lets tentative flatheads monkey with a bait without feeling resistance. Perhaps glass prevents a few more fish from rejecting the bait, and the soft tip also enhances castability of extra-large baits.

Rod length is a factor in battling big fish, because rod length determines rod leverage. Freshwater anglers, who deal with fish like largemouth bass, walleyes, and even stripers and muskies, rarely find the rod a critical factor. The fish just aren't that large and powerful.

In saltwater, though, where fish like sharks and tuna grow large and incredibly powerful, rod length becomes critical to success. Shorter rods provide more leverage with less torque and are therefore better for horsing fish with less strain on the angler— thus, the short rod used by the angler dealing with a 10-foot bull shark.

Catfish anglers needing to winch big cats from cover also need to consider rod length. Consider the shortest rod that still allows for casting big baits into position. Most catfish anglers choose 6½- to 8-foot rods.

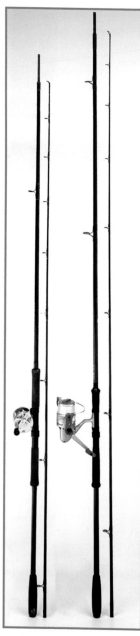

Graphite muskie sticks also are good options for moving big flatheads away from wood. Top choices are St. Croix muskie rods: a 6-foot 9-inch Avid AM69HF and a 7-foot Premiere PM70HF2, both matched with Abu Garcia 7000s.

If you're setting into a 50-pound fish that's close to a big snarl of roots, you want to be holding a rod that doesn't give much anywhere in the blank. Lose the first few seconds of that battle, and you've lost the match. Big cats never come easy, which is the way it should be. Best to be prepared.

LONG RODS AREN'T RADICAL

Longer rods are a fundamental element in better catfishing, most places, most times. They allow for casting farther, an option that ranges from just a little bit handy to absolutely critical, depending on the situation. Once a longer cast has been made, longer rods also allow more sweep on the hookset, to remove stretch from line and set the hook into a catfish.

Longer rods also help reach around bank obstructions to present baits. And when drift-rigging, particularly with floats, long rods allow more line to be held high—off the water—so current doesn't drag a bait out of position. Anglers in pursuit of record fish also prefer longer rods because they distribute stress on line more evenly over the length of a rod. Finally, a case can be made that longer rods provide the sort of left-right, up-down, rod-tip maneuverability at boatside or bankside that allows more options in fighting and landing fish.

But longer isn't always better. Rods are levers—tools to leverage or pry fish from their lairs. The perfect lever depends on the situation but usually is a compromise. A shorter lever provides more leverage with less torque (or strain) on the fisherman. Shorter rod, more leverage on fish, less torque on you. This means shorter is better when trying to drag a fish from heavy cover, or when trying to wrench something up off bottom.

But catfish, even the monsters, aren't sharks or tuna. Anglers after big saltwater fish in "stand-up gear" use a body harness hooked to a 5-foot boat rod. That's leverage, baby. Use your legs, buttocks, and back to work the short lever. That's power. That's heavy-duty pressure with a minimum of torque.

Cat anglers need to compromise in choosing power rods for catfish. We need just a little bit longer rod

Euro-style rods are offered in casting and spinning models. The casting model (left) is a Cabela's Predator rod, while the spinning model is from Euro Tackle.

Surf rods make great tailwater catfish rods. Their length and beefy nature allow long casts into the fast water below dams.

so we can pitch baits into place, but not so long that we can't handle the rod and apply enough pressure to drag cats from cover. Most of the power rods designed specifically for catfish are from 7 to 8 feet long.

EURO RODS

Longtime readers of *In-Fisherman* magazine know that we pioneered the use of 11-foot-class European-style rods—both casting and spinning—for fishing for catfish and other species. Such long rods aren't power tools so much as they allow long casts from the bank in lakes and reservoirs, and more perfect drifts when fishing baits below a float in a river. Euro-style rods work well for making long casts in smaller tailwaters below dams. Many styles are still available from specialty sources that sell carp tackle.

STEELHEAD STICKS

Steelhead rods measuring 9 to 12 or 13 feet tend to be too limber and light-powered for most but not all situations. Again, the quarry usually are channel cats away from cover. Lean on these rods, and you can put a surprising amount of pressure on an average fish. Flyrods fit this category, too. And so too the lighter Euro-style rods often billed as "zander rods." Zander (European walleye) sticks usually run 9 or 10 feet long.

All of these rods work well with lighter line, say from 6 to 12 pounds. Anglers who drift cutbait and dipbait over and around shallow wing dams in big rivers like the Mississippi during summer often use such light rods. Those boys mostly fish with 10-pound line. Often they use a float like the Thill Center Slider in combination with the rigging to help drift the bait.

EXTENDO STICKS

A bass flippin' stick remains a versatile rod choice for many situations. These rods pack well, breaking down as they do from 7½ or 8 feet when extended, to about 6 feet. They handle 30-pound-plus class fish. We've had them break at the joint while pressuring a fish at boatside or while wading, but most of these breaks happened in the course of filming TV programs, when we're called on to horse fish to the surface. Most rod companies offer several styles of flippin' sticks.

REELS FOR CATFISHING

The catfishing world's age of enlightenment began in the 1980s. Historians of angling pinpoint the genesis of this phenomenon as pivoting around the writings about the art and science of pursuing catfish by *In-Fisherman* Editor In Chief Doug Stange, Editor Steve Quinn, and Toad Smith. This trio compiled a book entitled *Channel Catfish Fever* in 1989.

In the chapter about tackle, they write that the Abu Garcia 6500C baitcast reel is the standard-bearer, calling it a delight to cast and sturdy enough to tame giant blue catfish. They also recommend the 7000C for extracting monsters from rootwads, logjams, and similar snag-infested lairs. In the years since the publication of that historic book, these reels remain the choice for scores of discerning anglers.

Phil King—winner of the 2003 Cabela's King Kat Classic and veteran catfish guide from Corinth, Mississippi—finds the Abu Garcia 6500 without peer for drifting and for vertical motifs. He's tamed blue catfish as large as 70 pounds with it and extols its durability, saying that all an angler has to do is "Oil the worm gear often, grease the main drive gears once a year, replace the pall every two years, and you're good to go catfishing." But King finds that his 6500 isn't stout enough to handle the rigors of the Mississippi River and its denizens. When King goes fishing there, he switches to the 7000.

Jeremy Leach, a 25-year-old tournament angler from Lexington, Indiana, is also an Abu Garcia aficionado. He says he started out using a 7000 on the Ohio River and has yet to find a big reel that equals its casting efficiency. Leach says the 7000 nearly equals the smooth casting abilities of the 6500. Also, it holds a lot of line for making long casts and probing deep-water coverts. He praises the 7000's reliability, too, saying that he's tested several other brands of reels and they've all suffered

TOP CHOICES FOR SPINNING

A plethora of big saltwater spinning reels can be used on surf rods, even exceeding the number of baitcast reels. Reels the size of Shakespeare's Tidewater SS4870 and SS4880 make up this category. Pfleuger, Daiwa, Penn, Mitchell, Quantum, Shimano, Okuma, Silstar, Bass Pro Shops, and others market reels that apply.

mechanical woes, unlike the 7000. The clicker system on the 7000 has worked unfailingly for plying swift currents with livebait, he says. Leach also likes the construction and design of the handle, noting it provides him with the leverage and power for manhandling big catfish in heavy currents below dams on the Ohio River.

Tim Smith—a grand master distance-caster and superb catfish angler from Drumright, Oklahoma—says there's no magic reel on the market, but he's praised the Abu Garcia 6500 and 7000 for years. By using either a BG7000 or 7000C3 with a 6-ounce sinker and a fairly large shad head, his average casts reach 175 yards. With a smaller piece of bait, he can hit 220 yards. Casts of those magnitudes are no small feat, but Smith says they're more a measure of the caster's technique, strength, hand-eye coordination, and of weather conditions than they are a gauge of the reel.

Across the years, Smith has made any number of 175-yard casts into the currents rolling out of the dam below Keystone Lake, Oklahoma, and other such tailraces. The mega-casters that fish the tailrace below Truman Dam, Missouri, have made similar numbers of very long casts, finding that the Abu Garcia 6500 and 7000 are more durable and repairable than comparable models made by other manufacturers.

James Patterson of Bartlett, Tennessee, says he's found another reel that performs well in the demanding waters of the Mississippi River near Memphis: Quantum's Cabo PT saltwater trolling reel. He uses the CLW20PTS model, which handles the river's blue catfish without a hitch. He finds it the most durable reel he's ever used on the Mississippi.

When anchoring and casting downstream, Patterson says the 4.1:1 gear ratio of the CLW20PTS is ideal for employing 6- to 12-ounce sinkers in the river's heavy currents—a faster gear ratio doesn't exert enough power to hoist those heavy sinkers upstream. Although it's designed as a trolling reel, he can make 150-foot casts with his Cabo.

But when Patterson drift-fishes, allowing his bait to bounce along bottom, he opts for a Quantum Cabo PT saltwater baitcast reel with a 5.7:1 gear ratio. He says a high gear-ratio is necessary for drifting, because an angler has to put a lot of line on the reel in a

Quantum Cabo CLW20PTS

Shakespeare Tidewater T15L

Shimano Calcutta CT700

Daiwa Millionaire-S 300

Pflueger Trion 66

Abu Garcia Ambassadeur 7000 C3

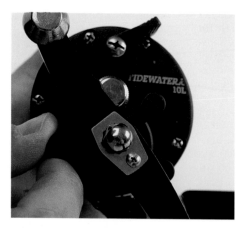

Tackle Tip—*Reduce drag tension at the end of a trip to extend the life of soft drag washers.*

hurry when a blue cat inhales a bait that's bouncing along bottom. His favorite model for drifting and bottom-bouncing is the CBC20PTS.

Since 1991, Shimano's Calcutta saltwater baitcasters have gradually been winning the hearts of some catmen. The CT400 and CT700, both with a gear ratio of 4.7:1, are two that most cat anglers employ. Users praise the reels' durability and Shimano's repair service, calling it "the finest in the industry."

Steve Brown, Warsaw, Missouri, is a full-time catfish guide on Truman Lake, and he would love to outfit his boat and clients with Shimano CT400s. In Brown's eyes, Shimano makes the finest reels for catching blue catfish, but they're too costly for the neophyte catfish angler who, he says, sometimes drops a rod and reel into the lake. So, he works with the Okuma Magda MA 20DX. It has a 5.1:1 gear ratio and is equipped with a line counter, which allows him to determine the most effective line-length when drifting mudflats for blue catfish. He's used these reels for three years without any malfunctions.

For decades, Rick Gebhardt of Glasgow, Missouri, has fished the Missouri River as a recreational and tournament angler and a catfish guide. And for the past four years, he's become a Pflueger baitcast reel devotee. His reel of choice for fishing fast currents for big blue catfish is the Pflueger Contender G30, a saltwater trolling reel. He says the G30 is a smooth caster, allowing him to place his baits far from his anchored boat. Moreover, he notes that the G30's 4.3:1 gear ratio is powerful enough to quickly tame a massive blue cat. The reel also sports a bait clicker.

Tackle Tip—*Use the correct lubricants in your reel. Some parts call for grease, others for oil.*

When pursuing channel catfish, Gebhardt opts for the Pflueger Trion 66 baitcast reel. He fills the reel's spool with 160 yards of 20-pound-test monofilament, easily casting more than half the line off the spool when using a 2-ounce egg sinker and a Cat Tracker dipworm. The Trion 66 has a bait clicker and a 5.2:1 gear ratio.

These reel selections by Patterson, Brown, and Gebhardt reflect the connection between inshore saltwater and catfish anglers that tackle manufacturers have been promoting over the past 10 years. Nowadays, Stange and other members of the In-Fisherman staff have become avid partners in this relationship, based on the fishing they do for In-Fisherman television, where Shakespeare,

Pflueger and, recently, Penn are the exclusive reel sponsors.

Doing television work, Stange and *In-Fisherman* Publisher Steve Hoffman have tamed an array of big flathead, blue, and exotic catfish from a variety of difficult waterways—including some along the equator—wielding Shakespeare's Tidewater T15L and T20L reels. They've also used Shakespeare's monster big-water reel, the Tidewater T30LA.

Hoffman and Stange call the T15L the most versatile reel of the lot. It holds about 270 yards of 20-pound-test monofilament, and its 4.2:1 gear ratio fills the needs of most anglers who pursue big blue and flathead catfish. If anglers need a stronger-test line for working logjams at close quarters, Stange says that the T15L does a good job of handling 50-pound-test monofilament. Also, an angler can purchase three T15L reels at the same price that he might spend on one high-end reel, the reason Tidewater reels are among the most popular on the market today.

When catfish anglers need a lot of line for making long casts, Stange says using a T20L on a long rod and filling the spool with 20- to 30-pound-test monofilament accomplishes that feat admirably. Moreover, when anglers have to extract big specimens from brush and logs, the T20L filled with 100-pound-test braided line is a good option.

Daiwa's Millionaire reels are also popular choices for serious cat anglers. The S, CV-X, and CV-Z series sport a 5:1 gear ratio and the Super Drag system. The Super Speed shaft makes for long, easy casts, and the CV-X and CV-Z series feature the Magforce V X-Treme magnetic backlash system.

For years, Penn has made saltwater reels for a reasonable price that fit many catfish anglers' needs.

***Tackle Tip**—Replace the stock handle on a compact casting reel with a larger power handle for more cranking leverage.*

***Tackle Tip**—Use a surfcasting reel with magnetic cast control when casting distance is important.*

***Tackle Tip**—Consider a lever drag reel when smooth drag performance or heavy pressure is necessary.*

Likewise, Bass Pro Shops and other reel makers offer a potpourri of heavy-duty reels that catfish anglers should examine.

SPINNING GEAR FOR CATFISHING

Discovering the perfect rod and reel has been a perpetual quest for scores of anglers, and across the years, many divergent opinions have surfaced about what constitutes an ideal rod and reel. Rick Clunn of bass fishing fame, for instance, began his pursuit for the perfect rod-and-reel combination well before most contemporary catfishermen wetted their first line. He contends that the best combo is one that works in a broad variety of situations, but it's also one that won't upset his rhythm, efficiency, and concentration—because if those three elements go awry, he says, his casting and presentation suffer.

Stange says the selection of a rod and reel for the serious angler is a matter of logistics and location. He points out that the needs of catfishermen are strikingly different from those of bass anglers. Because the size of the catfish can range from a pound to a 100 pounds, Stange asserts that catmen require a diverse range of rods and reels—that they can't work with the one-rod scenario Clunn desires. Clunn agrees, saying that's a difficult proposition even for bass anglers.

Although Stange is a proponent of diverse tactics, he often shuns spinning outfits for catfishing, saying that casting tackle is the way to go 95 percent of the time. Likewise, Hoffman, who also favors casting tackle, says: "I know guys who pursue flatheads with spinning tackle, but none I would consider serious. The

light-tackle gear they use in Missouri and Kansas makes sense, but at some point most flathead anglers realize that baitcasting gear is better suited to big fish in heavy cover. Even English anglers fishing for giant wels catfish usually prefer casting tackle, and they're as hardcore spinning fans as you're likely to find."

Jeff Williams, Grove, Oklahoma, has considerable experience catching trophy blue cats from Lake of the Ozarks in Missouri and Grand Lake, Oklahoma. For years, he says, most of his fellow catfish anglers have been wedded to the notion that baitcasting is better than spinning. He says they have a bias in favor of baitcasting, probably because few have given spinning outfits serious consideration.

Williams says that spinning tackle has always been the best option when pursuing gargantuan blue cats at such reservoirs. He agrees with Hoffman's assessment about the effectiveness of casting tackle when dealing with flatheads in heavy cover. What's more, in heavy current situations on some rivers, he notes, the winch-like power of a lower-gear-ratio casting reel works better than a spinning reel. But those are the only situations wherein he opts for casting paraphernalia rather than spinning.

Stange lauds the effectiveness of spinning tackle at tailraces: "Spinning does well in areas where flatheads are taken from the deep water spilling out of a scour hole. This is done with a jig-and-minnow combo, in the same fashion as vertical jigging for walleye or sauger. Light casting tackle would work there, but probably not quite as well as spinning tackle."

Besides the effectiveness of spinning tackle at tailraces, shorebound anglers at Lake Texoma regularly use spinning reels and 14-foot surf rods to make extraordinarily long casts. Cody Mullennix of Howe, Texas, for instance, used such an outfit to land the former world record 121.5-pound blue catfish at Texoma.

Although Williams fishes from a boat, he says spinning tackle allows him and his clients to make long and accurate casts—even into the wind—without worrying about backlashes. He finds that casting into the wind with baitcasting tackle is always difficult, and when anglers use lightweight baits, it's even more of a problem. By constantly executing long, accurate, backlash-free casts, Williams says catfishermen can approach those elements of rhythm, efficiency, and concentration that Clunn hopes to achieve with his bass-fishing tackle.

Williams notes that making lengthy pinpoint casts is critical to properly presenting baits from an anchored boat when anglers target blue cats on shallow mudflats. When anglers are working with large livebaits such as gizzard shad, it's essential that the bait isn't harmed during the casting process. To coddle his bait, Williams makes a lob cast, and he's found it easier to make

a long and gentle lob cast with spinning tackle than with baitcasting gear. Blood-bait aficionados also find that spinning outfits do a stellar job of placing their bait, which is often a tender morsel, into a catfish's lair.Williams also drifts baits for blue catfish, using the same spinning outfits he casts with, finding them superior to baitcasting equipment. Hoffman agrees, saying that drift-fishing is easier with a fixed spool reel. Whether Williams is casting or drifting, he uses a 7550X Pflueger Contender Saltwater Spinning Reel, mounted on a 7-foot medium-action BWS 2200 Shakespeare Ugly Stik Tiger rod. During the past decade, more reel manufacturers began producing saltwater spinning reels that fitted the needs of anglers like Williams. Hoffman finds that the bait-clicker system on most of these spinning reels is better than those on baitcasting reels. In addition to the Pflueger that Williams uses, Stange and Hoffman suggest that catfish anglers examine the reels produced by Penn, Quantum, Shimano, Daiwa, Shakespeare, Silstar, and Mitchell, among others.Because Williams uses circle hooks, he doesn't employ the spinning reel's bait-clicker system; rather, he prefers the line to tighten as a catfish takes a bait, which helps set the hook. He likes the retrieving speed of spinning reels, saying that they do a better job of quickly putting line on the spool than baitcasting reels do. When there's a hot bite and a blue cat steals a bait, it's important to get the empty hook back to the boat, rebaited and returned to the water quickly.

Fishing guides work in an excellent arena for scrutinizing the effectiveness of various products. But because Williams focuses only on using spinning tackle for catching big blue cats in reservoirs, it's important to consider the spinning rods and reels of guides who fish for channel catfish and smaller blue cats.

Jerry Martin hails from Stephenville, Texas, and is the proprietor of J Pigg Stink Bait. When he and his clients pursue channel and blue catfish in the reservoirs of central Texas, they use spinning and baitcasting equipment. But Martin readily confesses that his favorite outfit is a 7-foot medium-light-action vintage Garcia spinning rod and a 2000RG Shimano Solstace spinning reel, spooled with 10-pound-test Ande monofilament. He describes it as his "search rod" because it's extremely easy to cast, making it a great tool for locating schools of suspended blue cats. He also calls his spinning outfit his "joy stick"—a delightful way to do battle with scores of 18-inch blue catfish per outing.

Clyde Holscher, Topeka, Kansas, guides on flatland reservoirs in eastern Kansas, and during summer his primary quarry is channel catfish. He agrees with Stange that spinning tackle is the best choice for vertical presentations, and he agrees with Hoffman that "the light-tackle stuff that guys do in Missouri and Kansas makes sense."

Holscher's a chummer, using fermented soybeans for channel cats. His favorite chum holes are usually situated on the edge of a hump, adjacent to a drop-off or along a submerged creek-channel edge. The depth of these locales ranges from about 12 to 30 feet. To fish these areas, he fishes from an anchored boat, vertically probing the chummed area with punchbait on a #8 barbless Gamakatsu treble hook.

Holscher's clients often catch and release fish at a hand-over-fist pace. Even though the action can be fast, Holscher describes the typical chum bite as a subtle one. To detect bites, he's found the best outfit to be an 8-foot medium-light action Pflueger DR 4780 rod paired with a Pflueger Trion 4735 reel, spooled with Shakespeare Supreme 8-pound-test blue line. He designed his outfit for catching oodles of small catfish, but says a deft angler can eventually whip a 15-pounder and have the time of his life doing it.

While Williams, Martin, and Holscher acknowledge that baitcasting equipment works in reservoir situations for blue and channel catfish, they all agree that spinning is the best option for the situations they fish. Carefully weigh the advantages and disadvantages of spinning versus baitcasting for the situations you fish, and you're likely to choose a winner.

DISTANCE CASTING
EQUIPMENT, RIGS, & TECHNIQUES

Coastal fishermen have long recognized the value of delivering their bait to the fish, even when the fish lie 100 yards or more offshore. Catfish anglers who fish below big river dams or from the shore of a big lake or reservoir also recognize the value of a long cast, but usually they don't have access to the equipment and information available to surf fishermen.

Rods—Most freshwater anglers assume that rod length is the most important attribute for longer casts. Truth is, rod power and action are as important as length. A rod must have enough backbone to transfer the energy from the caster to the cast. The ideal action begins with a soft tip that firms up in the middle of the blank and ends in a powerful butt section.

Design elements like stiffness, whiplash, and recovery also are important. Each of these attributes can be measured by holding a rod by the handle with both hands and shaking it up and down a time or two. A tip that continues to bob up and down more than a couple times indicates whiplash, which increases line friction and decreases distance.

Distance-casting benefits anglers fishing tailraces closed to boaters.

Picture the movement of the rod tip during a cast—moving backward as the rod is loaded, straightening toward the middle of the forward cast, then bending forward during the forward flick. On a poorly designed rod, the tip continues to bob, while on a good distance rod, the tip recovers quickly. Selecting a rod with adequate backbone, minimal whiplash, and good recovery is the first step toward longer casts.

Reels—In the hands of the best distance-casters, conventional or casting reels usually produce more distance. The difference usually is small, though, and with sinkers weighing less than about 2 ounces, spinning reels tend to perform better than casting models. If your goal is tournament casting, use a casting reel. If your goal is pleasant fishing, any type of reel you're comfortable with is ideal.

A decade or two ago, most surf fishermen avoided casting reels with level winds. Many of the reels equipped with this feature were unreliable, and none could cast as far as those without level wind. Modern reels are built to such tight tolerances, however, that few casters notice any difference in performance. Reels equipped with centrifugal brakes also are more forgiving, especially for novice casters.

On any reel, follow the manufacturer's lubricating instructions. Many anglers assume that more oil or grease results in a smoother reel, but loss of control is more likely. Reels also should be cleaned regularly to remove dirt and sand particles that create friction and limit distance. Finally, be sure to fill any reel to within 1/16 inch of the top of the spool.

Before casting a spinning reel, the drag should be locked down tight. If the drag is in the normal fish-fighting position, the spool may slip during the cast, resulting in a loss of energy and distance. Line slipping across your fingertips also may cause a cut. Remember to loosen your drag after the cast, or you risk breaking the line while fighting a fish or having an unattended rod pulled into the water by a fish.

Line—Use only premium monofilament lines. The best brands are more consistent from spool to spool than bargain lines and usually have a thinner

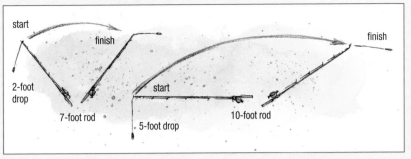

The Power of Arc and Leverage

start

finish

finish

2-foot
drop

start

7-foot rod

5-foot drop

10-foot rod

Nine feet of leverage and a 60-degree arc result in little distance.

Fifteen feet of leverage and a 150-degree arc result in greater distance.

diameter for a given break-strength. Smaller-diameter lines offer less air-resistance during the cast, and less water-resistance when the rig is anchored on the bottom.

Powerful casts with line testing less than 20 pounds or so require a shock leader—a length of heavier line added to the end of your mainline. Shock leaders should be long enough to wrap around the reel spool 5 times, travel up through the guides, then back down the blank to the spool. Most surf fishermen prefer about 10 pounds of break-strength for every ounce of weight, but they rarely use line heavier than 40 pounds, even with 6- to 8-ounce sinkers.

Mechanics—Outfitted with the right equipment, most anglers can increase their casting distance by 50 percent or more by understanding how to maximize leverage and arc. Leverage is a combination of rod action, length of rod, and distance from rod tip to sinker. A 7-foot rod and a 2-foot drop, for example, would translate to 9 feet of leverage; a 10-foot rod and a 5-foot drop would deliver 15 feet. A rod with adequate backbone also increases leverage, but the effect is difficult to measure.

The arc of a cast refers to the path traveled by the sinker. The larger the arc, the greater the distance. If you begin a cast at 11 o'clock and end the forward flick at 1 o'clock, the cast achieves an arc of 60 degrees. Increasing the arc allows the rod to fully load for maximum energy and, in turn, greater distance. Most beginning distance-casters find a 150-degree arc that begins at 9 o'clock and ends at about 2 o'clock comfortable and effective.

Technique—The overhand thump is the most popular casting technique, though it provides less distance than more advanced casting styles, is the easiest technique to master, and the best for light tackle and crowded fishing situations. Begin with the rod tip pointed back and down, your elbows up. Right-handed casters should pull the rod butt toward the hip with the left hand, as the right hand pushes straight forward then stops suddenly at the forward flick.

Watch the best tournament casters and you'll notice that all their casts seem to begin in slow motion. Speed gradually increases as the rod approaches the midcast position, then explodes so quickly at the forward flick that the blank appears as a blur. Notice, too, that weight is shifted from the back foot to the front

Long Ranger Pulley Rig

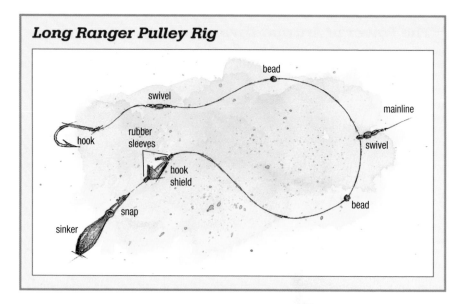

foot during the cast, but no forward step is taken. Stepping toward your target usually results in a loss of power and control.

Starting a cast with the sinker on the ground increases leverage, arc, and acceleration. Begin as before with the rod tip pointed down and behind, but with the sinker laying on the ground. The length of the drop can be increased for better leverage, which also increases the arc, since the sinker travels a greater distance. The drag created by the sinker dragging on the ground at the start of the cast also loads the rod more quickly.

Rigging—Most freshwater anglers shorten the length of their leader or use no leader at all, when trying to increase their casting distance. This is a fine option in many situations but may not result in a natural presentation in others. Baits tethered on short leaders in slow current or still water may lie motionless on the bottom, while baits with a longer leader may move slightly to attract a fish's attention.

The Long Ranger Pulley Rig allows anglers to use long leaders while achieving greater distance, keeping baits in good condition. The key feature of this rig is the hook shield that holds the baited hook tight against the leader during the cast, then releases it as soon as the rig hits the water. This results in less air-resistance, since the bait isn't flailing around the leader, and it keeps baits from flying off the hook.

Using the right sinker also can add as much as 10 yards to a cast. Aerodynamic bank sinkers, with most of their weight concentrated at the bottom, cast much farther than round or oval designs. The Breakaway sinker by Breakaway Tackle features an aerodynamic shape and grip wires that dig into the bottom for anchoring, then fold back so the rig can be retrieved.

Baits should be as streamlined as possible. A large chunk of cutbait might be appealing to a big channel or blue cat but also flail about wildly during the cast, resulting in less distance and perhaps a lost bait. A small shad head, on the other hand, tucks nicely behind a hook shield and can be cast a long distance accurately. Better to have a small bait in the fish zone than a big bait on the beach.

Hooks, Lines and Sinkers

CRITICAL COMPONENTS

Hooks are the critical link between angler and catfish. Whether you're after a stringer of eating-sized channel cats or a trophy blue or flathead, a hook is what makes your catch possible. The right hook for a particular fishing situation presents the bait in a natural manner and then hooks and holds the fish throughout the duration of the fight. The wrong hook might perform one or two of these tasks well but seldom results in a landed catfish.

When faced with thousands of hook styles and sizes, choosing the right hook can be intimidating. Much of this process is based on personal experience—a preference for a particular hook design or a prejudice against others. Unfortunately for many catmen, this kind of thinking often has a negative effect on fishing success. Explore the possibilities and then decide which hook style is right for you.

ALL-AROUND HOOKS

No single hook design is suitable for every catfishing situation, but some hooks come close. *In-Fisherman* Editor In Chief Doug Stange has recommended the same basic hook style for more than 20 years. During that time he's caught many thousands of catfish up to 50 pounds on the Eagle Claw 84 and the Mustad 92671, hooks so similar that most folks can't tell them apart.

The Eagle Claw 84 and Mustad 92671 are sturdy and economical hook designs that cover most catfishing situations.

Most major hook companies offer a hook of somewhat similar design. Compared to the classic O'Shaugnessy hook, these models have a slightly shorter shank and are constructed of lighter wire. They also feature an offset beaked point, which grabs catfish flesh better than a straight point that's not offset—at least for rod-and-reel fishing.

"The advantages of this hook design are many," Stange says. "First, this hook style is among the most popular ever offered, so it's easy to get. I've walked into bait shops, tackle stores, and supermarts across the country and never failed to find either or both in sizes up to about 3/0.

Parts of a Hook

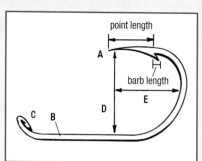

point length

A

barb length

E

D

C B

(A) The Point—Must be very sharp. A few strokes with a file sharpens a dull point, ensuring quick penetration.

(B) The Bend and Shank—Shank wire gauge and weight and hook size must match line weight. A thick-shanked #1 won't sink past the barb if the hook-set is fueled by a light-action rod and

4-pound line. Some steel shanks have less torque or bend during a hook-set. Others bend easily. Which you choose depends on the situation.

(C) The Eye—Eyes are straight, turned down, or turned up. The design determines the knot you use and the rigging application. Hooks with turned eyes are usually snelled. Use conventional knots for straight eyes.

(D) Hook Gap—Critical. Small gaps don't grab and hold as quickly or efficiently as large gaps. Use the largest gap you can get away with. Bending the base of the shank of a hook out 5 to 10 degrees opens the gap enough on some hooks to improve hookups.

(E) The Throat—It must be just deep enough to allow flesh to pass the barb.

"The 3/0 size is my favorite all-around choice for most situations with cutbait. Even for smaller channel cats, I rarely go smaller than 1/0. When fishing for flatheads with live baitfish, I use at least a 7/0 and up to a 10/0 hook. Only serious catfish shops in flathead country stock hooks this large. But again, this hook design is so readily available that bait-shop owners can easily get them if you ask.

"Economy is another major advantage. Catfish anglers lose lots of hooks. In quantities of 100, these hooks rarely cost more than a dime apiece, while chemically sharpened models might cost 10 times that much. Run a file a few times along the point and barb, and these hooks sink easily into soft flesh and also slide easily through baitfish and cutbait.

"These hooks aren't designed to pull stumps, although often as not, you might get the job done," Stange concludes. "They would not, however, work well for large fish on setlines, where a catfish can get leverage against a stiff limb. Still, in all the years I've fished these hooks—often around heavy cover—I've never straightened a hook."

WIDE-GAP HOOKS

The classic wide-gap design is one of the most popular catfish hooks in many areas of the country. The unusual design of this hook style, sets it apart from all-purpose hooks like the Eagle Claw 84 or Mustad 92671. As you might expect, these hooks work superbly in some situations, modestly in others.

This design is often called a Kahle. The name Kahle applies only to the wide-gap design offered by Eagle Claw and is the registered trademark for their wide-gap hooks. So, the "wide-gap" designation is more accurate for the range of hooks that fall within this category.

Most companies offer a range of wide-gap hooks. Eagle Claw makes the Lazer Sharp L141 in sizes up to 10/0. Mustad offers the 37140 (and 37160 with an upturned eye) in sizes from 14 through 6/0; Gamakatsu offers their Shiner Hook from 6 through 6/0.

In smaller sizes for use with nightcrawlers, minnows, or grasshoppers, a wide-gap hook is a better choice than a light-wire Aberdeen. It's also sturdier and hooks fish better. In larger sizes, the wide-gap also is the best design for presenting several smaller chunks of cutbait on the same hook.

This design isn't the best choice for presenting a single strip of cutbait, especially in current. A small square chunk is okay, but a longer strip often doubles itself back over the point, making it difficult to set the hook into a catfish's mouth. But some anglers, including master catman Ed Davis of Fayetteville, North Carolina, argue that the wide-gap is the finest all-around design.

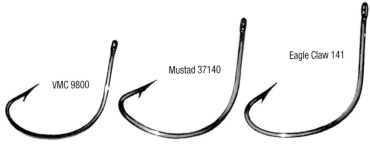

Eagle Claw 141

Mustad 37140

VMC 9800

Smaller wide-gap hooks are a good choice for crawlers and minnows, while larger sizes excel for live baitfish and multiple cutbait chunks.

"My favorite hook, the one I use for 90 percent of my fishing, is a 6/0 Mustad 37140," Davis says. "I've heard many good anglers speculate that this hook bends straight under the strain of a large fish, but I never had a problem with it. In fact, I've put the hook in a bench vise and tried to straighten it. I managed to break a length of fresh 80-pound line, but I couldn't break the hook.

"I haven't had the same success with some of the hook styles traditionally used for big cats," Davis continues. "I have a fair collection of fractured and straightened stainless-steel O'Shaugnessy hooks all the way up to 12/0. Anyone who has used a hook like this knows that no freshwater fish should be able to break it. What most folks fail to realize is that the temper and design of a hook are more important than wire thickness."

Gamakatsu
Octopus Circle

CIRCLE HOOKS

When most anglers look at a circle hook for the first time, they can't believe that it catches fish. Unlike standard J-hooks, where the point is almost parallel to the shank, the point on a circle hook is nearly perpendicular to the shank. A more precise definition probably is warranted, since many of the circle-hook designs on the market today aren't actually circle hooks—they more closely resemble modified wide-gap hooks.

The point on a circle hook drops to about a 45-degree angle from the shank. The gap—the distance between the point and the shank—matters little, since it doesn't change how the hook functions. The bend might affect hooking performance, but again, it doesn't determine whether or not a particular model is considered a circle hook.

A circle hook has been described as self-setting, driving itself into the jaw of the fish without much angler assistance. After a catfish engulfs a baited circle hook and its jaw begins to close, the hook rotates in the direction of the point of penetration. As the line begins to tighten, the point drags along the inside of the fish's mouth until it reaches the jawbone and begins to penetrate.

"Setting the hook with a circle hook is different than setting with a standard design," says George Large, a noted expert from his days at Eagle Claw. "Many anglers have been taught from an early age to sweep hard when a fish picks up the bait. Since determining the position of the hook within the fish's mouth is impossible, enough force must be applied to drive the point through the jaw, be it soft tissue or hard bone. For many veteran anglers, this type of set is instinctive.

"But a sharp, swinging set with a circle hook probably is the surest way to miss a fish. The correct set is accomplished with pressure rather than force. As the hook rotates in the fish's mouth, line pressure drives the point through the lip. Once the point penetrates, it's difficult for the fish to throw the hook, even if the line goes slack.

"Remembering not to set is the most difficult aspect of using circle hooks," Large says. "That's probably the reason some experts recommend them for beginning anglers, who aren't programmed to swing when a fish grabs the bait. Hook manufacturers have developed slogans to help fishermen overcome this instinct, such as, 'Work 'em, don't jerk 'em', or 'Crank before you yank'. Whatever the mantra, the point is the same: Allow the hook to rotate and penetrate on its own."

Circle Hook Science

A study of circle hooks by S. J. Cooke and C. D. Suski reveals findings that should interest catfish anglers.* The authors combine their own results with those of 43 other studies, including data from 25 fish species. In all cases, circle hooks were tested against standard J-hooks.

Post Release Mortality Rates: Mortality was higher for fish caught on J-hooks in the majority of studies:

Percent mortality

Fish species	Circle Hooks	J-hooks
Red drum	3	7
Striped bass	3-5.9	15.5-18.2
Chinook salmon	0	15
Coho salmon	3	24
Bluefin tuna	4	24
Smallmouth bass	3	6
Largemouth bass	5.1	6.6
Bluegill, pumpkinseed, rock bass	0 to 1.3 percent spread equally among circle hooks and J-hook types (baitholder, widegap, and Aberdeen.)	

Hooking Depth and Location:
- Circle hooks embedded shallower than J-hooks about 80 percent of the time—equally shallow in 20 percent of instances, deeper in none.
- Circle hooks lodged in the jaw roughly 85 percent more often than J-hooks, less often in about 10 percent of cases.
- Circle hooks became gut-hooked 80 percent less often than J-hooks; 20 percent equally often, relative to conventional hooks.

Offset versus Non-offset Circle Hooks: Offset refers to the degree of deviation in the plane of the hook point, relative to that of the shank.
- Bleeding and deep-hooking rates of striped bass caught on offset circle hooks were 7.8 percent and 12.5 percent, respectively. Rates fell to 0 percent and 5.9 percent, respectively, for non-offset circle hooks.
- Deep-hooking in Pacific sailfish was nearly 3 times more prevalent in severely offset (15 degrees) circle hooks compared to minor offset (4 degrees) and non-offset hooks.

Findings:
- Hooking mortality rates were reduced by roughly 50 percent by using circle hooks instead of J-hooks.
- Gut-hooking and deep-hooking were generally rare for fish captured on circle hooks.
- Some fish showed increased tissue damage, especially to the eye region, from the use of circle hooks. Mouth structure, it appears, determines tissue damage from circle hooks.
- Circle hooks occasionally caused more damage to tissue than J-hooks, as they can be more difficult to extract.

*Cooke, S. J., and C. D. Suski. 2004. Are circle hooks an effective tool for conserving marine and freshwater recreational catch-and-release fisheries? Aquat. Conserv.: Mar. Freshwat. Ecosys. :299-326.

Eagle Claw
L702

MODIFIED CIRCLE HOOKS

Classic circle-hook designs like the Eagle Claw 190 and Mustad 39960 are popular with setliners. These heavy-wire saltwater hooks are well suited to loglines and limblines, when a fish pulls against a short line anchored to a solid log; but they're too heavy for rod-and-reel fishing.

Most catmen prefer modified circle hooks, which are constructed of lighter wire and feature a wider gap than those mentioned earlier. Thinner wire results in a more natural presentation with live- or deadbaits, and more easily penetrates catfish flesh when the hook rotates into the jaw. The wider gap also makes these hooks easier to bait and easier to remove from fish.

Modified circle hooks like the Gamakatsu Octopus Circle and Eagle Claw Lazer Sharp L2222 are available in a range of sizes for different fish, from small-stream channel cats to record-class blues and flatheads. When selecting a circle hook, we usually choose a size or two larger than the all-purpose hook we'd normally use in the same situation. Instead of a 2/0 Mustad 92671, for example, we might use a 3/0 Gamakatsu Octopus Circle.

Circle hooks can be substituted for other styles in almost every situation. Again, the key is to not set the hook. Instead, apply steady tension by slowly lifting the rod tip, or let the fish set it by pulling against a limber rod anchored in a sturdy holder. It takes time to overcome your instinct to set the hook, which leads some anglers to wonder whether circle hooks are worth the effort.

Most catmen prefer modified circle hooks, which are constructed of lighter wire and feature a wider gap.

"If there's a problem with circle hooks from my perspective," Stange says, "it's that setting the hook is no longer part of the equation. It's almost like setlining with a rod and reel. And I haven't decided whether or not I like that. After all, the moment when line comes taut and the hook snaps forward, splitting lip and bone, sending the mighty whiskered quarry digging deep and hard, is perhaps the most magical moment in fishing."

Stange notes that one of the most important aspects of using circle hooks is being in the right position: Not only where you are relative to the bait, but also the angle of the rod. "When fishing from a boat in rivers, anchor upstream from where baits will be presented. Rod positioning is important to this system, as rods set pointed directly at baits or at too high an angle won't load properly," he points out. "Anchor from the bow of the boat and position rods in sturdy holders off the stern. Point rods downstream at the baits, up at about a 45- to 60-degree angle. Rods off either side of the boat should be positioned at about 45 degrees to the baits.

"Wading is a fine way to fish channel cats in smaller rivers. But it's important to be ready and in the right position. Again, hold the rod up at about a 45-degree angle to the downstream or slightly cross-stream bait. Once a fish takes it, resist the urge to immediately drop the rod tip and set the hook. Quick hook-sets usually result in the hook rattling free. Instead, keep the rod steady as it loads, then begin reeling as you steadily lift the rod tip."

SELECT CIRCLE HOOK SCENARIOS

Channels and blues in rivers—In-Fisherman Publisher Steve Hoffman has tested circle hooks in countless fishing situations, greatly refining the program. "I can now say with certainty that circle hooks shine in moderate to heavy current situations, particularly when pursuing channel cats or blues," he says.

Which Circle Hooks When?

Industry standards for circle hook sizes are not uniform: Gap distance, bite, throat, angle of hook-point bend, eye size, offset angle, and total length vary greatly from circle hook to circle hook (even within one manufacturer's line). Each model must be fished and examined separately. Even the definition of circle hook has been blurred, as some styles more closely model beaked points than the perpendicular in-turned points seen on original circle hooks.

Given the lack of clearly defined terms, as well as how function relates to specific hook features, top cat anglers remain on the lookout for great circle hooks, working through every model on the market to reveal top performers for each situation. Here's a sampling of preferred circle-hook applications:

Cutbaits for Channel Cats and Blues: In-Fisherman Publisher Steve Hoffman prefers a 4/0 to 6/0 Eagle Claw Lazer Sharp L2222. This octopus-style circle hook sports an upturned eye for snelling and a slight offset, facilitating easier hook-sets for rod and reel uses. Minnesota River guide Dennis Steele likes Gamakatsu's Nautilus, size 5/0 to 6/0. *In-Fisherman* contributor Cory Schmidt favors Daiichi's Circle Chunk Light, a modified wide-gap style hook.

Livebaits for Flatheads: As baitfish girth increases, so should hook gap. Hoffman likes the 9/0 and 10/0 Lazer Sharp L2022 when using live bullheads and suckers. Steele prefers the 8/0 Gamakatsu Octopus Circle. Schmidt's choice remains a 10/0 to 13/0 Daiichi Improved Circle.

Larger Cutbaits for Big Blues: For working with sectioned cutbait like skipjack herring, Hoffman opts for an 8/0 Gamakatsu Octopus Circle or 8/0 Lazer Sharp L7228.

Leopard Frogs for Big Channel Cats: Hoffman opts for a 6/0 to 7/0 Lazer Sharp L7228. Steele uses an 8/0 Gamakatsu Octopus Circle.

Smaller Baitfish, Grasshoppers, Crawlers: Schmidt prefers a 2/0 Lazer Sharp L702 or a 3/0 Daiichi Circle Chunk Light. For nightcrawlers, try a Lazer Sharp L787.

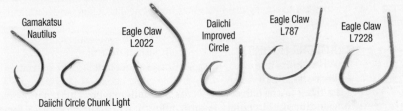

Gamakatsu Nautilus — Eagle Claw L2022 — Daiichi Circle Chunk Light — Daiichi Improved Circle — Eagle Claw L787 — Eagle Claw L7228

"We usually position above a snag or a hole, baits set to contact catfish moving upstream. What often happens here," he says, "is that catfish move forward, take the bait, turn, then head back downstream. Perfect scenario for a circle, because the retreating fish loads the rod, which pivots and sinks the hook point neatly into place in the fish's jaw. Unlike blues or channel cats, flatheads don't always move so predictably in current, so I often substitute a wide-gap hook when targeting them."

Drifting—Another pattern Hoffman helped popularize is drifting with circle hooks in reservoirs. Although he once preferred circle hooks whenever drifting, he's now refined his thinking. "Drifting with circle hooks works well on bigger blue cats—say, when you're into numbers of fish 8 pounds and up," he says. "Smaller blues or channels, though, often don't get enough of the bait into their mouth fast enough to fully take the hook. As the boat continues moving, the bait slips out before the hook can pivot and set. Only way to combat this is to slow your drift, but at this point you're normally better off switching to J-hooks."

River flatheads—Catfish guide Dennis Steele echoes Hoffman on current applications for channel cats. "I use circle hooks 80 percent of the time when fishing channels," Steele says. "I also like them when targeting flatheads. In rivers, choosing a rig or a hook often depends on the direction catfish move within different currents or near cover, relative to your position. When setting baits for active flatheads near snags," he says, "circle hooks work because fish frequently move back toward cover after eating a bait. Lock down the drag and be ready to grab the rod quickly—an aggressive flathead can overload a blank in a hurry.

"Circle hooks aren't always the answer for flatheads," he notes. "I prefer other styles of hooks when it's necessary to let flatheads run, or when you're not concerned with the fish getting tangled in wood. I also like standard hook styles when fishing the tail of a hole, as flatheads here move upstream toward your position after taking a bait. Tough to get a circle hook to set on slack line," he says.

Freelining stillwater—Frequently, anglers find themselves amidst various suburban fisheries—artificial golf-course lakes, park ponds, small residential reservoirs. Many of these waters, which pepper urban regions in surprising density, contain impressive catfish populations—lots of channel cats from 2 to 10 pounds, fair numbers of blues with a few mammoths, and the odd bull flathead. Catfish of all species roam shallow water near inlets, at corners, or beneath stands of shoreline trees where drifting pollen or falling bird droppings accelerate the food chain. The best spots, then, often lie within a short cast of shore.

Experienced catmen might make a case for slipsinker or float rigging, saying that traditional hooks and hook-sets are best in stillwater situations. But if you're working additional rods with different baits or for different species while your cat rod sits unattended—or if you've set aside an afternoon for a little family fishing—circle hooks are the answer. Toss out a bunch of baits, rods secured in bankside holders, and return to the family. Throw a football, eat a picnic lunch, read a story. Race your kids to the lurching rods. Marvel at those fat handsome catfish and harvest selectively.

SNAGLESS HOOKS

When In-Fisherman co-founder Ron Lindner first began experimenting with snag-resistant rigs, he thought that circle hooks would be the answer. "Circle hooks didn't work well for walleyes, mackerel, or other species that grab or slash at baits," he says. "But they're almost foolproof for catfish, bass, and any fish that feeds by engulfing baits."

Confining his experiments to predatory fish with big mouths, Lindner set out to see how well the hooks performed in cover. "I was amazed how snag-resistant circle hooks are in big cover like downed trees," he says. "Straightpoint hooks often stick into downed trees and similar cover and only sink deeper when you pull on the line. The perpendicular point on a circle hook, on the other hand, almost never pierces wood."

Lindner was disappointed, though, when he tried to fish circle hooks in woodcover consisting of numerous small limbs and in heavy weeds. "Once the hook bend is around a limb it's almost impossible to free," he says. "With a traditional hook design you can sometimes shake a hook loose, but that trick doesn't work with circle hooks. They also don't perform well in small rocks or shell beds, where the hook point tends to catch and hold."

Lindner eventually teamed with Greg Bohn, a guide and Lindy pro-staff member from Wisconsin, to evaluate other hook designs. "We tried the same type of fiberguards used on bass jigs, loops of stiff monofilament line looped over the hookpoint, and even small rubber bands stretched between the hookpoint and the eye," he says. "Everything worked reasonably well for certain applications, but nothing worked all the time."

The major problem with weedless hook designs is making the guard stiff enough to resist snagging cover, yet soft enough to hook fish. "Fiberguards do a good job of deflecting wood, but they also prevent many hook-sets. It's tough to achieve the right balance with either of these options," he notes.

For years, Bohn had been making jigs with a wireguard that proved to be equally effective for hooks, not the standard loop of single-strand wire found on most commercial weedless hooks but a length of multistrand wire similar to fiberguards. "Stranded wireguards are just as effective as fiberguards at protecting the hook point but give more easily when a fish slurps the bait," Lindner points out. "They're the best solution I've found, and Lindy Legendary Fishing Tackle manufactures No-Snagg Hooks to complement their No-Snagg Sinker."

The No-Snagg Hook comes in sizes more popular with walleye fishermen than catfish specialists, but it's easy enough to make your own. Start with a piece of 27-pound-test Sevenstrand wire slightly shorter than the hook shank. Thread the wire down through the eye of the hook about 1/4 inch, and use fly-tying thread to lash the wire to the hook shank. Bend the wire down to cover the point, trimming the ends if necessary.

The major problem with weedless hook designs is making the guard stiff enough to resist snagging cover, yet soft enough to hook fish.

A LINE ON CATFISH

Finding a reliable, functional catfish line is simple, as so many excellent lines exist. Of course, this same abundance of riches can also make line choice a bit tricky. But you don't have to work through intricate on-the-water tests with every line in order to make the right choice.

Before spooling up, consider your surroundings—current or stillwater, heavy cover or open water, and the size of fish you're after. Look, too, at the rods, reels, hooks, sinkers, and baits you've chosen for the way you fish. Each variable might call for a different line type, or at least small jumps up or down the break-strength scale.

MONOFILAMENTS

Monofilaments are surely the most popular catfishing lines. Most of the best mono lines for extreme catfishing scenarios—flatheads in timber, channel cats in riprap, big blues in dam tailraces—continue to be best met with lines made to target saltwater fish. If saltwater-rated lines such as Berkley Big Game, Stren High Impact, and Ande Premium stand up to sharks and coral reefs, then they're a good bet in even the harshest catfish settings.

Other lines like P-Line CXX X-TRA Strong and Berkley Trilene Big Cat consist of an even tougher outer shell to better resist damage from underwater objects. Premier Pro-Cat and Mason Big Cat also offer extra resistance to line damage. Two more tough monos are Sufix Siege and Shakespeare Supreme Super Tough.

Siege claims to have improved its abrasion-resistance by a factor of 15, while offering near-zero line memory. Super Tough maintains high abrasion-resistance with low stretch. Shakespeare's Cajun Red Lightnin' is red, reportedly becoming less visible underwater. Berkley Trilene XL is also offered in a red color, remaining highly visible to the angler above water. Berkley's Big Game Supreme has smooth castability with improved shock strength, often a factor for battles with giant head-thrashing flatheads.

Another line consideration, somewhat related to shock strength, is stretch. While stretch sometimes gets a bad rap, particularly among users of braided superlines, this feature can provide several advantages. Mono's stretch cushions powerful jolts from big cats, saving wear on the rod and the angler, and also prevents the hook from tearing loose. The rising ranks of circle-hook users increasingly find that give—not only in the rod but also in the line—plays a key role in hooking catfish. A long, soft-tip rod coupled with a relatively stretchy monofilament moves the hook gradually within a catfish's mouth, rather than popping it loose, as can happen with a low-stretch braid.

Relative to selection of specific break-strengths, the rule remains: Use the lightest line with which you feel comfortable. Lighter lines are thinner, which not only slices current and wind for better rig control and bite detection, but also yields longer casts with less weight. But thinner lines also mean more damage from sharp rocks and wood. Even if you're only chasing 2- to 5-pound channel cats, if they're holding near a tangle of downed timber, a 20-pound line becomes a wise choice. Faced with 20- to 50-pound flatheads swimming amid snags, the range jumps to 50-, 60-, even 80-pound test.

Tough-Skin Monofilaments

Company	Brand	Break-strengths
Ande	Premium	2-400
Berkley	Big Game	10-125
	Big Game Supreme	10-180
	Trilene Big Cat	20-40
	Trilene Hi-Test	10-130
Cajun Line	Red Lightnin'	6-200
P-Line	CXX X-TRA Strong	2-125
Stren	High Impact	20-100
American Premier	Pro Cat	10-40
Maxima	Chameleon	2-40
Triple Fish	Camo Perlon	4-100
Mason	Big Cat	10-40
Sufix	Siege	4-30
Shakespeare	Supreme Super Tough	2-30

So it's not about cats being line-shy—usually not the case in common dark-water environments, anyway—it's about which line best performs the job at hand, with current speed, cover, rig weight, and fish size all being factors. Mono lines excel when fishing near heavy cover and when stretch and shock absorption are important. Mono is also generally less expensive than braided superline, although it breaks down more rapidly, requiring frequent respooling.

Berkley IronSilk offers another viable option for cat anglers requiring superior toughness in heavy cover. Berkley calls it a super-polymer—it uses a molecular reinforcing network to strengthen nylon molecules, the way steel rebar reinforces concrete. The result is a line that is said to be 2 to 3 times more abrasion-resistant than other tough lines. It's super limp and manageable, too, never coiling and rarely twisting.

BRAIDED AND FUSED SUPERLINES

The same factors guiding mono line choices also determine superline selection. Unquestionably, superlines—Berkley FireLine and Big Game Braid, Stren Super Braid, Spectra PowerPro, Spiderwire Stealth, P-Line Spectrex IV, and Shakespeare Ugly Braid, among others—offer break strengths that far exceed any mono at similar line diameters.

Superlines excel in moderate to heavy current and for drifting, when minimal line drag means better rig control, bite detection, and hook-setting capacity. These lines also yield longer casts and more power to horse big cats with confidence. Rarely does a superline break arbitrarily. What can happen, however, is that even light contact with a sharp, solid object can slice the line.

Some anglers debate whether or not to use superlines near heavy cover, but the braid faction says they'd rather have the low stretch and sheer pulling power to turn a big cat before it reaches that cover. The key when fishing superline near cover is to go heavier than normal, which adds line thickness and abrasion-resistance. Instead of 50-pound Spiderwire, go with 100. The 100 still has less diameter than most 50-pound monos.

Still, most of the innovations in fishing are with superlines. Newer processes for joining multiple microfibers into what amounts to a single "super" strand seem to be the objective. P-Line Spectrex IV, for instance, combines 60 fibers of Spectra into a single carrier, and this unites with three other carriers to produce a rounded line, which enhances strength and casting distance.

Superlines

Company	Brand	Break strengths
Ande	Premium	2-400
Berkley	FireLine	4-30
Spiderwire	Original	10-80
Spiderwire	Stealth	6-100
Stren	Super Braid	8-130
Spectra	PowerPro	8-250
P-Line	Spectrex IV	10-200

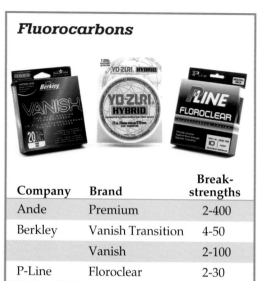

Fluorocarbons

Company	Brand	Break-strengths
Ande	Premium	2-400
Berkley	Vanish Transition	4-50
	Vanish	2-100
P-Line	Floroclear	2-30
	Fluorocarbon	2-20
Seaguar	Fluorocarbon Premier	18-200
	Carbon Pro	2-20
	FW	2-40
Yo-Zuri	Hybrid	4-30

Berkley FireLine, on the other hand, uses thermal bonding rather than a braiding process to fuse multiple strands of a material called "micro Dyneema." Spiderwire Stealth also offers a smooth surface and good manageability. Spiderwire Original is perhaps the thinnest braid on the market, while Stren Super Braid and Spectra PowerPro also are popular among catfish anglers.

Superlines certainly belong on the spools of at least a few of your reels. Couple these reels, though, with slower-action glass composite rods capable of absorbing some of the shock low-stretch lines deliver. Superlines excel in current for wrenching big cats to the boat fast. They work great for drifting reservoirs, for casting and setting hooks at long distances, for float-fishing and, finally, for improved bite detection in all situations.

FLUOROCARBONS

The biggest advantage of fluorocarbon line—that it disappears underwater—isn't a huge factor in most catfishing situations. Still, it also offers good abrasion-resistance (better than most monos), low stretch, and quick-sinking properties. While rigging livebaits for flatheads near snagpiles, some catfish anglers run a heavy braid mainline with about a 30-inch leader of heavy fluorocarbon. The mainline superline allows you to muscle fish and, because it's so thin, it also reduces any line bow caused by current. The thicker fluorocarbon adds the right measure of abrasion-resistance near cover. Another option is a heavy monofilament leader.

Today's exceptional fishing lines offer catfish anglers many advantages. Once you find some good lines for the situations you face, you can stick with them and probably be set for the rest of your life. Then again, you might be surprised at the comparative performance of another line in the same situation. Make time to test at least a couple of new lines each season.

KEY KNOTS FOR TACKLING CATS

Well-crafted knots are slick works of wonder. Using the best one for the situation might be the reason you land rather than lose that monster catfish. The right knot is what knotting is all about—and why there are so many to choose from. It's why great anglers know and regularly use a half dozen or more.

Understanding how different lines react to knotting yields a clearer idea of the best knot for each situation. Monofilament stretches and gives, allowing line to grip itself and prevent slippage. These qualities make mono (and fluorocarbon) vulnerable to friction burns when cinching knots dry. Braided superlines neither stretch nor contract, providing a rock-solid connection, yet they're susceptible to slippage should the wrong knot be applied.

Another overlooked consideration is the number of wraps tied into knots. Too many wraps may cause excess friction, letting the line play against the knot until it breaks. Too few might mean line slippage or knot failure. It's wise to learn a few methods of joining line to line and how to snell a hook—remembering to also moisten lines before tightening knots to prevent knot damage, and to tightly cinch down each knot from both the tag and mainline ends.

MONOFILAMENT TO HOOKS AND SWIVELS

TRILENE KNOT

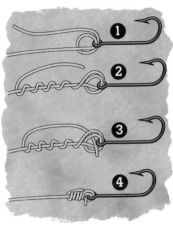

The Trilene knot provides a reliable connection that tests at about 95 percent break strength. Although this knot works best with monofilament, threading the tag end back through the large loop also secures superlines.

1. Run the line end through the eye, reinsert the line back through the eye, forming a double loop.
2. Wrap the tag end around the standing line 5 to 6 times.
3. Pass the tag end through the double loop at the eye.
4. Moisten the knot, hold the tag end firm, and draw the mainline tight.

THE UNI-KNOT: ONE FINE ALTERNATIVE

The uni-knot is a knot system encompassing several variations, all of which secure different portions of your rigging. The basic uni-knot is an excellent option for tethering mono or superline to terminal tackle.

1. Insert the tag end through the eye. Double the line and form a loop with the tag end toward the hook eye.

UNI-KNOT

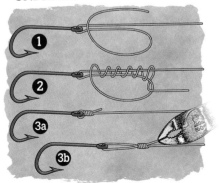

2. Wrap the tag end around the doubled line through the loop 6 times for light monofilament, 3 to 5 times for heavy mono, and 3 times for superlines.

3a. Grip the tag end, pulling slowly to draw the knot up semi-tight. Moisten the line, pulling gradually on the mainline to snug the knot tight against the eye.

3b. To leave a loop, grip the tag end firmly with pliers, tightening the knot down in place. This option works well with straight-eye circle hooks.

PALOMAR KNOT

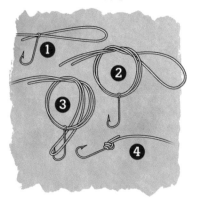

SUPERLINE TO HOOKS AND SWIVELS

Line manufacturers agree that the Palomar knot is a top option for tying braided and fused superlines. Slipping the hook through a loop locks the knot in place, preventing line slippage. This knot also works with fluorocarbon lines. Moisten the line before gradually cinching tight.

1. Double approximately 4 inches of line and slide the loop through the eye.
2. Tie an overhand knot in the doubled standing line.
3. Slip the hook through the loop.
4. Moisten and pull both ends of the line to snug the knot in place.

HOOKS WITH UPTURNED EYES

Snelling hooks that have upturned eyes keep hookset pressure straight in line, while providing an exceedingly strong connection. The uni-snell knot works just like the standard uni-knot, except the tag end is wrapped around the shank of the hook, as well as the doubled line. The uni-snell works well with all line types.

1. Thread the line through the hook eye, pulling through at least 6 inches. Form a loop and hold it tight against the hook shank with your thumb and finger.
2. Make 4 or 5 turns around the shank and through the circle.
3. Pull on the tag end to draw the knot almost closed, and moisten. Finish by holding the standing line in one hand, the hook in the other, and pulling in opposite directions.

UNI-SNELL KNOT

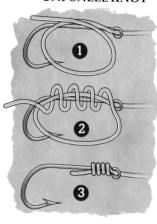

DOUBLE UNI-KNOT

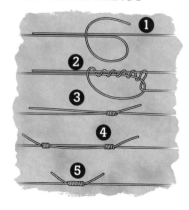

JOINING LINES OF NEARLY EQUAL DIAMETER

Yet another variation of the uni-knot system, the double uni-knot, connects two lines of similar or equal diameter. This knot tests at around 90 percent break strength and is one of the strongest, most reliable connections between two lines of similar diameter.

1. Place two lines together, ends running in opposite directions. Form a loop in one line.
2. Wrap the end 5 or 6 times around both lines, through the loop.
3. Tighten by pulling on the tag end.
4. Repeat the process using the second tag end.
5. Finish the knot by moistening the lines between knots, sliding both knots together, and snugging in place.

JOINING LINES WITH DIFFERENT DIAMETERS

Among a host of alternatives, two knots best known to surf casters, the Albright knot and the shock-leader knot, both provide strong connections between mainline and leader. A common scenario in saltwater involves a lighter mainline tethered to a heavy monofilament shock leader. While some catfishing situations call for a similar setup, other instances may necessitate a thinner superbraid leader. Both of these knots work well in either case. The shock-leader knot is the easiest to tie, while the Albright may offer a slightly higher break strength.

Albright

1. Form a loop in the leader and run the mainline through the loop, parallel to the leader, giving yourself 10 inches of extra line to work with.
2. Wrap the mainline back around itself and the leader.
3. Wrap 10 turns of the mainline over the other three strands and run back through the loop.
4. Pull the tag end of the mainline tight, then pull the standing end of the mainline tight.
5. Pull standing lines of mainline and leader and cinch tight.
6. Trim close to knot.

Shock-Leader Knot

This is similar to the double uni-knot, except you form just one uni-knot connection in the mainline, wrapped around the leader.

1. Form an overhand knot in the leader, pass the mainline through the knot, then form a 6-turn uni-knot atop the leader.
2. Snug down the overhand knot, then tighten the uni-knot against the overhand leader knot.

ALBRIGHT KNOT

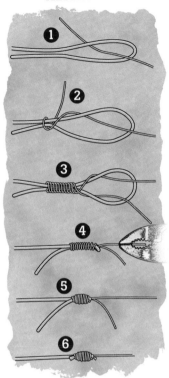

SHOCK-LEADER KNOT

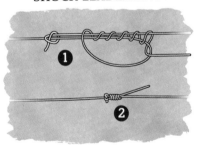

FORMING LEADER LOOPS FOR TROTLINES, JUGLINES, AND LIMBLINES

In building rigs, catfish setliners (also rod-and-reel anglers) commonly employ loops at the ends of their leaders for convenience. Although the Bimini twist is a great knot for heavy duty applications, the spider hitch does big fish nearly as well, and it's much easier to tie. In a pinch, the surgeon's end loop also forms a reliable loop connection point.

SPIDER HITCH

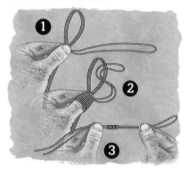

SURGEON'S END LOOP

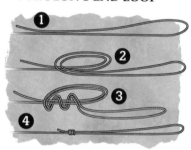

Spider Hitch
1. Double the line, forming a 10- to 12-inch loop. Form a small loop in the doubled line near the base of the large loop. Pinch the small loop between your thumb and index finger.
2. Wrap the large loop around the base of the small loop 3 times.
3. Hold the tag end and the mainline secure while you pull on the large loop until snug. Clip the tag end.

Surgeon's End Loop
1. Double the end of the line.
2. Make a loop in the doubled line.
3. Pass the doubled line back through the loop twice.
4. Pull the doubled line and standing line in opposite directions to tighten.

SINKERS & SINKER SYSTEMS

Sinkers are the workhorses of catfishing rigs. Yet, compared to other rigging components such as lines and hooks, matching the functional attributes of sinkers to the fishing situation is often overlooked. Whether you're leashing baits on bottom with setrigs, bouncing over bottom while drifting, working floatrigs, or finessing cats with a lighter touch, using the right sinker is the easiest way to improve your presentation.

Consider pouring your own sinkers. You'll save money, and you'll always have your favorite sinker on hand. With the right equipment, molding sinkers is an easy process. Plus, you get the satisfaction of fishing with your own home-crafted tackle, but be sure to follow safety precautions provided by the manufacturer when working with lead.

Environmental note—Because lead tackle can pose health risks to the environment—including ingestion by waterbirds—some states, particularly in the northeastern U.S., have banned the use or sale of some lead tackle. There's also a ban on the use of lead sinkers in 13 U.S. national wildlife refuges. Because laws concerning the use of lead tackle vary by state and over time, we suggest you check current regulations in your area.

In jurisdictions where lead bans are in place, most regulations prohibit using lead sinkers of a small enough size to be potentially ingested by waterbirds. Most catfishing, however, involves using heavier and larger sinkers, so catfishermen aren't affected as much by the regulations as are anglers of panfish and trout.

Alternatives to lead are materials such as tin, bismuth, brass, steel, and tungsten. Several companies, such as Bullet Weights, Lake Fork Tackle, XCalibur, Outkast Tackle, Penetrator Weights,

bell sinker

Tru-Tungsten, and Water Gremlin offer lead-alternative sinkers, with most styles developed for the bass fishing market. Heavy bullet sinkers, used primarily in bass fishing, are available in lead-free materials and can serve the same purpose as a sliding egg sinker in catfishing. Water Gremlin offers tin split shot that works well for riggings requiring smaller sinkers.

SINKER CHARACTERISTICS

The primary consideration when selecting sinkers for a particular rig is the shape of the sinker. A sinker determines how far and accurately a rig can be cast, how fast it sinks through the water column, and how well it holds or drifts across the bottom. Matching the right sinker shape to the conditions you encounter on the water is the easiest way to improve your presentation.

Casting—Catmen who fish small rivers or ponds usually aren't too concerned with casting distance or accuracy. Cast a bait out onto a shallow flat or toward the face of a snag, and cats holding in the general vicinity eventually find it. It's a different story for shore anglers fishing a big river tailrace or a major arm in a large reservoir. They often need to launch baits 100 yards or more to reach active fish.

Hook shields secure leaders while casting, to protect baits and allow greater casting distance and accuracy.

Sinker weight directly affects how far a rig can be cast, but again, sinker shape also is important. Take a look at the weights used by surf fishermen to make monster casts into strong coastal winds. Bank sinkers and similarly shaped models, with most of the weight concentrated in the bottom half of the sinker, are preferred. These weights offer maximum distance with the least amount of weight.

Casting distance also is reduced by the resistance of the bait, hook, and leader flailing through the air during the cast. Most anglers can immediately improve casting distance by using a hook shield—a small plastic clip held in place on the sinker dropper with silicone sleeves. The baited hook is inserted under the clip, and the weight of the sinker keeps the leader tight and streamlined during the cast. As soon as the bait hits the water, the hook pops free and the rig functions like a normal paternoster rig. Some distance casters claim a 30 percent increase in casting distance by using a hook shield.

Sinking—Most catfishing takes place in water shallower than about 20 feet, so most catmen don't think too much about the sinking efficiency of their sinkers. In deep or fast water, though, a sinker design that drops quickly through the water column can be as important as casting accuracy. If the rig is carried downstream 20 feet before hitting the bottom, for example, fish holding near the target area may never detect the bait.

No-Roll sinker

The same bank sinkers used by surf fishermen for improved casting distance also are preferred by fishermen who probe wrecks and reefs directly below the boat in 200 or more feet of water. The same characteristics that allow the sinker to pass efficiently through the air also allow it to drop quickly through water, even in heavy current. Bell sinkers and pyramid sinkers sink efficiently, especially when compared to flattened models.

For years, catfish guide Stu McKay used a flattened design called a snagless sinker to fish below the swift waters of the Lockport Dam on the Red River of the North. The wide profile kept the sinker from rolling around on the bottom in current as round or oval sinkers do, but the wider profile caused the weight to turn like a spinner blade as it dropped to the bottom. McKay eventually settled on a roll-less sinker with a hole running through the center instead of a separate line attachment eye.

Molding Your Own

With larger sinkers costing up to several dollars each, you can save some money by making your own. There's an initial equipment investment, but if you run through a lot of sinkers, this may be the way to go.

Lead stock can be purchased, but with a little investigation you can find less expensive or even free sources. Check recycling centers or municipal solid waste facilities. Used tire-balancing weights can be found at certain local service stations or tire stores. For shot and pinch-on sinkers, pure, soft lead—available from some tackle manufacturers, bulk lead distributors, and plumbing supply houses—works best.

For pouring your own sinkers, you need a melting-pot setup and molds. Some pots are equipped with spouts for pouring molten lead directly into the molds; pouring sinkers over about 2 ounces requires a melter and a ladle. When working with lead, be sure to follow all equipment instructions and recommended safety precautions.

Do-It Corporation offers a full tackle-craft product line, including the sinker molds mentioned here, and more; melting equipment; tools; accessories; and tackle tips. Do-It also has teamed up with In-Fisherman to create the DVD *Tackle Crafting Today*, providing a step-by-step demonstration of how to make your own tackle. It covers how to find lead, melting equipment, available molds, provides tips on safety, and more.

Contact: Do-It, *do-itmolds.com*.

One of the most useful sinkers for bottom-rigging in rivers is the No-Roll sinker by Do-It. With its flat, low-profile design, this sinker holds in place better than egg or bass-casting shapes. Its weight-forward, teardrop shape allows for long casts and helps reduce snagging in woody cover. The flat shape causes it to sink more slowly than casting-type sinkers. The sinker's carried more in current because of its large surface area, making the No-Roll a good option for walking baits and rigs along bottom in current.

Gapen Bait Walker

Holding—It doesn't matter how far a sinker can cast or how fast it drops to the bottom, if it can't hold your rig where you want it. Again, in lakes and ponds with a clean bottom, almost any sinker style works. The same is true when fishing directly behind a boat anchored in current. But when you're fishing cross-current, either from shore or from a boat, sinker design can make a difference. And different designs hold well on different bottom types.

A clean silt or sand bottom often is more challenging to hold to than a broken bottom. Four-sided pyramid and elongated storm sinkers have long been popular with surf fishermen forced to contend with heavy tides and sand or silt bottoms. The problem is, these designs often hold too well, especially at long range. Grapnel sinkers with flexible wire arms are popular in coastal areas. The wires dig into the bottom, then bend straight under pressure so the rig can be retrieved.

Of course, the bottom of many catfish rivers more closely resemble a junkyard than a beach. Holding in broken rock or dense piles of timber usually isn't the problem, but getting the sinker back out is. Bell and bank sinkers can be pulled out of tight cover, especially from a boat positioned directly above the snag. Long, thin designs like pencil sinkers also are easy to pull out of cracks and crevices, but don't hold as well as other styles. Another option is to use a grapnel sinker with the wire arms bent out so the sinker can't drop between branches or rocks.

Drifting—Some catfishing situations call for a bait to be slowly drifted or trolled near the bottom instead of anchored near fish-holding structure. Sinkers designed for drifting must be heavy enough to keep the rig down in the fish zone, but light enough that the rig can move with the current or follow a drifting boat. These weights also must be snag-resistant so they don't hang up on bottom structure. The most popular option is a three-way rig weighted with a heavy bell sinker.

Wire-legged bottom bouncers skip and bounce over rocks, logs, or clean bottom, and they excel in situations requiring coverage or snag-resistance. Tie your mainline to the bend in the wire frame just as you would tie on a spinnerbait. Attach a leader to the snap or snap swivel at the top of the wire arm. The leader stretches back one or two feet to your bait. Legless bouncers like the Gapen Bait Walker also can be still-fished directly behind a boat anchored in current. Keep just enough tension on the line to stand the lead base upright, and set the hook as soon as a fish mouths the bait.

To feed line to a fish while retaining the snag-resistant features of a bouncer, try a slip bouncer. Much like a sliding slipsinker, the wire-legged lead weight clips into a clevis that slides down the line until it hits the barrel swivel at the end of the leader, positioning it a set distance ahead of the bait. When a fish takes the bait, follow it back with the rod tip a foot or two, and set. Should you need a heavier weight, just snap the bouncer out of the clevis and insert a heavier weight.

Balancing—This is not really a sinker characteristic so much as a specialized sinker function. We use 3/0 lead shot to balance slipfloat rigs, designed to keep baits moving along the bottom with the current. Pinch enough shot on the line a foot or so above the hook so about two-thirds of the float is submerged. Properly balanced, slipfloats are easily pulled under when a fish strikes, but buoyant enough to keep the bait moving.

Removable and reusable split shot, such as those by Water Gremlin, have tiny wings to bend the shot open and remove it from your line. Many anglers feel, however, that round shot provide a more natural presentation in current. We prefer ultrasoft round shot like Dinsmores that can be pried open with a fingernail. Dinsmores offers an egg-shaped shot made from tin that they claim casts, sinks, and drifts as well as round lead shot. The weights also feature a "fingernail divot" for easy removal.

To anchor larger livebaits for big flatheads and blue cats, add a swivel about a foot above a 3/0 to 7/0 hook. Depending on the size of the float, a sliding egg sinker weighing 1/2 to 2 or more ounces may be needed to balance the float. Several manufacturers also offer quick on-off rigging via an internal rubber grip that fits inside a slot in the sinker. Insert your line into the slot, twist the ends of the rubber strip, and your line is gripped without a swivel or a knot. These sinkers allow you to adjust weights to fine-tune buoyancy as you change baits.

Sinkers are a key component to most catfish rigs, but few catmen consider which sinker is best for the task. Get yourself some sinkers. Better yet, get yourself a catbag full of sinkers of different sizes and styles and find out which ones work best for you. You'll quickly learn that using the right sinker in the right situation is one of the simplest ways to improve your presentation.

Chapter 3

Tackle Topics

Catfishing Rigs

BASIC SETUPS TO ADVANCED SYSTEMS

As selective as catfish might be about where they live and what they eat, they're seldom choosy about rigs. So most catmen favor simple rigs, which are easy and inexpensive to construct and have fewer components to interfere with a natural presentation.

Indeed, some catfishing situations require nothing more than a baited hook. Most conditions, though, call for added weight to aid casting distance or to anchor baits in current. A lead shot or two pinched on the line 6 to 12 inches above the hook might suffice for cats in shallow, still water, but a bank sinker weighing 6 ounces or more is needed for some big-river tailraces.

The point is that no single rig is suitable for every application. The best cat-men—those who consistently catch fish when others complain about poor fish-ing—adapt their rigging to conditions. Learning to do the same will help you catch more and bigger catfish.

FREELINING

The best rig in some situations may involve using no sinker at all. Cast a baited hook onto a shallow flat in a lake or reservoir or into a quiet eddy in a river, and allow the bait to slowly drop to bottom. Unweighted baits also can be drifted in moderate current, tumbling slowly across the bottom until catfish find them.

This is particularly true when drifting slowly over shallow water, or over deeper water with large baits. Nebraska anglers, for example, often drift for channel cats over 20- to 30-foot flats with big chunks of bloodbait. The weight of the bait alone usually is enough to stay near the bottom. California blue cat anglers use a simi-lar strategy, though most substitute half a mackerel or other large baitfish for the bloodbait.

Freelining small pieces of cutbait also can be effective in current, either from a boat or from shore. One high-water technique for channel cats is to drift a large chunk of cutbait through shallow eddies, letting the current bounce the bait along bottom where active cats are most likely to find it. Many anglers use a slipfloat rig in this situation, but freelining often is more effective in shallow slackwater, as long as snags aren't a problem

SPLITSHOTTING

If the weight of the bait alone isn't enough to keep it near bottom—either because the bait is moving too fast or the water is too deep—a lead shot or two pinched on the line may be the best solution. This is especially true in lakes and reservoirs, where tentative cats often reject a bait when too much pressure's on the line from a heavy sinker. A single 3/0 or #7 shot usually is enough to keep the bait in the strike zone, but not so heavy that a cat rejects the added weight.

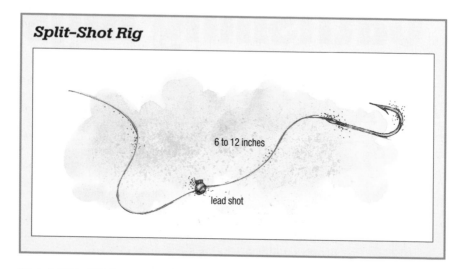

Split-Shot Rig

6 to 12 inches

lead shot

Basic Sliprig

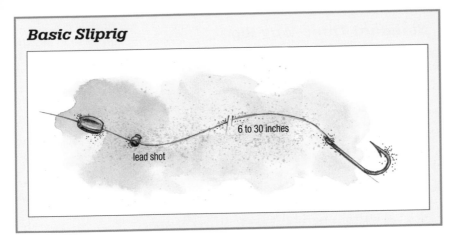

6 to 30 inches

lead shot

This rig also is a top choice for river fishing situations that usually would call for a slipfloat rig. Pinching lead shot on the mainline about 6 to 12 inches above the hook results in a rig that can be drifted through riffles, shallow holes, and even around the edge of visible cover like snags and boulders. Round shot, as opposed to the removable type with ears, tends to drift better in current and doesn't twist as much while drifting in still water. Soft lead shot also is less damaging to lines than lead substitutes like tin or shot poured from hard lead alloys.

SLIPRIG SAVVY

Many catfishing situations call for a livebait or piece of cutbait to be still-fished on the bottom. The most popular bottom rig for all catfish species is the simple sliprig. This rig consists of an egg sinker sliding on the mainline, held in place above the hook by a lead shot. The objective is to anchor the bait near the bottom, and then allow a catfish to swim off with the bait without feeling too much tension. The idea is sound, but this rig doesn't accomplish either objective well.

The success of trotlines and limblines illustrates that catfish—particularly big cats—aren't timid feeders. Let a trout or walleye run with the bait before you set the hook, but don't wait for cats. When a decent-sized cat picks up the bait, he has it. Most of the time, you could set immediately without giving any line. But your chances of a solid hook-set increase if you let the fish turn first. When you feel the thump of a fish grabbing the bait, follow him with your rod tip for a foot or two, then set.

Another problem is the egg sinker. These sinkers work well when pitched directly behind a boat anchored in current. When cast across current, though, they tend to roll along the bottom and snag more often than other sinker designs like bell, bank, or flat sinkers. Slip your mainline through the top of a slipsinker and replace the split shot with a swivel to improve the effectiveness of this popular rig.

Leader length is another concern, especially for novice anglers. Don't use a longer leader just because it separates the bait from the sinker. Rather, adjust the length of the leader to vary the amount of action and movement imparted to the bait. A piece of cutbait tethered on a 12-inch leader may lie motionless on the bottom of a lake or pond, but would flail about wildly in heavy current.

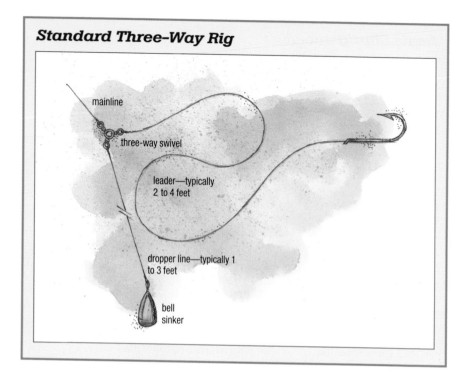

Standard Three-Way Rig

mainline

three-way swivel

leader—typically
2 to 4 feet

dropper line—typically 1
to 3 feet

bell
sinker

Use just enough leader for your bait to attract fish without hanging up. That might mean a 3- or 4-foot leader for drifting cutbait across the clean bottom of a reservoir for blue cats; a 6-inch leader for holding big livebaits in front of a snag for flatheads; or no leader at all for probing the broken bottom of a tailrace for channel cats.

THREE-WAY LEEWAY

The three-way rig is another option so versatile that it should at least be considered in most catfishing situations. It's an effective rig for presenting static baits in the heavy current of a tailrace or the still waters of a lake or pond. But it's unparalleled for slipdrifting on big rivers like the Mississippi, Missouri, and Ohio, and for drifting windblown flats in big reservoirs like Santee-Cooper.

The three-way rig consists of a dropper line 6 to 24 inches long, anchored by a bell sinker of sufficient weight to keep the bait near bottom. A half-ounce sinker might be sufficient in still water, but 3 to 8 ounces are needed to drift around the tips of wing dams for blue and channel cats. The leader should be slightly longer than the dropper line—usually 2 to 3 feet, depending on current velocity.

Three-way rigs also excel at extracting fish from areas where other rigs can't hold or return from. Say you're fishing for channel cats over a broken-rock bottom below a lowhead dam. Use a three-way rig with a 20-pound mainline and a 17-pound leader. Secure a 2- to 4-ounce bell sinker to the remaining rung of a three-way swivel with 6-pound line. When cast into place, the sinker hangs, anchoring the rig until a fish strikes. Big cats sometimes grab a bait hard enough to hook themselves and break the light dropper line. When a smaller fish strikes, a sharp snap of the rod tip breaks off the sinker and sets the hook.

Adjustable Three–Way Rig

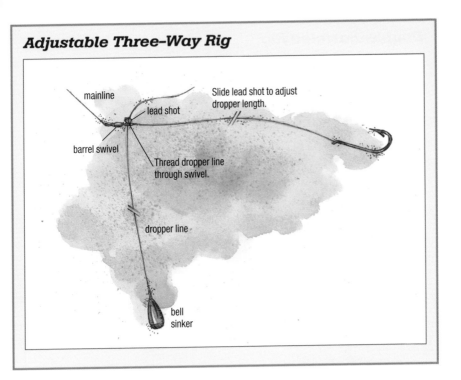

mainline

lead shot

Slide lead shot to adjust
dropper length.

barrel swivel

Thread dropper line
through swivel.

dropper line

bell
sinker

Another versatile rig is an adjustable three-way that doesn't require a three-way swivel. Instead, tie on a standard barrel swivel between your mainline and leader. Next, thread a long dropper line through one of the swivel rungs and clamp a lead shot somewhere on the dropper opposite the sinker and swivel.

The lead shot functions like a bobber stop. Where you set it determines the distance the swivel rides above bottom, and thus the depth the bait runs. To adjust the distance from bottom, simply slide the shot up or down the dropper. Should you snag, a firm pull slides the shot off your dropper line, once again losing only the sinker and saving the rest of the rigging.

DOUBLE-BARRELED SLIPRIGS

These rigs are a combination of a sliprig and a three-way rig. They're worth the extra time they take to construct—particularly for presenting livebaits to flatheads. The low-frequency vibrations emitted by a struggling baitfish attract catfish by stimulating their sensitive lateral lines. Baitfish of all sizes must first be wild and super-lively, and second be presented in a way that allows them to advertise these seductive qualities. Keep a wild bait suspended over cover and it feels exposed, vulnerable, and will panic.

Begin with a terminal leader as you would for a sliprig: A 12-inch section of monofilament or braided line with a hook on one end and a barrel swivel on the other. Before tying the swivel to your mainline, add a sinker dropper consisting of a lighter piece of monofilament with a bell sinker on one end and a swivel on the other. Thread the dropper swivel on the mainline so it slides above the leader swivel. The length of the bottom dropper determines how high the bait is held above the bottom.

Double-Barreled Rig

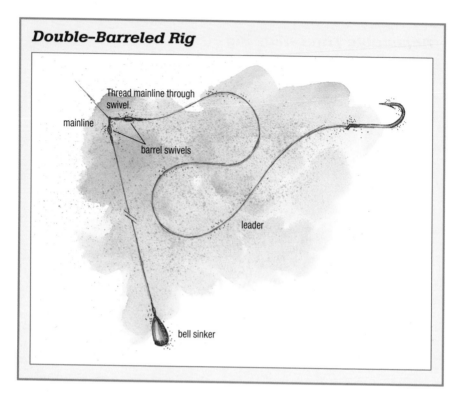

Thread mainline through swivel.

mainline

barrel swivels

leader

bell sinker

This rigging is most effective when you maintain a 30- to 90-degree angle on your line, from rod tip to sinker. Fishing the head of a hole from a boat anchored slightly upstream, fishing the edge of a flat from the sandbar on an inside river bend, or fishing the scour hole behind a bridge abutment from the top of the bridge are all top situations for double-barreled sliprigs.

Adding a slipfloat is a good option for fishing big livebaits close to cover. To construct this variation, begin as you would a standard slipfloat rig—stop knot, bead, and then slipfloat. Unlike a standard float rig, the sinker rests on the bottom, and the float need only suspend the weight of the bait and keep it swimming. This allows for the use of a smaller, more sensitive float. Next, add the sinker dropper, bead, and leader. Adjust the float stop for a little play in the leader, allowing the bait to swim in a big circle. A tightly tethered bait doesn't swim as vigorously as one that thinks it's going somewhere.

FLOAT RIGS

As much as floats aid strike indication, their true worth lies in the unique ways they present baits to catfish. Given that catfishing remains a game of delivering the right bait the right way, float rigs ought to play a major role in every angler's lineup. This is increasingly true as we discover how well cats respond to drifting, as well as to off-bottom presentations. A float is simply a bait-delivery tool similar to a sinker, and catfishermen ought to consider it just as important.

Regardless of which catfish species you're fishing for, the basic slipfloat rig is constructed in the same way. Before tying on a hook, cinch on a pre-made stop-knot, or tie a five-turn uni-knot around your mainline with the same or slightly

Double–Barreled Float Rig

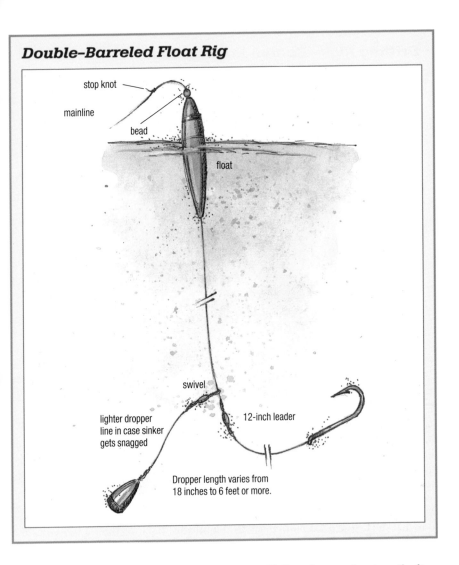

stop knot

mainline

bead

float

swivel

lighter dropper
line in case sinker
gets snagged

12-inch leader

Dropper length varies from
18 inches to 6 feet or more.

heavier line to serve as an adjustable float stop. Sliding the stop-knot up the line makes the bait run deeper, while sliding it down allows for a shallower drift. Next, slip on a 5-mm bead followed by the slipfloat. Anchor cutbait and smaller live-bait rigs with a few lead shot about a foot above a hook, ranging from a #2 for small baits to a 3/0 for bigger baits. To anchor larger livebaits for flatheads, add a swivel about 20 inches above a 3/0 to 7/0 hook. Slide a 1- to 2-ounce egg sinker on the line above the swivel to balance the float.

FLOAT SITUATIONS

Drifting Stillwater—In-Fisherman Editor In Chief Doug Stange notes: "Early in the season, and at certain other times throughout the open-water season, chan-nel cats in lakes, reservoirs, river backwaters, and ponds move shallow to feed. Particularly when vegetation carpets the bottom, a slipfloat rig keeps a bait snag-free

Drifting Rigs—Bottom Bouncer Rig

Fixed sinker rigs usually are favored for steady drift speeds or heavy current, since active cats tend to hit moving baits fast and hard. Fish often are hooked on the strike, but always set anyway to ensure a good hookup—unless you're using a circle hook. Another advantage of fixed-sinker rigs is that the leader slackens and tightens as the weight pivots along the bottom. When pulled behind a boat moving at a steady speed, the bait slows then darts forward, often triggering a neutral fish to strike.

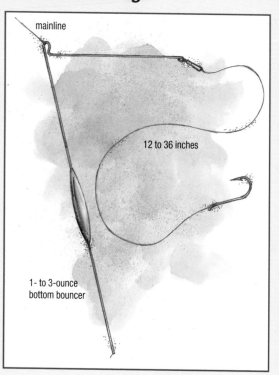

mainline

12 to 36 inches

1- to 3-ounce
bottom bouncer

and visible to feeding catfish. At times, it's a superior presentation when catfish wander about over shallow flats."

Set to run just above bottom with a stop knot, a pear-shaped slipfloat such as Eagle Claw's Oval matches well with a small chunk of cutbait or a dipworm. Above the hook, one to several lead shot balance the rig, keeping the bait drifting along with the wind. This rig also works well with the wind at your back. Set one float about 30 feet from shore, another out 50 feet, and so on. Occasionally, reel one float up to the other float, then let it drift back again with the wind to its original position. You're both fishing stationary, and covering water.

In calm waters or in light breezes, traditional slipfloats work fine—although given extra wind, a waggler-style float is a wiser option. Wagglers, such as Thill's TG Bodied Waggler, remain stable and won't blow wildly across the surface, as the bulk of the device runs underwater with just a tip of stem poking above. Some anglers dip the rod tip into the water, which keeps line below the surface, eliminating line bow.

Another slick float that works in wind, particularly if your bait's too heavy for a sensitive waggler, is Thill's Brute Force model. In either case, a breeze works in your favor, gently whisking the rig across flats, showing your offering to many more roaming cats.

Drifting Rigs—Slinky Rig

Slipsinker rigs usually are a better choice for slower drift speeds and lighter current. Standard slipsinkers like the walking sinker are fine over a relatively clean bottom, but more snag-resistant designs like the Lindy No-Snagg or Slinky sinkers are better in heavy cover. No sinker design is completely snag-free, but these designs glide through tangles that would devour egg and bell sinkers. Adding a panfish-sized float to the leader and using weedless hooks make the rest of the rig more snag-resistant, too.

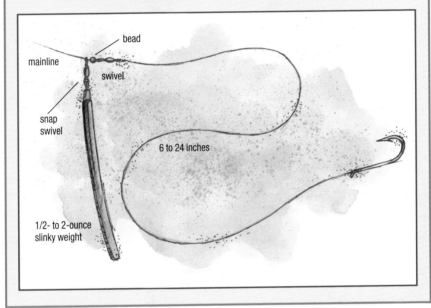

mainline

bead

swivel

snap swivel

6 to 24 inches

1/2- to 2-ounce slinky weight

The principle behind this basic rig also applies to other stillwater situations, including drifting large reservoir flats for springtime channel cats or blues. Simply modify the components, matching the float to wind speed and bait size.

Consider, too, float-rigging large livebaits for flatheads, an ideal task for a bulkier cigar- or tube-shaped float. Little Joe's Pole Float or Betts Billy Boy Pole Float, both available in sizes up to 12 inches, easily suspend large, vigorous baitfish. Thin tube shapes like the Billy Boy work best in calm waters, offering relatively little resistance to catfish.

Thill's Big Fish Slider, also a good choice for delivering hefty baits, lends extra stability in current or wind, while its squat shape provides added buoyancy. At night, add a Thill Glow Stick Float Night Light or use a Little Joe Nite Brite Lighted Pole Float. In each case, the float's main purpose isn't so much to provide bite-detection as it is to deliver a suspended moving target to prowling catfish.

Drifting Streams—In rivers and small streams, floats perform similar tasks. "Many years ago on a favorite small Iowa river," Stange says, "my old buddy Toad Smith showed me how well floats caught channel cats. By adding an old red-and-white bobber above his rigging, which kept his bait dancing along the

Slipfloat Rigging

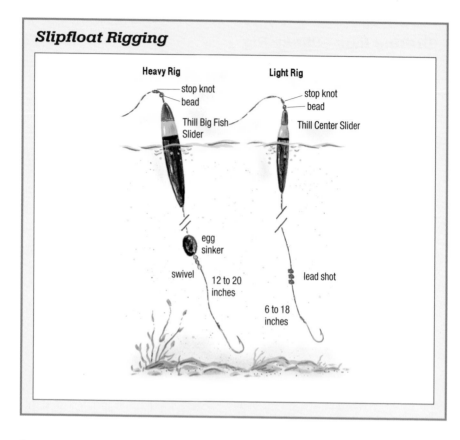

bottom, Toad was drifting baits downstream past lots more active fish. Meanwhile, I'd be tied to one spot with a sliprig, watching Toad hoist cat after cat. Luckily, I learn quickly," Stange chuckles.

"Of course, eventually the red-and-white bobber had to go," he says. "Just too wobbly in current, too apt to get blown right through a run. Today's cigar shapes are much more stable, drifting perfectly with current speed and providing the right buoyancy to suspend a piece of cutbait." In rivers and streams, Thill Center Sliders drift baits well in slow to moderate current, while a Thill Power Float matches heavier flows.

Another key part of current-drifting is the rod. "As Toad and I began experimenting with European match rods," Stange says, "it was apparent that these longer rods improved the quality of each drift. We could lift slack line off the water, steer rigs along current edges and snags, and solidly set a hook from well upstream. As the years passed, though, these rods were often hard to find, so most of the time we ended up fishing with flippin' sticks—which are 7½ feet long. They're one of the best all-around rods for all kinds of catfishing situations.

"With a longer rod it's possible to execute 100-yard drifts, coursing baits through entire segments of potentially good water. Such a sustained drift also reveals key feeding positions in each piece of water. This is opposed to casting a set rig just right, then waiting, often snagging bottom; then casting and setting, again and again. Floats can offer an advantage when targeting cats."

Tying a Stop Knot

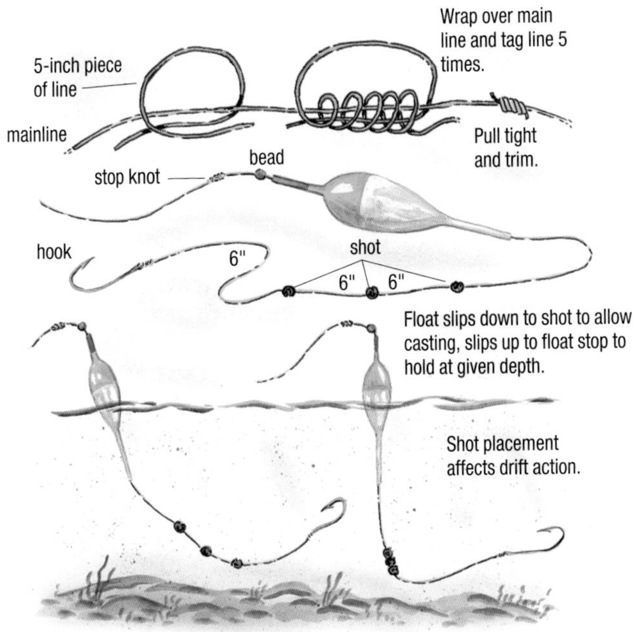

5-inch piece of line

mainline

Wrap over main line and tag line 5 times.

Pull tight and trim.

stop knot

bead

hook

6"

shot

6"   6"

Float slips down to shot to allow casting, slips up to float stop to hold at given depth.

Shot placement affects drift action.

Floats that Don't—Certain other float rigs not only don't drift, they don't even float on the surface. Consider the float paternoster rig. Essentially a three-way rig held erect by a large float, the paternoster shines in many applications. One obvious use relates to sneaking a livebait near specific cover objects that hold flatheads. Plunge the rig in place precisely at the head of a snag, for instance, and it stays put, hovering a lively baitfish a set distance above bottom.

The paternoster is a wonderful rig in areas of relatively consistent depth. The problem is, as depth changes with cast placement, you need to adjust stop-knot position to keep the rig running properly. To some extent, the float acts like a sail, too, catching wind and riding current at speeds exceeding that of water moving below the surface. In significant current or wind, the float may drag the top of the rig into trouble spots or, occasionally, dislodge the entire rig from its position.

Again, we need to change the way we regard floats on a fundamental level. Floats aren't only bite indicators, just as they don't necessarily have to remain on the surface. Consider the pop-up paternoster rig. Rather than presenting the float above the rig on the surface, slide the float onto the dropper line between the swivel and weight, typically a 1- to 5-ounce bell sinker. Streamlined floats, such as Betts' Billy Boy or Little Joe's Pole Float, catch less current, reducing downstream drag. By submerging the float, you've eliminated worries about adjusting stop knots to changing depths. At rest, the float "pops up" the dropper line, holding

Catfish Float Primer

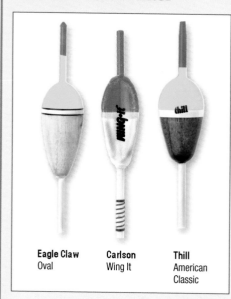

Eagle Claw Oval   **Carlson** Wing It   **Thill** American Classic

Classic Pears

Specifications
- moderately buoyant (moderately sensitive)
- moderate stability in current and wind
- widely available

Applications
- channel cats and small blue cats
- drifting in low current or suspending in stillwaters
- smaller livebaits, dipworms, cut baitfish, crawlers

Terminal Rigging
- traditional slipfloat rigging: stop knot, bead, float, one to several splitshot, hook

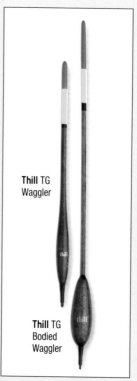

Thill TG Waggler

Thill TG Bodied Waggler

Wagglers

Specifications
- lightly buoyant (very sensitive)
- excellent stability in current and wind

Applications
- channel or blue cats
- suspending smaller baits in windy conditions and drifting in deep fast current

Terminal Rigging
- traditional slipfloat rigging
- space one to several micro or BB shot above the hook for superior sensitivity

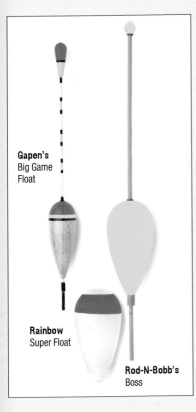

Gapen's
Big Game
Float

Rainbow
Super Float

Rod-N-Bobb's
Boss

Big Game Pears

Specifications
- moderately buoyant relative to size
- moderate stability in current and wind

Applications
- channels, blues, flatheads
- drifting in slow current or suspending in stillwaters

Terminal Rigging
- traditional slipfloat rigging

Rod-N-Bobb's **Boss Bobber** has a stem wrapped with an extra-sensitive stainless-steel spring, allowing the stem to move freely up and down through the body of the bobber. The body of the Boss serves as a platform that slowly submerges as the stem is gradually pulled down, after a fish inhales the bait. With the Boss, any resistance spreads gradually from the surface of the water to the top of the stem, exactly the opposite of traditional floats.

Modified Cigars

Specifications
- light to moderately buoyant (more sensitive)
- more stable than pear floats

Applications
- channel cats and small to medium blue cats
- drifting in slow to moderate current or suspending in stillwaters
- medium livebaits, ideal for cut baitfish

Terminal Rigging
- traditional slipfloat rigging

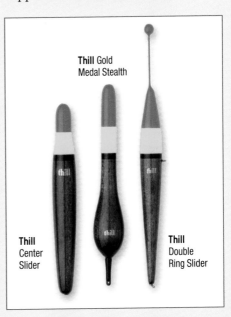

Thill Gold
Medal Stealth

Thill
Center
Slider

Thill
Double
Ring Slider

Catfish Float Primer (continued)

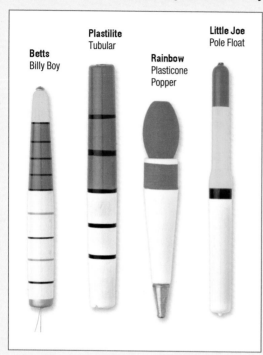

Betts
Billy Boy

Plastilite
Tubular

Rainbow
Plasticone
Popper

Little Joe
Pole Float

Tubes

Specifications
- light to moderately buoyant relative to size (more sensitive)
- poor to moderate stability in current and wind

Applications
- large channel or blue cats, flatheads
- suspending in stillwaters
- large live baitfish and heavy cut baitfish

Terminal Rigging
- traditional rigging with upsized components
- replace lead shot with a 1/2- to 2-oz. egg sinker above a swivel and short leader

Cigars

Specifications
- moderate to highly buoyant (less sensitive)
- moderate to solid stability in current

Applications
- large channel or blue cats, flatheads
- drifting in strong current rivers or suspending in stillwaters
- large live baitfish and heavy cut baitfish

Terminal Rigging
- traditional rigging with upsized components
- replace lead shot with a 1/2- to 2-oz. egg sinker above a swivel and short leader
- a good choice for float-paternoster rigging

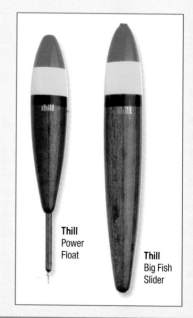

Thill
Power
Float

Thill
Big Fish
Slider

"Pop-Up" Paternoster Rig

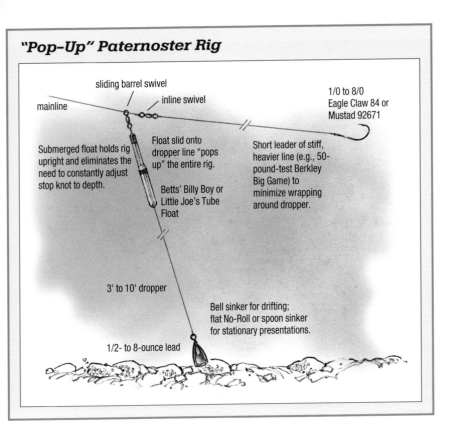

sliding barrel swivel

inline swivel

mainline

1/0 to 8/0
Eagle Claw 84 or
Mustad 92671

Submerged float holds rig upright and eliminates the need to constantly adjust stop knot to depth.

Float slid onto dropper line "pops up" the entire rig.

Betts' Billy Boy or Little Joe's Tube Float

Short leader of stiff, heavier line (e.g., 50-pound-test Berkley Big Game) to minimize wrapping around dropper.

3' to 10' dropper

Bell sinker for drifting; flat No-Roll or spoon sinker for stationary presentations.

1/2- to 8-ounce lead

the rig erect above bottom. The depth is a function of dropper length. Finally, by running back-to-back barrel swivels rather than a single three-way swivel, striking catfish run free with the line, similar to the action of a slipsinker rig.

EUROPEAN SURFACE RIGGING

In-Fisherman has long covered European strategies for tackling giant catfish abroad and their applications in the U.S. Here, catfish angler Keith Lambert, who lives in Hertfordshire, U.K., and is editor of Whiskers magazine as well as an In-Fisherman contributor, discusses Euro methods for catching wels catfish. These rigs can be applied in the U.S., too, and should particularly appeal to flathead catfish anglers.

Lambert: Tradition has it that European wels catfish, like many species of catfish worldwide, are predominantly bottom feeders. They've been considered scavengers and opportunistic feeders, and baits and rigs have been used to suit. These days we know differently about how catfish feed, and it's well accepted that these marvelously adaptable fishes feed and can be caught at all depths.

Although it's true that the European catfish is indeed a scavenger—consuming just about any food item that you care to imagine—it's also a highly efficient hunting machine. Its speed and efficiency coupled with a well-developed olfactory system make it one of the world's supreme predators. Possessing a mouth the size of a bear trap is pretty useful, too.

Keith Lambert, of Hertfordshire, U.K., with a European wels catfish. Lambert is a contributor to In-Fisherman publications on Euro tactics for catfish.

Because, at times, catfish can be caught at all depths including at or just below the surface, consider the types of rigs best suited to presenting baits in these areas and in such a way that they encourage a take. Like most rigs, there's always one that's more suitable in a particular situation. This can vary depending on conditions and the areas fished. Here, the focus is on rigs designed to present baits on or near the surface.

SURFACE RIGS

Simple Rig—The easiest way to present a catfish bait at or near to the surface is simply to hook a floating bait and anchor it in position. There are several baits that float naturally, such as dead fish with their swim bladders intact, day-old chicks, and certain types of sausage and meat products with high fat content. Simply run the mainline through a large-diameter ceramic ring (mine are mostly about 1/3 inch), which is attached to a sinker, and then tie on a hook. Cast the rig and allow the buoyancy of the bait to bring it to the surface on a slack line.

If your bait doesn't float naturally, add a float on the line near the bait, or insert a balsa-wood stick cut to the right length for the bait. Care should be taken to ensure that the buoyant material is properly fixed to the rig so that it can be recovered after a catfish has taken the bait.

Dumbbell Rig—A rig that has proven especially successful is the dumbbell rig. This rig is made by sliding a large-diameter ceramic ring onto the mainline.

A sinker of at least 2 or 3 ounces is attached to the ring with a weak link of 6- or 8-pound-test monofilament, which can be broken off easily if snagged. Next, slide a large rubber bead down the line, followed by a dumbbell float and then a strong swivel.

Readymade dumbbell floats are sold online or are easily constructed using a length of stiff boom tube between 9 and 15 inches long, with a poly or foam ball glued at each end. The diameter of balls depends on the size of the bait used, but 1¼ to 1½ inches suits most baits. Leave about 1/2 inch of the stiff tube extending beyond the foam ball at one end of the float. A tight-fitting piece of silicone tubing about 1 to 2 inches long is then pushed over the extended piece of boom tube. The mainline is locked into place by pulling the swivel into the silicone tubing after the swivel's been tied on with a strong knot.

The dumbbell rig is completed by tying on a leader of about 20-pound-test monofilament to which the hook is tied. The length of the leader determines the maximum depth that the bait is presented and should be shorter than the length of the float, usually between 6 and 10 inches. Forget braided lines for leaders; this is where many anglers go wrong. A stiffer line is required to avoid tangles made by energetic livebaits. Circle hooks are effective for nearly all surface-rigging applications.

Regardless of hook style, the dumbbell rig is a useful addition to any catfish angler's armory, if only for the fact that it isn't widely used on hard-fished cat waters. This rig is most effective when presenting a livebait close to surface weeds and lily beds. Casting along reeded banks can also be a productive method. Simon Clarke, Secretary of the Catfish Conservation Group in the U.K., has had great success using the rig in open water.

The dumbbell can be fished on water of any depth, although the nature of weedbed fishing means that it's most often used in water about 4 to 6 feet deep. After casting, allow the float to rise to the surface on a slack line before tightening the line. Once in position, the dumbbell float lies flat, occasionally dipping at the hook end as the bait swims. The tighter you have your line to the rig, the less area the livebait can cover but the more positive the takes should be. A glow stick can be inserted into a float for nighttime visibility, but make sure that it sits on the top of the float.

Bites are indicated by watching the float or by using an electronic bite alarm. A bobbin or line clip indicator isn't required with this rig. It's best to fish a

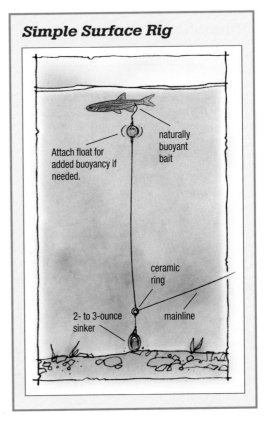

Simple Surface Rig

Attach float for added buoyancy if needed.

naturally buoyant bait

ceramic ring

mainline

2- to 3-ounce sinker

Dumbbell Rig

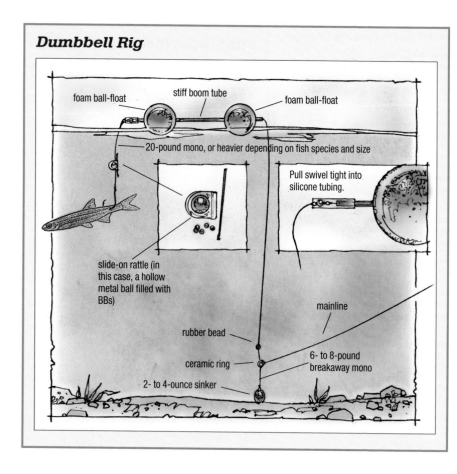

foam ball-float

stiff boom tube

foam ball-float

20-pound mono, or heavier depending on fish species and size

Pull swivel tight into silicone tubing.

slide-on rattle (in this case, a hollow metal ball filled with BBs)

mainline

rubber bead

ceramic ring

2- to 4-ounce sinker

6- to 8-pound breakaway mono

tight line to a dumbbell rig with the reel's bail arm closed and the baitrunner engaged. Runs are usually explosive and are often preceded by a burst of activity from the bait.

The dumbbell rig has one restriction—it can only be fished effectively on the surface. If conditions should change, such as heavy rain or a developing wind, it might be better to present the bait below the surface. The poly-ball rig is far more adaptable to these conditions.

Poly-Ball Rig—The poly-ball rig, as its name suggests, was originally developed with a polystyrene (Styrofoam) ball or egg, lifting baits off bottom to any desired depth. The original design had a poly ball attached to a short length of mono, which was tied to the eye of the hook. Often, letting the float pop a bait right to the surface works best.

The rig allows you to vary the depth (within a foot or so) that the bait is fished below the surface, while still having the float visible. The advantage is being able to check that the bait is still lively. My version is also virtually tangle-proof and fishes the bait on a sort of "mini-boom," which aids the take-to-hooking ratio, especially when coupled with my favorite circle hook. If a cat is hooked deep inside its mouth, unusual with circles, then the hook link is doubled up for the first few inches, giving greater protection from the abrasions of the catfish's teeth.

To make a poly-ball rig, start with a 30- to 36-inch piece of heavy mono. It should be stiff and memory-free—when stretched, it straightens fully and kinks are removed. Tie on a circle hook with an upturned eye about halfway along the line, using a knotless connection. Then take the tag end, about 14 to 17 inches long, and pass it back through the eye so that the leader is doubled. Next, slide a large rubber float stop over both lengths of line, making sure that it's well lubricated, and slip it down the two lines until it's about 4 inches from the hook. The two lines can now be separated and a large strong swivel tied to the end that connects to the mainline. The other end has the poly ball attached.

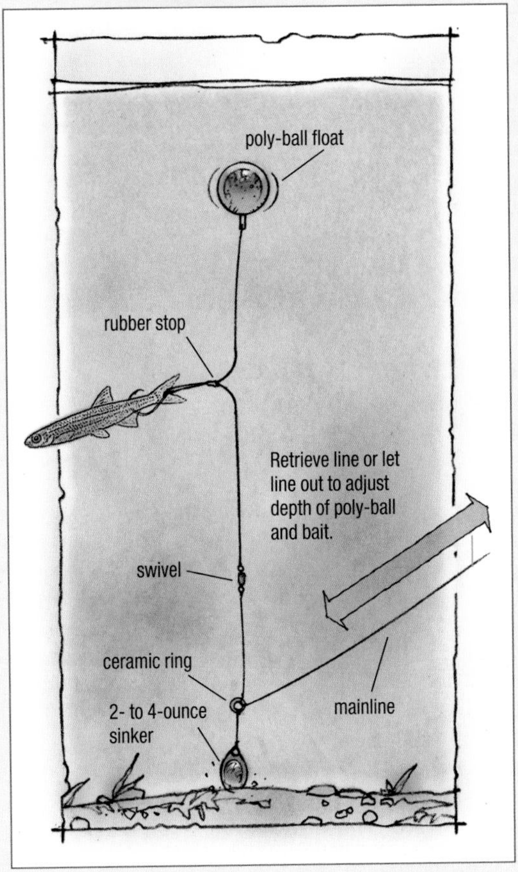

Before attaching the rig to the mainline, slide on a ceramic ring with a sinker attached. Once the rig is cast, allow the float to rise on a slack line

Poly-Ball Rig

poly-ball float

rubber stop

Retrieve line or let line out to adjust depth of poly-ball and bait.

swivel

ceramic ring

2- to 4-ounce sinker

mainline

above the sinker. The distance between the float and the rubber stop determines the depth below the surface the bait fishes when the poly ball is on the surface. For sub-surface fishing, crank the rig down in the water to the required depth. If you hold the rig up as if it's set, you see that the hook extends at right angles on a mini-boom created by the double lines. This is adjustable by sliding the float stop along the lines.

RATTLES AND BEADS

The movement and panic emitted from a tethered livebait is a predator attractor in itself, but there are other methods of increasing the vibration and noise of your baits. An inline float positioned a few inches from the hook always reaches for the surface, but can't get there unless line is released from the reel. The effect is a pull against the swimming motion of the bait, causing it to put more energy and vibe into its activity. This gives out more distress vibrations and hopefully attracts more catfish.

Another trick is to incorporate sound. This isn't a new idea but it might just give us an extra edge in some situations. The simplest way to do this is by using rig rattles and beads. Most of these are small hollow tubes or balls that are threaded or attached to the leader. They have a few small shot inside and rattle like mad every time there's any movement on the line. As a lively baitfish moves about, there's a lot of agitation to the rattle. Beads and beaded swivels are available that have micro shot in them.

SURFACE FISHING PERSPECTIVES

Everyone has his own opinion as to the best depth to fish livebaits for wels catfish—in truth, nobody is right or wrong. Such is the fickle nature of the feeding habits of the wels that logic and experience usually go out the window. I have a few theories that may offer some benefits.

Generally, I find that our catfish are sluggish below about 50°F. A mild spell in the spring often prompts them to feed, especially in shallower waters that are quick to warm. There are few deep catfish waters in the U.K., so we can virtually discount thermoclines. It's possible that turnover might come into play in early spring or late autumn, though I'm undecided whether it's relevant or if there's anything that needs to be changed in my methods at these times.

The deepest lake I fish is less than 30 feet and most are between 3 and 10 feet. In shallower lakes, surface fishing is generally better in the early part of the season. While I like a nice ripple on the water, strong winds and heavy waves are the kiss of death for surface fishing. I'm not a fan of catfishing in heavy rain, but humid and muggy weather can be excellent and many good cats are taken in flash thunderstorms, especially in midsummer after long periods of hot weather (not that we get much). If the water temperature is cool or if it's rainy or windy, I fish livebait deeper.

The majority of the rigs I use have been tried and tested over many years while targeting cats in the lakes and pits of southern England. Many of my rigs have been adapted for fishing for the real monster cats living in some of the major rivers of mainland Europe. Many of these rigs, methods, and presentations could easily be used or adapted to catch catfish Stateside, especially flatheads, similar to our wels. Try U.K. rigs—you may be pleasantly surprised.

RIG IS A JIG

A basic rig needs a hook and a weight, but consider leaders and the reasons fishermen cite for using them. Livebaits have more room to swim and thump, attracting catfish from greater distances; cats are less likely to shy away from or drop a bait the farther it is from a bulky sinker; cutbaits and deadbaits have wider swing angles in current and when drift-fished, allowing them to move more naturally and send out more visual and vibration signals to catfish.

So much has the thinking about leaders been pored over that it's become a habit to use leaders in just about every situation. For reasons described above, long leaders tend to be used more than short ones, yet there are many scenarios when going shorter can be better, even to eliminating the leader altogether. Zero it out—and you're left with a rig called a jig.

JIGS IN THEORY

"Few catfishermen use jigs, but there are situations when they can be just as or more effective than traditional rigs with leaders," says Doug Stange, among the first to experiment with jigs for catfish, praising their effectiveness in In-Fisherman books, magazines, and television. In Stange style, then, you first should understand the theory behind the thinking, in order to put it to best use.

Lindy No-Snagg
Timb'r Rock Jig

"There's a fundamental relationship that exists between leader length and how connected you are to your presentation," Stange explains. "A long leader results in less feel and less-precise bait positioning. The longer a leader is, the more control you sacrifice. Shorten the leader from 2 feet to 6 inches and the presentation becomes a tighter package, giving you a more direct connection to the bait. Eliminate the leader altogether and you're in direct and constant contact.

"Anglers generally don't equate a jig with a rig," he says, "but a jig is really nothing more than a fixed sinker rig with the weight directly molded on the hook, rather than positioned somewhere above a leader. It's the most compact a rig can get."

One of the reasons more catfish anglers don't consider using jigs is that they fear that the added weight of the head might cause a fish to drop the bait. Most jigheads, though, weigh less than the items catfish usually eat; and if walleyes and other discriminating species from panfish and bass don't mind the added mass, neither do cats.

Worrying about catfish being cautious around a jig is often unnecessary. Rarely does a catfish nose up to a bait and sample it with a *pick-pick-pick*. More often, a cat grabs it quickly. Flatheads like to mouth a bait before they run—that's typically the initial thumps you see or feel with the rod. Channel cats tend to grab and run right away. Strikes on moving baits tend to be aggressive, which is why drifted baits are usually hit hard. With jigs, often enough you can set right away, but you sometimes need to let cats mouth the bait to allow time for the hook to get in the right spot for setting.

"The greater feel and control you get with jigs is important across all water types," Stange says. "Considering water clarity alone, the ability of jigs to work on a catfish's visual sense is greatest in moderately clear to clear conditions. Most anglers don't realize how well catfish can see. Stationary rigs work across clarities, including big muddy rivers, because they tempt cats with scent and vibration," he notes. "Jigs become a better visual trigger in cases where sight plays a larger role in feeding, which is mostly in the clearer conditions of bigger reservoirs and some small- to medium-sized rivers."

JIGS IN PRACTICE

The same sliprigs, float rigs, and other rigging approaches you've been using for years might be good ways to approach given situations. But add jigs to your list of possible rigs and you might find them a better match.

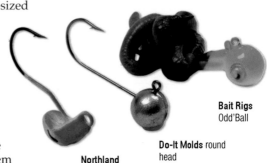

Bait Rigs
Odd'Ball

Do-It Molds round head

Northland Fire-Ball

Jig Pairings

Jigs have a variety of baiting options, perhaps more than plain hooks. Tip jigs with standard options like cutbait, live baitfish, dead minnows, nightcrawlers, grasshoppers, and more.

Doug Stange, *In-Fisherman* Editor In Chief, finds that a single piece of cutbait or a single minnow always slides down a jig's hook, preventing it from fishing effectively. To remedy this, he cuts a minnow into thirds. The midsection is added first so the long axis is perpendicular to the hook. The tail section is added next, followed by the head, which keeps the pieces from sliding down the hook. This baiting method gives the jig a larger profile and enhances its swaying action on the drop.

Jigs also open the door to using soft plastics such as curlytail grubs, shad-bodied baits, and creature designs. Scent- and flavor-enhanced softbaits provide added attraction. Try Berkley's biodegradable Gulp! lineup, such as a Gulp! Shrimp threaded onto a jig with a baitkeeper; or try FoodSource lures, which are made from all-natural ingredients.

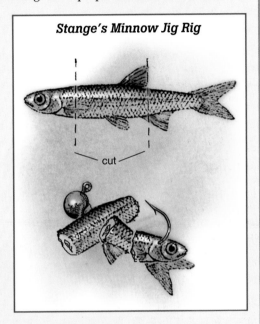

Stange's Minnow Jig Rig

cut

Tailraces—A three-way rig baited with a piece of cutbait is a common presentation for plying tailrace areas for cats. The rig consists of a three-way swivel, with the leader (usually 18 to 24 inches) connected to one eye of the swivel, and a 12- to 18-inch breakaway dropper with a sinker tied to the other eye.

"One of the biggest mistakes catmen make in this situation is worrying about the length of leader between the hook and sinker," Stange says. "This is needless worry because no leader is necessary. Too much leader causes a loss of feel, lack of control, and subsequently snags. A better option is to let the sinker slide right up against the hook. The resulting rig looks, casts, and fishes almost like a leadhead jig, which is exactly what you want.

Owner Saltwater Bullet and **Berkley** PowerBait Swim Shad

"Use current to move the jig along the bottom," he advises. "If your jig's just heavy enough and you hold your line just tight enough to stay in constant contact with current, your jig moves through prime current spots so you can feel everything down there. Lift the jig over rocks and slide it through sand and gravel pockets. Snags are minimized, presentation maximized.

"But the most important part of this process is the acquired ability to judge more than bottom content. Bottom content is secondary to current in determining where fish are. Current's the key, and you can use a jig to judge current conditions—specifically, to feel for current tunnels catfish use."

Vertical jigging—Slipsinker rigs and three-way rigs are often used to catch channel and blue cats from deeper structure in reservoirs. Baits are presented vertically from an anchored boat or while slowly passing over structure with an electric trolling motor.

"Again, jigs are a good option in this situation because you have precise control over your presentation," Stange says. "A lot of times catfish are on or just

Colorado River Catfish Rig

To the bend of a circle hook, attach a smaller hook using a section of braided line. The small hook serves to hold the bait, leaving the circle hook unobstructed.

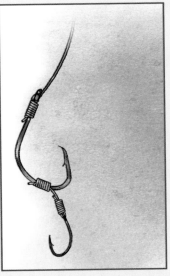

Hooking baits in the dorsal area works well on float rigs or other vertical presentations. Baits hooked near the anal fin or pelvic fin area retain the ability to swim upright, even with the added weight of the detached circle hook, making them good options for bottom rigs.

off bottom. With a jig you're in direct contact with the bottom, so it's easy to adjust depth and stay in a productive zone.

"Get the jig down to bottom. Take up slack so the rod tip's at the water's surface: When the rod tip's lifted to a specific height, you know exactly how far off bottom the jig is. You can't get that precise with a leader. Drop and lift as you move along, constantly checking for depth as you move up and down the slopes of humps and channel edges. Watch for depth on your electronics. Anticipating depth changes lets you adjust accordingly."

Vertically jigging a heavy leadhead jig dressed with a shad plastic like a Berkley Power Swim Shad or Lunker City Shaker often entices big flatheads when they won't respond to a baited sliprig. We've had good success with this tactic during fall when flatheads begin concentrating in wintering areas. Move slowly downstream using a trolling motor against the current, and drop the jig to bottom. Pop it off bottom, then follow it down with your rod tip on a semi-tight line. When it touches bottom, pop it again. The jig coupled with braided line gives you great feel for bottom content, cover, and strikes.

Ice fishing is an overlooked option for catching channel cats. Though you're limited to vertical tactics through a hole, an aggressively worked jig attracts catfish, while a slice of fresh cutbait on the hook triggers them to strike. The same type of presentation works from a boat anchored over a deep wintering hole in lakes, rivers, and reservoirs.

Small streams—A day spent on a small river can provide a fine day of catfishing, much of which can be done using jigs. "Most of my small-stream fishing is either wading or walking the bank," Stange notes. "Find a productive spot like a deeper bend hole, and it's hard to beat a baited hook weighted with a split shot a foot up the line. But often, a jig is more productive and easier to use in tighter quarters.

"With a 9- or 10-foot pole, vertically dabble a roundhead jig baited with cutbait, nightcrawlers, or crickets around woodcover—or make a short cast and allow the jig to drift along bottom next to cutbanks and through neckdowns. Jigs also work great on float rigs," he says.

Around cover—A lively baitfish on a long leader is like a dog on a long leash: Both tangle in whatever they can find. When fishing livebaits around logjams and fallen trees for flatheads, it's better to be shorter than longer, as far as leaders go. It's not necessary to use leaders longer than 6 to 8 inches around wood, and sometimes you can just let the sinker slide right up to the hook.

"Jigs are another option for flatheads around heavy cover," Stange says. "The best situation would be working jigs in an area clear of timber within a logjam or along the perimeter. A big livebait on the strong hook of a heavy jig could be fished stationary or worked along bottom. Cut-up deadbait like chunked shad or sucker also works on a jig. As a largely untried alternative, dress jigs with soft plastics."

A big weedless jig like the J-mac or Lil' Hustler Musky Jig paired with a livebait or soft plastic could be effective for flatheads around wood, as long as the current's not too strong. They have a stiff brushguard to reduce snags while probing around wood.

Jigs sporting weedguards take channel cats around snaggy cover. *In-Fisherman* Publisher Steve Hoffman had good success with Lindy's No-Snagg Timb'r Rock Jigs on the Red River of the North, fishing them with a piece of cutbait around wood. The stranded wireguard resists snags when it's pulled through wood, brush, rock, and weeds.

This is just a short list of situations to encourage you to experiment with jigs. Others might include using a football-head jig for dragging baits over bottom as your boat's propelled by wind or an electric trolling motor. If stillfishing's your game, try jigs with stand-up heads with a cutbait or small livebaits. For dipbaiters, there's the Jig-A-Cat by Apex, a dipworm on a stand-up jig head.

Consider how jigs can make your presentations simpler and more effective. Try a zero rig, and you might find yourself with more catfish.

Potential refinements to these and other rigs are endless. A minor modification made at the right time in the right place might mean the difference between not catching fish and catching lots of them. Begin with the basics, but don't hesitate to make a change if it improves your presentation.

Chapter 4

The "Natural" Choice for Cats

**LIVEBAITS,
CUTBAITS, WORMS
AND MORE**

What passes through the tiny brain of a catfish sitting in a hole on a river bottom, as the current passes along its streamlined form? Prior to the spawn, it might consider finding a fine mate with long barbels and a sleek tail. At all other times, though, a catfish uses its uniquely powerful sensory systems to sample the water for potential prey.

Scientific studies show that channel cats can detect several amino acids (which comprise all foods) at concentrations of just one part per 100 million. This sharp sense of olfaction also occurs among bullheads, whereby they can identify and remember other bullheads through unique odors emitted by their mucous coating. So, catfish can smell and taste the difference between a creek chub and a baby carp at 50 paces. In rivers, current carries both attractive and displeasing scents and tastes to cats. In still water, cats tend to move more, sampling the water for potential food. They disregard most sensations, just as our ears, eyes, and noses tune out most incoming stimuli.

What grabs their interest are preferred prey or certain flavors that may hold innate attraction for certain catfish species. Channel catfish are omnivores, consuming nearly all forms of animal and vegetable matter of appropriate size. Yet all savvy catmen know that the right bait can mean the difference between a few fiddler cats and loading the boat.

In our travels around the country, perhaps the most constant rule for bait selection is to use live or cut fish native to the river or reservoir we're fishing. That's what the cats are accustomed to feeding on. Yes, at times hot dogs, chicken livers, soap, and Uncle Stinky's gua-run-teed formula outproduce nature's own, and we can't, from a scientific or angling perspective, say why. But knowing about natural baits and how to present them is essential to being a well-rounded catfisherman.

CUTBAIT VERSUS LIVEBAIT

When choosing natural baits, one constant question is whether to use a whole live critter or cut sections. Many predators at times clearly prefer active livebait. Among catfish, flatheads, particularly big ones, often prefer livebaits that live for hours on the hook and struggle to escape. Bait like that attracts the big bites.

Sure, we've caught flatheads on deadbaits and cutbaits, but some of the season that's a low-percentage call. Channel, blue, and white cats, however, seem to prefer baits that are easy to catch over those that are lively. Channel cats dine on the stenchiest of winterkilled shad and carp, in addition to artificial formulas that imitate those aromas.

Cutting a baitfish frees the proteins and amino acids in the flesh, along with blood, a sure attractant. Similarly, inserting hooks in worms, frogs, crickets, crayfish, and maggots lets natural juices seep out to be sampled by the olfactory and gustatory organs of nearby catfish. Cats, sensing something they like, approach the source, then use taste buds located on their barbels and throughout their skin, as well as in the mouth, to make a final assessment of edibility.

Catfish accustomed to eating a particular prey type quickly detect its scent and taste, readily accepting it as food. They seem to innately prefer certain baits, though—cats raised in ponds on artificial feed quickly turn to goldfish, suckers, and other unfamiliar prey, if made available.

ANADROMOUS BAITS

On Atlantic and Pacific coast rivers, each spring brings a fresh influx of prey from the sea. Anadromous species live their adult lives in saltwater, returning to freshwater to spawn. When their eggs hatch, fry and fingerlings may spend from a few months to a couple of years in the river or estuary before entering the ocean.

American shad ascend rivers from Nova Scotia to Florida in spring when water temperatures rise into the mid-50°F range. A similar migration occurs in the

Columbia River on the West Coast. Adult shad, which run from 3 to over 6 pounds, may run many miles upstream, or spawn where obstructions block the migration.

American shad

In the Cape Fear in North Carolina and other rivers, giant flatheads and blue cats eat adult American shad, while spawning mortalities provide forage for smaller blues, channels, and white cats. Cut shad is a prime bait in coastal rivers through spring and summer, and young-of-the-year shad, which migrate to the sea in fall, are fine though delicate baits.

Blueback herring and alewives, which follow a similar pattern, also are prime baits. Skipjack herring aren't truly anadromous since adults don't move into saltwater, yet their spring upstream migration is a focus of catfish feeding. Large 10- to 15-inch herring attract the big guys, while chunks call in cats of all sizes.

Eels follow a reverse migration, called catadromous, as adults live in freshwater and migrate to the sea to spawn and die. Our contacts on coastal rivers assure us that catfish love eels, either young (10- to 18-inchers) that striped bass cherish too, or chunks of large eels.

When cut, the eel's nervous system continues to produce movement, a turn-on for flatheads that like live prey. Eel skin also exhibits excellent motion in current, so leave an extra flap on the chunk. For big fish, try chunks 3 to 4 inches long and 1 to 2 inches in diameter.

Certain marine fish also have a strong appeal. Atlantic mackerel roam nearshore waters, and cuts of these bloody, oily fish make prime baits for cats of all kinds. Mullet also make fine baits in southern rivers, where they occasionally stray from the ocean or the Gulf of Mexico.

STREAM SMORGASBORD

North American rivers contain hundreds of native and introduced fish, ranging in size from tiny shiners to buffalo, carp, and the big cats themselves. Nearly all are fair game for catfish, depending on the habitat they occupy. But catfish seem to savor some over others. Young carp, for example, are gourmet fare for big flatheads, who may follow them onto flooded pastures at night.

The closely related exotic goldfish also makes a fine bait on setlines or rod and reel. Surprisingly, cut carp doesn't rank nearly as high for channel, white, or blue cats. As a caution, be sure to check state regulations on which baits are legal and how they may be obtained. Rules vary.

Across North America, white suckers are a can't-fail bait, as this most common species is suitable in size for yearling channel cats and up to 40-pound flatties. Slice 'em and dice 'em for float or bottom rigging for blues and channel cats, or tail-hook a 2-pounder to lure a mother flathead from her lair.

Note the difference, though, between pond-raised bait suckers and wild ones. Cultured baits don't flee, a movement which often triggers a lethal attack from a predator. Seine baits or catch suckers on live worms, instead. We've found that keeping pond-raised suckers in a tank with a big flathead quickly trains the suckers in survival, making them better baits.

Smaller members of the catfish clan—stonecats, madtoms, and bullheads—make excellent baits. Indeed, studies of catfish show this species to be quite cannibalistic. In some waters where flatheads have been introduced, bullhead populations have plummeted.

Some prey preferences come as a surprise. Big blue cats often chomp bowfin before they sample more tender morsels. Observations in aquariums show that the big fish love 3- to 4-pound dogfish. On the other hand, freshwater drum (sheepshead) make a poor snack, despite the drum's fine white flesh and relative defenselessness.

Wherever gizzard and threadfin shad abound, catfish prey on these aromatic, abundant species. Catfish guides on Santee-Cooper and many other southern reservoirs use cast nets to gather a tank full of livebait to start the day. Skewering several 4-inch threadfins through the eye socket provides a tasty bait for channel cats, blues, and flatheads. Cutting larger gizzard shad in half and rigging them on the bottom also brings action.

In early spring and fall, 3-inch shiners and redtail chubs from bait shops make fine baits for channel cats. These selections follow the general rule: Smaller baits in colder water, big stuff for summer nights.

Sunfish make great baits, remaining lively on the hook or when cut. Toughest and liveliest of all is the green sunfish, a prime flathead bait on line or rod and reel. Bluegills, pumpkinseeds, redears, and the rest of their clan are appetizing, too.

INVERTEBRATES

Flathead catfish share with bass an innate love of crayfish. Often just rubbing a cat's belly reveals their lumpy remains. Tail-hook live craws and bottom rig them. But as flatheads grow, they're less likely to take these smaller baits, or maybe they have a harder time beating their 5- to 10-pound kin to the forage.

For channel cats, craw tails make a fine bait for bottom drifting or float-fishing in summer. When using a whole craw, try crushing the head a bit to release those tasty brain morsels that Cajun crawdad fans can't resist.

Catfish eat clams—freshwater mussels, Asiatic clams, snails of various sorts, even zebra mussels. Blue cats are notorious for foraging on mussel beds. Shake their bellies and you can almost hear the shells rattling.

Success with clams as bait is less than spectacular, however. Crushing the shell and impaling it just isn't natural, and the cat's preference for clams may be linked closely to abundance and location of other prey or seasonal availability.

Larvae of the dobsonfly, commonly known as hellgrammites, stay in small rocky streams throughout North America. After hatching, they remain in these streams for 2 to 3 years before moving onto land for their metamorphosis into adult flies. They are ferocious predators, using their two strong pincers to prey on worms, insects, and small

Crawlers for Cats

1 Some nightcrawler aficionados have discovered that covering the lens of a flashlight with a piece of red cellophane reduces the intensity of the light, which prevents the crawlers from becoming startled and eluding an angler's grasp.

2 An opportunity for city folks to quickly collect several hundred nightcrawlers occurs when a warm and substantial rain falls during an early spring or mid-autumn night. As the water begins to gush down the gutters of the street, a large piece of wire screen is placed across the mouth of the storm sewer inlet and checked every 15 minutes. During the best spring rains, massive handfuls of crawlers can be extracted from the screen at each 15-minute interval. This method works best in older urban neighborhoods, where yards slope towards the street and homeowners don't use heavy doses of pesticides and fertilizers on their yards.

3 The Schmidtlein family of Topeka, Kansas, gathers night-crawlers by flooding them out of their boroughs in the late afternoon or early evening. They install a flushing meter on a fire hydrant and flood a large section of soil in an area known to propagate large numbers of crawlers. "Within 10 minutes of thoroughly soaking a good area, the ground looks like spaghetti," Dave Schmidtlein says. "It's not uncommon to gather 40 to 50 dozen per hour per person."

Nightcrawlers can't tolerate the chlorine added to the city water supply, according to Schmidtlein. Therefore, the captured crawlers are immediately washed in fresh well water. After sickly and smaller crawlers are discarded, he places the remaining crawlers in a container filled with shredded paper and places them in a refrigerator.

fish. Gamefish, including bass, walleyes, rock bass, and catfish, turn the tables by rooting for these meaty morsels. Rig hellgrammites by hooking them under the collar and drifting them on a split-shot setup or on a floater head.

Nightcrawlers remain a great bait for all cats, sometimes unequaled for channel cats. Even the biggest cats can't resist worms. Drift 'em, float 'em, or bottom rig 'em. A ball of about six crawlers on a 3/0 hook is a fine bait for flatheads early in the season. The aroma and wriggling action seem to attract the big cats. In Kansas reservoirs, catmen dabble treble hooks adorned with several juicy crawlers for spawning flatheads, targeting undercuts and rock crevices along riprap walls where cats have holed up.

Catalpa worms are a highly regarded bait in parts of the South, where they're common. These meaty green worms apparently become a focus for many fish species, where they feed on lakeside trees and tumble into the water. Freeze 'em for future use. The worm's flavor is said to be so irresistible that several artificial bait manufacturers use essence of catalpa or crushed worms in their pastebaits.

Throughout the northcentral U.S. and in southern Canada, walleye and panfish anglers treasure leeches for bait. These flat worms swim with an undulating motion on jigs and plain hooks when hooked through their large sucker.

Bait leeches, collected in ditches and swamps, also make good catfish bait when drifted in small streams on floats or bottom rigs. Cats also eat larger bloodsuckers and horse leeches that inhabit northern lakes.

OTHER TERRESTRIALS

The unwary mouse that falls from a vine over a catfish hole has made its last mistake. We sometimes find rodents and snakes, as well as water-dwelling amphibians like frogs and salamanders, in the guts of catfish.

Frogs and waterdogs are locally popular and usually productive baits. Frogs can be hooked through the nose or through one leg. Some anglers cut off the lower legs to make a more compact bait. Dead frogs usually work as well as live ones. As with fish and crayfish, cutting or crushing them allows the attractive amino acids to flow toward the catfish's sensitive olfactory and taste organs. Forget tadpoles, though. They apparently secrete a substance or aroma that's noxious.

Waterdogs are the aquatic larvae of tiger salamanders that many species of gamefish relish. They're widely available in bait shops in Texas, the Southwest, and other regions, where bass anglers pay up to a couple of dollars apiece for them. Hook them through both lips and fish them on a jig or bottom rig in prime holes.

Again, there's little a catfish (particularly whites and channels) won't eat. They take advantage of any food seasonally available, including cottonwood fluff, berries, and other fruit and vegetable matter. And there's no denying the appeal of human food like marshmallows and hot dogs. Still, using baits that are natural to the system and familiar to the fish, or commercial baits that duplicate natural baits, works best most of the time.

MORE ABOUT CUTBAITS AND SOURS

Cutbait offers several advantages over other traditional catfish baits, not the least of which is being economical, since it's relatively easy to net, trap, or catch the bait needed for a day's fishing from the water being fished. And with the exception of sour cutbait, it's also cleaner to handle and easier to maintain than many other baits. Cutbait also is easy to size.

Most importantly, cutbait is effective on a range of fish sizes—on small fish and also large channel cats and blue cats, and in some situations, flatheads. This again is because cutbait is familiar to these fish.

According to *In-Fisherman* Editor In Chief Doug Stange, in clear water, vision is an important part of a cat's feeding strategy. In most environments, their hearing and lateral-line senses also are used to find prey. But in turbid rivers, where visibility is limited and rushing water somewhat distorts the transmission of sound waves, catfish rely heavily on smell and taste to locate food. The blood and oils from a fresh piece of cutbait allow cats to easily home in on the bait. Oily flesh is the key, according to many top catmen.

Depending on where you live and the waters you fish, locally available cutbaits tend to be the favorites and easiest to procure. Here we cover details for collecting and preparing three popular cutbaits—skipjack herring, suckers, and mackerel—along with a recipe for sourbait (any type of cutbait turned sour). Whatever species you use for bait, follow these general guidelines to make the most of bait preparation and storage.

SKIPJACK BY THE NUMBERS

Cumberland River catfish guide Jim Moyer's favorite time to catch skipjack herring is in winter, when concentrations of shad in warmwater discharge areas attract massive schools of skippies. As the water begins to warm, skipjack migrate toward dams, where they spawn then mill about until late summer. When the water starts to cool in early fall, herring concentrate near creek mouths and even ascend larger tributaries, until they're drawn once more to warmwater discharges.

To catch skipjacks, Moyer favors a 7½-foot medium-power spinning rod and medium-capacity reel spooled with 14-pound FireLine. He ties a small barrel swivel to the end of the mainline, then ties on a 3-foot length of 25-pound Berkley Big Game. Three 1/8-ounce jigheads sporting 1/0 hooks are tied about 10 inches apart, then tipped with 1½-inch red and white tube bodies. A small silver spoon may be more effective in early spring, and a Sabiki rig is a good choice when the fish hold deep during late fall and early winter.

"Try it high, low, fast, and slow," Moyer says. He advises that if fish are breaking near the surface, work your lure fast in the upper foot or two of the water column. If not, let the jig fall on a three-count before beginning an erratic retrieve.

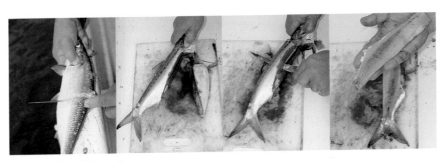

Cleaning Skipjack

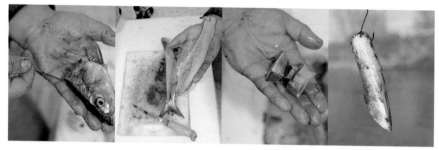

Rigging Options for Skipjack

Work progressively deeper until you contact fish, then stick with what succeeds. The school is always on the move, so continue to fancast the area if you stop catching fish. When the fish aren't in the mood to chase (this is rare), pause the retrieve to allow the lure to flutter and fall.

Moyer uses about 25 to 30 skipjack a day for catfish bait, or 2,000 to 2,500 fish during an average season. Some clients have so much fun catching bait that he has a hard time talking them into fishing for blue cats. "It's not easy to sit still and wait for a fish to bite when you've been catching 50 or more fish an hour all morning," Moyer says. "On a slow catfish day, some clients just want to go back and catch more skippies."

Cleaning begins as soon as the catching's done. Start by scaling the fish over the side of the boat. Remove the gut pocket by cutting from behind the head and under the backbone to the anus. Then remove the fillet from each side by sliding the knife along the backbone. Pack the flesh in Ziploc bags in a cooler of ice to use the same day, or store in the refrigerator for up to a month. If you freeze baits for later use, it's best to vacuum-seal them.

Moyer says skipjack heads are effective during spring and early summer, but not when the water's cold. Long strips of meat are the best option through most of summer and into early fall, except when the current is exceptionally fast. Multiple cubes of bait threaded on an 8/0 to 10/0 hook don't spin like long strips, making them a better choice in heavy current. Gut pockets are a good option during the middle of winter, but are quickly devoured by smaller fish when the water warms above 40°F.

SPRING SUCKERS

Suckers, in their many varieties, are everything a sportfish should be. A bullet-shaped, muscular redhorse pushing 3 pounds quickly peels off 15 feet of drag if you're running 6-pound line—enough to make you wonder if your rig will hold. Then it burrows and shakes, runs another time or two, and perhaps jumps, if the water's warm enough.

Redhorse are beauties to behold, too—perfectly scaled packages of sunset gold and vibrant red, with dark, deep eyes. Fish from clean, cold water are wonderful tablefare. Often smoked or pickled, they're even better ground and mixed with mashed potatoes for fish patties. And as much as you may like the taste of fresh suckers, channel cats relish them even more.

Redhorse and white suckers prefer relatively clean streams with mostly sand and gravel bottoms and moderate current. Most such rivers in the eastern half of

Suckers are as much fun as catching catfish— almost!

the U.S contain fishable sucker populations, with the exception of coastal states in the South and Southeast. If a stream looks like trout or smallmouth bass water, suckers probably are there, too.

Spring is the best time for numbers because the fish are concentrated in and around tributary streams to spawn. The first strong runs of fish often pack tightly into eddies at the mouth of feeder streams, below dams that block upstream migration, or below shallow riffles in smaller feeder creeks. Best of all, the fish are usually eager to eat any edible morsel drifting in the current.

RIGGING & TACKLE

A 6- to 7-foot light-power spinning rod usually is sufficient for sucker fishing. Longer rods, say 8½- or 9-foot models designed for light steelhead applications, allow for longer casts and better line control on larger streams. Match the rod with a medium-capacity spinning reel spooled with 6-pound-test monofilament line.

Water temperature and bottom composition dictate rigging. When fish first begin concentrating in prespawn staging areas, they may not be willing to chase fast-moving baits. Use a sliprig constructed with a 3/8-ounce bell sinker and a 12-inch leader to pin half a nightcrawler in the center of an eddy or the tailout of a riffle.

Once the water temperature begins to warm and sucker metabolism increases, drift rigs are a better choice. Pinch a 3/0 or #7 lead shot onto the line about 6 inches above a #4 hook and let the rig drift through riffles and eddies. If the rig hangs up frequently, put the shot on a short dropper constructed with a surgeon's knot, or use a snag-resistant slinky or sandbag sinker.

Keep suckers in a cooler of ice so the flesh remains firm and fresh.

Penetrating a sucker scale with a hook point is almost impossible. Remove the scales when you clean the fish, or bait hooks with care.

Fillet the fish and cut into bait-sized chunks.

SLICING & DICING

Hold the suckers you intend to keep for bait in a cooler of ice to keep the flesh firm and fresh. To prepare a sucker for cutbait, scale it with a knife, spoon, or other tool. Sucker scales, especially red-horse, are quite large and easy to remove. Or leave the scales intact, but be sure the hook point passes between the scales to ensure a good set.

Next, fillet the fish by carving through the rib bones and along the backbone to the tail. Be sure to keep the belly meat,

Pack the cubes in freezer bags for storage.

too, as it seems to have special appeal for channel cats. Cut the fillets into bait-sized chunks so no cutting is required while catfishing, or put the whole fillets on ice. This allows for cutting larger or smaller portions when the fish show a preference for a particular size offering.

Now you're ready to fish. Fresh sucker meat can be used immediately or frozen in Ziploc bags and used for most of the summer without losing its effectiveness. And it doesn't take as many fish as you might think. One 3-pound sucker provides enough bait for two anglers to fish a good bite all day.

MACK ATTACK

In southern California, cut mackerel is the most popular bait for channel, white, and blue cats. The few legal livebaits such as shad, crawfish, mudsuckers, and waterdogs produce well under certain conditions, but more and bigger cats are caught on cut mackerel than on any other bait. Mackerel has caught on in other parts of the U.S., too.

Throughout most of California, the only legal cutbait is dead saltwater fish, and mackerel usually is the species of choice. Of the commonly available saltwater species, mackerel excels because it has a strong fishy flavor combined with a high oil content that appeals to catfish.

The two most common mackerel species are the smaller, milder-flavored Spanish mackerel and the larger Pacific greenback mackerel. Some experts swear by ultrafresh, sushi-quality chunks of the thin-skinned Spanish variety, but the thicker-skinned greenback is the most popular and readily available, either fresh or frozen.

THE TROUBLE WITH MACKEREL

Mackerel is anything but user-friendly, especially for those who shorefish and have to cast a baited hook any distance. When cut and placed on a hook, whether fresh or slightly thawed, the soft meat easily separates from the skin and flies off during the cast. Warm flesh turns to mush, rendering it useless.

Old-time surf fishermen were among the first to take advantage of salt-cured baitfish such as anchovies and mackerel. The curing process involves varying amounts of rock salt and brown sugar, which preserves soft baitfish and toughens the meat, making it more durable for casting beyond the waves. To this day, cured mackerel is a mainstay in the surfcaster's arsenal and also has possibilities for catfishing.

Although frozen mackerel is available at most bait shops and marinas, many cat anglers keep a few in their freezer until needed. Just before a trip, frozen mackerel go into the ice chest with plenty of ice to keep them frozen during transport.

When it's time to bait up, take a mackerel from the cooler, slice half-inch-wide strips off its side, and thread a strip onto a 2/0 to 6/0 octopus-style hook. The rest of the bait is then returned to the ice chest.

A BETTER WAY

Tons of catfish have been taken with this simple method, but many improvements are possible. One problem with the traditional method is that you may lose half your bait if you cast far. If you don't lose it, it's probably because you've learned to pack a big wad of bait tightly on the hook to prevent it from flying off. The trouble is, when using a big wad of bait you may inadvertently obscure the hook point, reducing the chance of a solid hook-set—critical on pressured waters where bites often are few and far between.

Unless you catch your own bait, your best bet is to visit a fish market. Markets serving Asian communities usually have fresh mackerel on hand. Select a few of the largest, freshest, and firmest greenback mackerel; their coloration often appears more blue than green. The larger 14- to 16-inch fish have a thicker skin, which is a plus for bait purposes. Place them in the freezer for a while to firm them before processing.

Fillet each fish, leaving the skin on, and cut the pieces into half-inch squares. Trim them so they're about a quarter-inch thick. The scraps make a good chum. The square pieces are the essence of the baitfish, containing the flavor of the skin and the fatty tissues just beneath it, including the blood-rich dark meat.

Bag the pieces in a Ziploc bag, and you're ready to fish with fresh bait or to freeze it for later use. Two 14-inch mackerel processed this way yield a sandwich bag about half full of bait chunks. Divide this into two or three bags and fish with one bag at a time, keeping the rest as cold as possible until needed.

RIGGING TIPS & TRICKS

Mackerel chunks work well when threaded onto a 2/0 to 5/0 wide-gap hook such as a Mustad 37140 or Eagle Claw Lazer Sharp L141. You can cast a country mile and still have your offering intact when it reaches the bottom of the lake or river. It's also more difficult for smaller fish to steal the bait, as the skin portions are tough. And most importantly, the hook point remains exposed.

Another advantage of this method is that after the hook is properly baited, you can drop it into a tub of your favorite dipbait and work it around without having the whole mess disintegrate before you cast. Catfish sometimes want only pure mackerel, and at other times or on different lakes, they prefer it enhanced with dipbait.

Anglers pursuing trophy blue cats sometimes use the head of the mackerel, cut an inch behind the gills, with a large hook inserted through both lips. Some use whole fillets hooked through one corner of the fillet, or three whole fillets hung on a big treble hook. Still others prefer to cut the baitfish into inch-thick steaks and pin them on a large hook.

In California, perhaps the most popular presentation for mackerel in calm waters is called fly-lining, a saltwater term describing the use of hook and bait only, with no sinker. The reel is left out of gear, and a catfish is allowed to pick up and run with the bait a short distance before the reel is engaged and the hook set. Whether from boat or bank, this technique requires fairly light tackle, usually 6- to 12-pound test.

If long casts are required, or if much wind is present, then the sliding sinker rig is the next best choice. When the fish are aggressive, or for fishing in moving water, the three-way rig can be a good choice, especially for tight-line methods with the reel in gear. In this case, circle hooks such as the Lazer Sharp L197 or L198 can be used; a 5/0 hook works well with chunked mackerel. A gritty, citrus-based hand cleaner like Fast Orange works well for removing mackerel smell from your hands.

Other saltwater species work well for catfish, too. Pacific bonito, another oily member of the tuna family, works just as well as mackerel, sometimes better. Their thicker skin is an advantage, and bonito fillets can be chunked in similar fashion. Cut anchovies, sardines, yellowtail, and barracuda, plus squid, shrimp, and clams also are well received by the catfish clan.

SOURBAIT

Sourbait is cutbait turned rotten, rancid, and ripe. Winter-killed fish don't decompose in the cold water, but when temperatures begin to rise in spring, the gases inside these fish expand and the fish float to the surface. These floaters are driven by wind and current to predictable places—coves on the windward side of a lake, cuts on a reservoir creek arm, and large eddies in rivers. Catfish concentrate in these areas, too, gorging on these springtime delicacies.

Eventually, the abundance of sours declines and with it the bait's effectiveness. Still, some baitfish are always dying, and during summer they quickly decompose, offering a somewhat constant although inconsistent source of sourbait. During summer, carp, in particular, tends to fish more effectively as sourbait than as fresh cutbait. It's just tough enough to hold together and be a presentable bait, even during the warmest weather.

Doug Stange's recipe for preparing sours: Start with a tough-skinned fish like carp. Other fish work, but some—like sour shad and shiners—too easily disintegrate when they hit the water. Such baitfish can be fished in nylon netting, but it's a messy process. Meanwhile, scale and fillet the carp (or try sheepshead, mooneye, goldeye) and cut the fillets into 1 x 2- or 3-inch pieces about half an inch thick.

Pack the pieces into a glass jar, leaving an inch open at the top. Add a few teaspoons of water, or any other liquid you want to experiment with, to accelerate fermentation. Screw on the lid loosely—not too tight or the expanding gasses may cause the jar to explode. Bury the jar in 6 inches of soil that receives some sunlight for most of the day. Direct sunlight tends to break down fish too quickly, although experiment if you need the bait in short order. It's best to let the bait fester for almost a week.

To use sourbait, hook it once through with the hook point exposed. The bait is just as effective rigged below a float as on a sliprig lying on bottom.

LIVEBAIT CARE

Cory Schmidt, Nisswa, Minnesota, is a longtime In-Fisherman *contributor whose articles also appear regularly in* In-Fisherman's *annual* Catfish In-Sider Guide. *An astute catfish angler, Schmidt has a knack for keeping live baitfish for catfishing. Here he offers advice for maintaining healthy baits at home and on the water.*

The choicest baitfish species are often the trickiest to keep alive long enough to present on hook and line. If keeping the best baits were easy, everyone would do it, and there would be fewer big cats swimming today.

A few forage species stand out from the masses of everyday baits. It's hard to beat a spry 4- to 6-inch gizzard shad for big blues, for instance. Yet, prized baits like shad are among the most difficult bait species to keep healthy.

Top catfish guides from the Mid-south say that live skipjack herring

Cory Schmidt

could be the king of all livebaits, if anyone knew how to keep this delicate, delectable baitfish alive. Legendary Cumberland River guide Ralph Dallas has cracked the skipjack code, though he won't

A well-aerated bait tank is one key to healthy baitfish.

tell us his bait-tank setup, worried that other anglers will use the information and harvest too many bull stripers, his favorite fish.

Consider yourself lucky if your catfish love bullheads, sunfish, or carp. These hearty species are the easiest to keep in captivity, as they tolerate warm water and dissolved oxygen as low as 2 to 3 ppm (parts per million). The reward's in keeping those fragile baits that few anglers know how to keep.

BAITFISH BIOLOGY

Oxygen and temperature are the two most critical factors affecting baitfish survival. In its dissolved form, oxygen is necessary for fish respiration. Levels of at least 5 ppm are suitable for most baitfish, with many species becoming oxygen-stressed at levels below 3 or 4 ppm and dying below about 2 ppm.

All fish have a preferred temperature range, but the most common baitfish species can survive over a wide range of temperatures. Many can survive near-freezing temperatures, while upper-temperature tolerance varies by species.

An important consideration with temperature, however, is its relationship to fish metabolism and dissolved oxygen. Cooler water holds more oxygen. It also slows fish metabolism, which lowers oxygen consumption. Slow metabolism reduces stress and calms baitfish, reducing injury inside your baitwell. In warm water, supercharged baitfish bang into walls, pumps, and hoses, losing scales and excreting waste products that foul water quality.

Even in a system with adequate oxygen, water flow, and temperature, poor water quality can have a devastating effect on baitfish. In longer-term home storage tanks, ammonia, a by-product of fish waste, is a common cause of baitfish mortality when it reaches toxic levels. Keeping water temperatures below 60°F reduces the potential for ammonia toxicity. Commercial additives, such as Sure

---

Life No-Mmonia, help reduce ammonia levels, as well as other factors contributing to poor water quality, like chlorine and nitrites.

Avoiding bait overcrowding, frequently replacing old water, and removing solid wastes are also important in maintaining good water quality. Agricultural mixing salts (non-iodized) help too, as they reduce fish stress, protect slime coats, and lower chances for disease. A good recipe is about a cup of salt per 20 gallons of water.

HOME BAIT SYSTEMS

Some anglers catch or buy enough bait for each day's fishing, while others collect and keep enough for several future trips. Bait dealers say that cool, recirculated water is key for holding baits long-term. Most bait dealers use commercial systems equipped with chiller units that refrigerate water, but refrigerated systems typically aren't practical or affordable for most anglers.

Some of the better home-fashioned bait tanks I've seen use the natural cooling properties of the earth. Placing tanks in an underground root cellar, for example, keeps water cool in the warmer months and prevents freezing during winter. My earth-insulated garage stays cool in summer and warm in winter, and for many years, it's where I've kept a 120-gallon livestock tank filled with dozens of different bait species.

Stock tanks are durable, relatively inexpensive, and constructed with a smooth oval interior that won't damage swimming baitfish. To soften rough surfaces, I coat the inside of my tank with the leftover contents of a spray-on truck bedliner. The dark color of the bedliner keeps baits calmer than does a brighter interior.

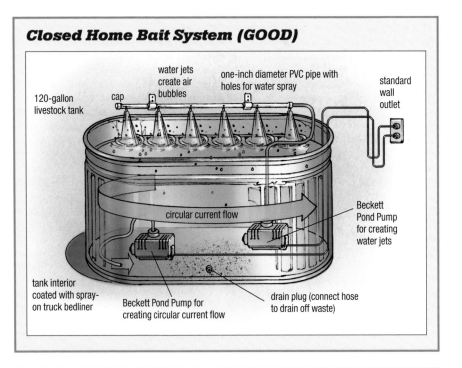

Closed Home Bait System (GOOD)

120-gallon livestock tank

cap

water jets create air bubbles

one-inch diameter PVC pipe with holes for water spray

standard wall outlet

circular current flow

Beckett Pond Pump for creating water jets

tank interior coated with spray-on truck bedliner

Beckett Pond Pump for creating circular current flow

drain plug (connect hose to drain off waste)

Open Recirculating Bait System (BEST)

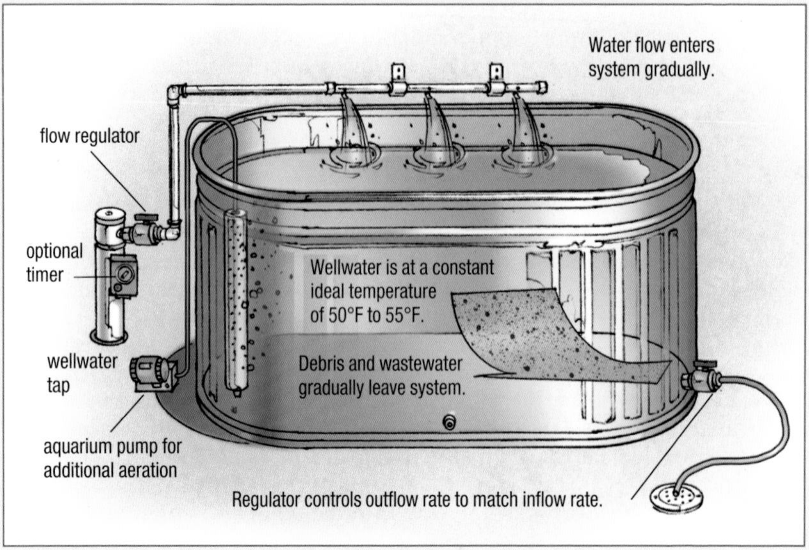

Water flow enters system gradually.

flow regulator

optional timer

Wellwater is at a constant ideal temperature of 50°F to 55°F.

wellwater tap

Debris and wastewater gradually leave system.

aquarium pump for additional aeration

Regulator controls outflow rate to match inflow rate.

Even if kept cold, all bait tanks eventually need replenishing with fresh water. A good way is to attach a pump and hose to your home's well-water system (if you have one). Tapped into an independent rural well, you can use a flow regulator to pump a slow, steady stream of fresh, cool, non-chlorinated water into the bait tank. On my tank, a drain on the bottom allows me to attach a hose that empties wastewater along with debris that collects on bottom.

If you can't connect to a well system, frequent water change is needed. Be careful when using city water, as it usually contains chlorine that can kill baitfish. If you have to use municipal water, let it stand in the tank for 24 to 48 hours before adding fish; let replenishing water stand in containers before adding it to an existing system, or use a dechlorinating additive such as Sure Life LCR.

During all but the two warmest months of the year, my system keeps bait healthy. When my garage exceeds 70°F, I completely flush and refill the tank weekly. This is also a good time to add mixing salt to the tank.

To meet the oxygen and waterflow needs of baits like wild redhorse suckers, I run two pumps (Beckett DP140) designed for decorative backyard ponds. They retail for around $80, cycle up to 160 gallons per hour, operate on a standard wall power supply, and connect to a foam filter kit that helps maintain water quality. At water temperatures above 65°F, it's necessary to monitor filters closely. Rotate badly soiled filters with clean spares that cost a few dollars each.

At the end of one pump is a 2-foot section of 1/2-inch tubing, which sits on the bottom of the tank to create a swirling current. The second pump shoots streams of water through a 3-foot piece of 1-inch PVC. The PVC has about ten holes drilled along its length, with a cap at the far end. This forces water out through the holes into the tank, creating lots of tiny aeration bubbles.

Depending on the bait species, it's often necessary to remove one of the pumps: Delicate bait such as shad thrive in tanks with a moderate circular flow but can

Oxygen Systems

In the process of caring for bait-fish, dissolved oxygen remains the most critical variable. According to David Kinser of Oxygenation Systems of Texas, "The problem with standard livewell pumps is that although they deliver high volumes of air bubbles into the water, fish don't breathe air—they breathe oxygen.

"Air contains only about 20 percent actual oxygen. In warm water (75°F to 85°F and above), even the highest-flow aerators may only raise dissolved oxygen levels by 2 to 3 parts per million." For delicate baits like gizzard shad or skipjack herring, this isn't enough oxygen. These species require at least 6 ppm and sometimes as much as 12 ppm to remain healthy for sustained periods.

The answer lies in using a system that infuses water with pure oxygen. A top option is the Oxygen Edge by Oxygenation Systems. The Oxygen Edge saturates bait water using tanks of pure compressed oxygen. According to Kinser, unlike other systems, the Oxygen Edge actually lets you regulate oxygen flow into your baitwell. "Oxygen concentration should chiefly depend on fish density, because ten dozen shad require much more oxygen than two dozen."

Use the simple formula in the instructions to achieve optimal

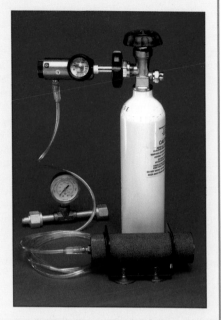

oxygen concentrations. In addition to longterm bait storage, this system lets you temporarily kick up oxygen dosage to "supercharge" baits with supersaturated water—an insider trick that saltwater anglers use to shift their baits into turbo mode.

Regardless of which oxygen system you use, it's vital also to agitate the water with an aerator to release potentially harmful carbon dioxide and nitrogen gas. A buildup of either of these can kill baitfish, even if the water is otherwise of optimal quality.

be killed easily by strong jets of water. For delicate baits, I replace the PVC sprayer pump with a large aquarium pump that adds gentle bubbles. If there's still too much current, I remove the current-producing pump and hose.

While my system has allowed me to keep up to 6 dozen 10-inch wild suckers and chubs for several months, it isn't without disadvantages. The pumps themselves get warm and can raise water temperature by several degrees. This makes frequent water changes even more critical, particularly in the warmer months.

BAIT IN THE BOAT

It's a shame to work hard keeping a cache of wild bait at home for months, only to have most of it die during your first hour on the water. Many good quality, affordable portable tanks are readily available to keep bait healthy while afield.

KeepAlive makes tank systems for boats from 10 to 30 gallons. Ruggedly built, the tanks use a submerged pump that draws air through a tube and mixes it into the current created by the pump. They also offer the Nite-Glo tank, which illuminates the tank interior with a glow to help find baits at night.

The AquaWorld Super Tank Plus, another good option, employs a Reverse Flow system that adds fresh water near the top of the tank, pushing harmful debris to the bottom, where it's flushed through an outtake and over the boat's transom. The Super Tank Plus is available from 8 to 24 gallons.

It's important to temper bait-tank water so that baitfish are acclimated to the temperature of water where they're fished. Holding fish in 60°F baitwell water and then casting them into a 75°F river almost certainly will shock and kill them. Fish slowly acclimate to changes in water temperature, so it's best to slowly cool or warm the tank water to avoid such trauma.

Gradually cooling the water with handfuls of non-chlorinated ice or frozen bottles of water can prolong bait survival. Still, it's critical to monitor water temperature, keeping the water in the bait tank within 10°F of the water body. A cheap aquarium thermometer can be used to measure temperatures.

Another item to try is AquaWorld's Superbag, a softsided, in-water baitwell that fits over the transom, leaving more room in the boat. It's supported by a rigid frame at the top and attaches to a recirculating pump.

In addition to a quality recirculating baitwell, one of the best bait-keeping tools is a soft, collapsible livebait bag. While fishing from an anchored position or on a slow drift, I often use Lindy Legendary Fishing Tackle's 30-gallon Bait Tamer to hold a dozen or so good-sized baits. When I need a fresh bait, it's easy to grab the Bait Tamer, drain the water, and snatch the bait I want. A bag keeps baitfish in the same water they'll be fished in, which almost guarantees a lively bait on the hook. Watch out for hungry turtles eyeing bait in softbags, though.

Keeping livebait healthy takes some effort and know-how, but the rewards are worth it. Take care of your soldiers, and they'll catch you more catfish.

Prepared Baits

DIPS, DOUGHS, CHUM AND BLOOD

Ask the manufacturers of commercial catfish baits, like Catfish Charlie, Cat Tracker, Bowker's, Sonny's, Sure-Shot, Magic Bait, and others, about their ingredients, and the universal response is a long silence. Persistent prying yields only generic hints like "shad flavoring" and "sour cheese," or mysterious codenames such as "TC Secret 7" or "Formula #148." Recipes are guarded as closely as Donald Trump's Swiss bank account numbers.

"I keep the formula pretty much in my head," says Bob Hosch, owner of Doc's Catfish Bait, Parkersburg, Iowa. "I think my secretary, Frances, could probably mix up a batch if she had to, because she's helped a lot over the years. Good

Bait Carriers

sponge rig

doughbait hook

fiber dip rig

plastic dipworm

luck trying to get the formula out of her, though. If I forgot it, I'm not sure she'd tell me what it is."

Even if an angler could deduce the secret ingredients, there's more to creating a successful catfish bait than its core components. "It's not just the secret formula," says Sonny Hootman, owner of Sonny's Catfish Traps and Bait, another Iowa manufacturer. "The specific flavors are critical, but how I make it is just as important as what's in it." Hootman followed the path of many commercial catfish bait manufacturers on his road to success. A self-described "river rat," he tinkered with homemade baits for years. As the efficacy of his baits evolved, so did their popularity with friends and local anglers.

An epiphany sent Hootman on a quest: "I got to thinking. If I could sell a pound or two a year to 40 or 50 local guys, why not sell a pound or two a year to 40,000 or 50,000 people around the country? So I started researching to figure out how to make the best bait possible. I studied books and pestered all sorts of people in the food industry, trying to learn not only what should be in the bait, but how to mix and process it to get the results I wanted. I finally hit it bigtime—I found a lady who told me some stuff about food processing that made it all work. She didn't know she told me the secret, because it was the way I used her information to make my bait that made the difference. But that lady made me a wealthy man."

Most bait manufacturers acknowledge that commercial catfish baits can be big business. Some companies, like Catfish Charlie or Magic Bait, are family operations that support extended families. "My grandfather and dad started the company in my grandmother's kitchen when Dad was 16 years old," says Scotty Hampton of Magic Bait. "Grandma was real happy when they got big enough to move it to their garage. Now we work out of a big plant, and the whole family is involved. It's an interesting business that's been good to us."

Another garage-born bait business is now the self-described largest prepared-bait manufacturer in the U.S. Rusty's Bait started out in Rusty Ryan's garage 54 years ago. Seventy-eight-year-old Ryan still fishes a lot to develop new baits. "Charlie" Poe, company manager, says their product line long ago outgrew Ryan's tiny garage. "It's a multimillion-dollar business," she says. "But we're still selling one of the baits that got him started, Rusty's Big Dipper Sponge Bait."

Rusty's takes a different tack than other catfish bait manufacturers and offers not only dough- and dipbaits but also preserved crawdads, minnows, shad, and other natural baits. "Other than blood coloring added to the Bloody Shad,

Dipworms and Sponges

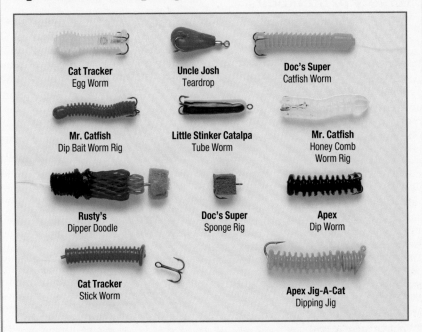

Cat Tracker
Egg Worm

Uncle Josh
Teardrop

Doc's Super
Catfish Worm

Mr. Catfish
Dip Bait Worm Rig

Little Stinker Catalpa
Tube Worm

Mr. Catfish
Honey Comb
Worm Rig

Rusty's
Dipper Doodle

Doc's Super
Sponge Rig

Apex
Dip Worm

Cat Tracker
Stick Worm

Apex Jig-A-Cat
Dipping Jig

■ The Apex Jig-A-Cat Dipping Jig is a single-hook jig method for catching big blue and channel catfish with stinkbaits. Apex also offers the Dip Worm.

■ Cat Tracker merchandises four styles of dipworms in a variety of colors: The Stick Worm is for lakes and average current flows in streams, Egg Worm is for heavy currents, Tubie Worm is for extra strong currents around locks and dams, and Tubie 2000 can be purchased with either a single or treble hook.

■ Doc's Catfish Bait Company sells the Super Catfish Worm in seven different colors and the Super Sponge Rig.

■ Uncle Josh manufactures the Little Stinker Catalpa Tube Worm, the Mr. Catfish Dip Bait Worm Rig, and the Little Stinker Teardrop. They also offer the Mr. Catfish Honey Comb Worm Rig.

■ Rusty's Bait Company has three devices for dipbaits: Dipper Doodle Sponge Rig, Stink Hole Rig, and Sponge Hook Rig.

they're all-natural baits," Poe says. "Convenience is the driving force behind those baits. People don't have time, or don't know how, or don't want the mess of getting their own live- or natural baits. We do all the work, so all they have to do is buy a package of our crawdads or shad and go fishing."

THE EVOLUTION OF STINKBAITS

Doughbaits—concoctions that are kneaded into balls and pressed onto treble hooks—are the grandfathers of all prepared catfish baits. The first commercial doughs appeared in the 1920s. Dipbaits and punchbaits are the second

Gallery of Stinkbaits

There are hundreds of manufacturers of prepared catfish baits in the U.S. Some work out of their garages and concoct 10 to 50 gallons of bait per year for friends and neighbors. Others, like Catfish Charlie, Magic Bait, and Cat Tracker, measure their monthly production in tons. Without preference for region or size, here's a sampling of well-known catfish bait manufacturers and their varied offerings:

MAGIC BAIT:
Both dough- and dipbaits are available in liver, cheese, Premo Super Sticky, Hog Wild, and Big Bite. King Kat Chicken Blood and other flavors are offered as cubed doughbaits. "It's about convenience," says Magic Bait's Scotty Hampton. "When I fish, I use our Big Bite doughbait, but then, it doesn't bother me to get it on my hands. Other guys like to use the preformed cubes—it's less messy and more convenient."
Contact: *magicbait.com*, 800/259-8040.

CATFISH CHARLIE:
Buddy Holub and his family continue to improve bait formulas and add new products. "Catfish Charlie Blood Dough Bait is still our number one bait, but Full Stringer Wild Cat Chicken Liver is getting popular," says

Buddy's wife Eileen, company VP. "We use real chicken livers to make the liver baits, in a cheese-bait base, so you get the best of two worlds." Catfish Charlie also offers shad, beef blood, and cheese in their dip- and doughbait lineups.
Contact: 641/673-7229.

BOWKER'S:
A regional favorite that has earned national recognition. Available as Original cheese-based, Blood-Added, Shad-Added, Shrimp-Added dipbaits, as well as pre-formed Catfish Bits. "The shad and shrimp flavors seem to do better in cooler climates and when the water is cool," says Roger Belohlavy, company owner. "It's not the consistency—it's something about the actual shrimp and shad ingredients that disperse better than cheese or blood when water temperatures aren't especially warm." **Contact:** *bowkersbait.com*, 402/826-2516.

DOC'S:
"Dr. Schaulk, a catfisherman and veterinarian in Alden, Iowa, developed the original Doc's catfish bait back in 1927," says Bob Hosch. Hosch's father purchased the company in the late '70s, and his son soon took over the business. "It's pretty much the same basic recipe, but we've added and refined things as we've found ingredients that make it better," he says. "Guys are pretty loyal to our product, and we don't like to tinker with something that already works really well."
Contact: *docscatfish.com*, 800/747-3627.

BERKLEY:
Berkley's Gulp! water-soluble softbaits are available in chicken liver and other catfish-attracting flavors. The flavor of real chicken livers, enhanced by unique oils and other flavors found to be attractive specifically to catfish, allowed

Gulp! baits often to outperform real chicken livers and other natural catfish baits in field trials. **Contact:** *berkleyfishing.com.*

UNCLE JOSH: The Uncle Josh brand includes Little Stinker and Mr. Catfish. Little Stinker products are designed as a catfishing system. Anglers use squeeze tubes of liver, shad, catalpa worm, and other flavors to inject the bait paste into a Little Stinker Catfish Lure, which is made from a soft rubber "egg" around a built-in hook. Slits in the egg allow the formula to bleed into the water; the soft rubber egg collapses and exposes the hook when catfish grab the bait. Mr. Catfish doughbaits come in cheese and other popular flavors. **Contact:** *unclejosh.com, 866/244-2277.*

EAGLE CLAW NITRO BAITS:
Nitro Biscuits are doughbait cubes in cheese, liver, shad, and other flavors. Nitro Gravy is a liquid that contains Nitro's secret formula, Factor X-2, as well as fish-attracting pheromones. Dip

Nitro Biscuits in Nitro Gravy and you serve catfish Biscuits and Gravy. Some anglers inject Nitro Gravy into live- or cutbait to enhance a bait's potency. "This isn't a guessing game," says Nitro Product Manager Lisa Villani. "Our catfish baits are designed specifically for catfish, with ingredients that we've proven attract catfish." **Contact:** *nitrobait.com, 303/321-1481.*

RUSTY'S:
While Rusty's offers doughbaits, their specialty is packaged natural baits: chicken livers, shad sides/cut shad, cheese-flavored chicken livers, baby shad, eels, minnows, crawdads, and other variations on natural baits. "We save people the time of catching and transporting their own natural livebaits," says Charlie Poe, Rusty's manager. **Contact:** *rustysbait.com, 620/842-5301.*

CAT TRACKER: The Mihalakis clan, based on the Mississippi River in Dubuque, Iowa, offers 8 or more varieties of dipbait,

including Wicked Sticky cheese bait, Sewer Bait, Blood Bait, Almost Illegal Shrimp Bait, and Shad Bait. They also offer a complete line of dipbait worms and catfish-specific tackle. **Contact:** *cattracker.com,* 888/248-9183.

SONNY'S:
Few catfish baits have followers more loyal or vociferous than Sonny's. Offered only as dipbait. "Guys that think dipbaits are too messy aren't real catfishermen," says Sonny Hootman, the colorful and somewhat opinionated founder and owner of Sonny's. **Contact:** 319/878-4115.

TEAM CATFISH:
Jeff Williams' new line of catfishing products includes TC-Secret 7 Catfish Dip Bait and Dead Red Blood Spray. "TC-Secret-7 is the ingredient that makes our dipbait so effective," Williams says. "A catfisherman who was also a chemist formulated the recipe. I developed Dead Red to reactivate cutbaits that get washed out." **Contact:** *teamcatfish.com,* 866/466-5738.

generation of prepared catfish baits, more liquid to get flavor into the water faster. Dipbaits require the use of dipworms, foam hook covers, or other devices to absorb or hold this juicier bait on a hook.

Punchbaits are a southern alternative to dip-baits, an answer to the bait-liquefying temperatures common to a hot summer day in the South. Punchbaits contain ingredients that stiffen their consistency, making them less prone to puddling at high temperatures. Anglers use a stick to punch a bare treble hook into a tub of punch-bait. When the hook is pulled from the tub, the glob of bait clinging to the hook is stiff enough to cast into the water, where it slowly dissolves to disperse scent and flavor.

Dip- and punchbaits have dominated the commercial catfish bait market in recent years. "The big challenge with dipbaits is keeping enough on the hook to satisfy the angler," says Mark Mihalakis, Cat Tracker manager. "If they reel in their line and there's no dipbait left on the rubber dipworm, they think it's not working. But the bait was washed off when they pulled the worm through the water reeling it in. All the bait manufacturers are now trying to make the stickiest baits they can, so they stay on the hook but are still liquid enough to milk off and put lots of flavor in the water to attract fish."

Doughbaits and preformed dough balls are popular with anglers who prefer not to deal with applying and maintaining dipbaits. Magic Bait's number one seller is chicken-liver-flavored dough cubes. Catfish Charlie's Blood Dough Bait is their top seller, too.

Berkley's Gulp! bait technology incorporates meticulously researched attractants incorporated into water-soluble, biodegradable softbaits. "We've done extensive research with catfish in tanks as well as with wild catfish, and identified flavors and chemicals they respond to," says John Prochnow, product innovation manager for Berkley. "We've created baits that not only have the attraction of chicken liver, shad, or other natural baits, but they've also got those extra fish attractants we've identified, in a formulation that disperses in the water better than real liver or shad. The result is baits that outfish liver or shad in many side-by-side field comparisons."

REGIONAL FAVORITES

There is no one-flavor-fits-all to catfish bait. Manufacturers are well aware of regional preferences. "In the Santee-Cooper area, we can't get them to use anything except our Sewer Bait," said Cat Tracker's Mihalakis. "Here in the Midwest, it's Wicked Sticky. Down in the Tennessee Valley Authority lakes region, they want shad-flavored bait."

Magic Bait's Hampton notes that anglers in Texas and Oklahoma prefer blood-flavored prepared baits, while California catmen opt for clam-formula Magic

Bait. Hosch, with Doc's, agrees that blood-based baits sell well down South, but says his cheese-flavored baits sell better in the Upper Midwest.

The search to develop a universally popular catfish bait is the Holy Grail for bait manufacturers. Hootman, Mihalakis, and Frances Krull do regular and exhaustive "research" to test and develop new bait for their respective companies.

Krull is the receptionist, secretary, and overall Girl Friday at Doc's Catfish Bait Company. "Some mornings, she's late for work because she's been down at the river fishing," says her boss, Hosch. "She takes a lot of long lunch hours, and it's nothing for her to walk into the office carrying a stringer of 3- to 5-pound channel cats. I'd name her chief of my Research and Development Department, if I had an R&D department."

> *"Taste it and tell me what you think is in it, and I'll tell you if you're right."*

Berkley's Prochnow notes that there are chemicals that could revolutionize commercial catfish baits. "Our research has uncovered a number of compounds that are attractive to catfish," he says. "One, in particular, would make a revolutionary catfish bait, but the product is so expensive that no catfisherman would pay the price we'd have to put on it."

Eagle Claw's Lisa Villani says her company also has discovered a powerful but pricey chemical that they'd like to add to their Nitro prepared catfish baits. "Experimental batches of bait we formulated using that product outfished our current Nitro baits, and were three times better than any of our competitor's baits in side-by-side, in-the-field testing," she says. "But that secret ingredient is currently just too expensive to incorporate in our baits."

So we're back to secret ingredients, the core of any prepared catfish bait. When it comes down to the exact formulas manufacturers use to make their specific baits irresistible, they offer few clues. Catfish Charlie's Buddy Holub, under pressure, finally conceded to helping curious anglers and competitors deduce his secret formula: "Taste it and tell me what you think is in it, and I'll tell you if you're right."

THE DIPWORM DILEMMA

What's the best size, style, and color of dipworm to use with dipbait? According to manufacturers of dipbait and veteran anglers who use it, the answer is: Never more than 1 inch in length, but never less than 4. The ribs on a dipworm should always be deep, except when they're shallow. The color of a dipworm makes absolutely no difference, unless it makes a difference.

Confused? Don't feel bad. Finding the best delivery system for the latest generation of dipbaits depends on a variety of factors and angler preferences. Here are some of the variables to consider.

RIBBED VERSUS SURGICAL TUBING VERSUS SPONGE

"A dipbait worm needs to match the viscosity of the dipbait you're using," says Berkley's John Prochnow. "If you have a thin, runny dipbait that dissolves easily in water, you need either a sponge worm or a tube worm. If the dipbait is thicker and stickier, you need a ribbed worm that sheds the bait easily."

Depth of ribs on dipworms isn't as significant as the type and condition of "rubber" that the worms are made of. Ribbed dipworms actually are made of PVC plastic, with plasticizers added to keep the worms supple.

Rigging Options for Dipworms

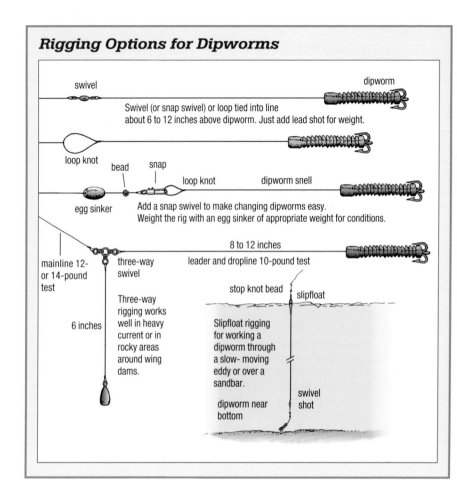

swivel

dipworm

Swivel (or snap swivel) or loop tied into line about 6 to 12 inches above dipworm. Just add lead shot for weight.

loop knot

bead   snap

loop knot   dipworm snell

egg sinker

Add a snap swivel to make changing dipworms easy. Weight the rig with an egg sinker of appropriate weight for conditions.

8 to 12 inches

mainline 12- or 14-pound test

three-way swivel

leader and dropline 10-pound test

stop knot bead   slipfloat

6 inches

Three-way rigging works well in heavy current or in rocky areas around wing dams.

Slipfloat rigging for working a dipworm through a slow- moving eddy or over a sandbar.

dipworm near bottom

swivel

shot

Tube-type dipworms are made of a different type of plastic, but both have shiny, oily-looking surfaces.

Those shiny chemicals on the surface of a worm can make it difficult for dipbait to adhere. Prochnow recommends washing shiny dipworms in a bath of warm water and a little dish soap. Rinse them in clean water to remove any traces of soap. In the field, he suggests blotting worms dry with a paper towel or cloth to remove any water, to improve dipbait adhesion when dipworms are poked into bait tubs.

Many dipbait manufacturers dislike foam dipworms because the sponge rubber tends to soak up water and releases the bait too rapidly. Wayne Scheffsky, owner of W-D-3 Baits in Geneseo, Illinois, agrees that foam dipbait worms must be selected carefully. "I make my dipworms from a special type of rubberized silicone sponge with fibers embedded in it," Scheffsky says. "I prefer that sponge material because it lets my dipworms float even after they've been loaded with dipbait. I want my bait floating right at eye level when catfish come cruising by, looking for the source of the scent and flavor particles released by the bait."

SIZE MATTERS

Length of dipworms is another source of discussion for dipbait manufacturers and users. "Some guys cut my worms in half because they want short worms, and others string two worms together because they want the longest worm possible," says Bob Hosch.

Everybody agrees that longer worms hold more dipbait, which puts more flavor in the water per cast. And everybody agrees that more flavor attracts more catfish. The argument is in the way catfish bite dipworms of various lengths. Buddy and Eileen Holub prefer a 1½- to 1¾-inch dipworm so a catfish can swallow it in one gulp. "If the worm is too big, cats will pick it up by one end and carry it before they swallow it," Eileen says. "They seem to pick up and gulp shorter worms in one bite, so they're easier to hook."

Rick Gebhardt of Glasgow, Missouri, chases catfish for up to 100 days each year on the Missouri River. He agrees that length of dipworms affects how catfish bite, but he swears that longer worms yield better hookups. "Cats tend to take dipworms in a big gulp," he says. "That means a longer worm puts the hook farther into their mouth when they take it. I've noticed that the

Does Color Matter?

Most dipbait manufacturers believe that color makes a difference. Many anglers think enough of color, though, that most manufacturers offer dipworms in a rainbow of shades. Experience suggests that water clarity is the most important factor in determining the effect of color, but confidence also plays a role.

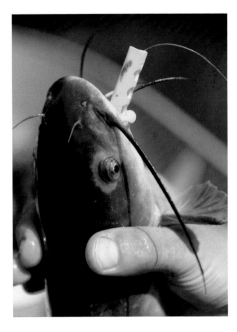

longer the worm, the deeper in the throat the fish tend to be hooked."

COLOR CATCHES CATFISH

Gebhardt also swears that the color of a dipworm makes a difference. He began using dipworms 30 years ago, when Devil Worms first hit the market. "Every package had two colors of worms, red and black," he recalls. "The black worms always outfished the red worms nine to one. It got to the point that when we got a package of those worms, we'd throw the red worms away."

He still favors dark dipworms in most situations, but notes that comparatively clear water conditions in the Missouri River last summer allowed white dipworms to outfish darker colors. "The fish were feeding on shad, and I think when the water is clear the fish learn to associate the color white with shad," he says. "I've also done well with chartreuse, and I've noticed in catfish tournaments that orange dipworms work better on cloudy days, for some reason I haven't figured out yet."

Mark Mihalakis isn't picky about what color dipworm he uses when he catfishes (and he catfishes frequently as he researches new baits), but offers dipworms to customers in a variety of colors because anglers [like Gebhardt] believe that color counts.

"If a dipbait is working like it should, about 20 percent of the bait washes off the dipworm before it reaches the bottom," Mihalakis says. "That's good, because it means that a lot of flavor is dissolved into the water to attract fish. But it also means that some of the dipworm is exposed, so color could become a factor."

Short versus long. Ribbed versus sponge. Dark versus light. It seems like modern dipbaits catch catfish no matter what configuration, color, or delivery system is used. The difference is what each angler believes works best—confidence remains a key factor for consistent fishing.

DIPWORM TRICKS

Looking for options, some anglers tinker to make their own blue-ribbon bait holders.

Stange's Modification: Years ago, *In-Fisherman* Editor In Chief Doug Stange proposed a simple modification to commercially available dipworms: Replacing the treble hook with a circle hook. "Dipworms with trebles work well to catch catfish, but catfish often take trebles deeper into their gullet, which can injure or kill fish, narrowing options for selective harvest," he says. "Most dipworms come snelled. It's just a matter of pulling the treble out, clipping it off, tying on a circle hook, and pulling the shank back up into the worm.

"Hookup rates are good with circle hooks," Stange notes, "and catfish are almost always hooked shallow, making for easier hook removal and greater

Stange's Modification

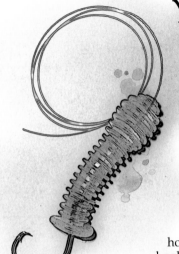

Years ago, *In-Fisherman* Editor In Chief Doug Stange proposed a simple modification to commercially available dipworms: Replacing the treble hook with a circle hook.

"Dipworms with trebles work well to catch catfish, but catfish often take trebles deeper into their gullet, which can injure or kill fish, narrowing options for selective harvest," he says. "Most dipworms come snelled. It's just a matter of pulling the treble out, clipping it off, tying on a circle hook, and pulling the shank back up into the worm.

"Hookup rates are good with circle hooks, and catfish are almost always hooked shallow, making for easier hook removal and greater survival. A 1/0 circle hook, like Eagle Claw's Lazer Sharp L7228, works well on most worms. I like hooks with a larger gap to handle the bulk of the dipworm and still leave room for hookups."

survival. A 1/0 circle hook, like Eagle Claw's Lazer Sharp L7228, works well on most worms. I like hooks with a larger gap to handle the bulk of the dip-worm and still leave room for hookups."

Marks' Bait Holder: Wally Marks, Greendale, Wisconsin, makes his own tubular bait holders with circle hooks. "I prefer tubular bait holders over dipworms," he says, "and a circle hook substantially reduces gut-hooking. I insert the hook into the lead end of the dipworm instead of on the back end. The hook should barely catch the leading edge. Tapering the end leaves a suitable hook gap without obstruction from the bait holder. "I make bait holders from soft latex tubing—3/8 inch outside diameter and 1/4 inch inside—available at home improvement stores. Pinch the tubing and cut out semicircles to make round holes, or make two straight cuts for diamond-shaped openings.

"I use the Owner #1 Mutu Light Circle hook. My overall experience in small Wisconsin rivers is catching as many 14- to 26-inch channel cats with the circle hook as I used to with trebles on the back end of the rig," says Marks. "I also catch fewer catfish under 14 inches than before. Catfish are rarely gut-hooked. Aside from the satisfaction of catch-and-release fishing, you also get fewer snags," he adds.

McKay's Dipworm: Kirk McKay, Winnetka, California, a contributor to In-Fisherman publications, says he's tried just about every kind of dipbait rigging out there. "I've had great success on a homemade dipbait rig for channel catfish. I save torn-up worms from bass fishing to make it. Ribbed soft-plastic worms tend to work best to hold dipbaits—I've found that channel catfish like baits soft and chewy.

"I often use Phenix worms for bass, and they work well on the dipbait rig," he says. "The worms are soft and salt-impregnated. Threaded on a circle hook as shown (I use a 4/0 Owner Mutu Circle hook), fished on a 3-way rig, and dipped in a nice warm tub of Hog Wild or Bowker's, it's the most consistent thing I've found for channel cats. A rod in a holder catches just as many cats as when I'm holding the rod."

CHUM DOCTORS

To most catfishermen, chumming means scattering fermented soybeans, wheat, or milo around a covert to attract catfish or to stimulate those in the area to feed. Besides fermented grains, some anglers in Texas opt for cottonseed cakes, which are manufactured from the residue of cottonseeds after most of the oil has been removed.

Cottonseed cakes are expensive, however, and at many locales, they aren't readily available. Consequently, some anglers use 20-percent range cubes, which

---

Marks' Bait Holder

Wally Marks, Greendale, Wisconsin, makes his own tubular bait holders with circle hooks. "I prefer tubular bait holders over dipworms," he says, "and a circle hook substantially reduces gut-hooking. I insert the hook into the lead end of the dipworm instead of on the back end. The hook should barely catch the leading edge. Tapering the end leaves suitable hook gap without obstruction from the bait holder.

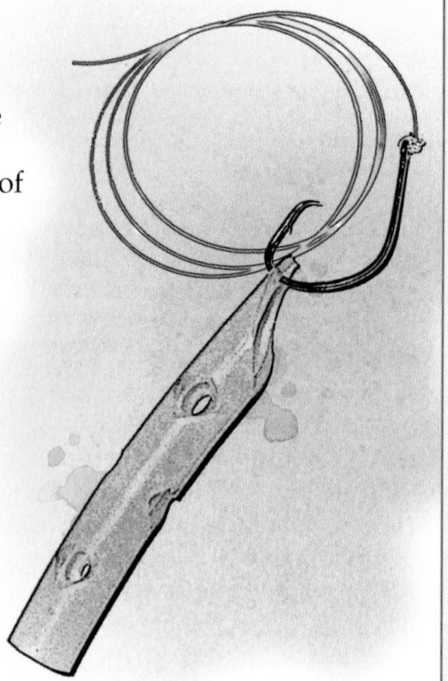

"I make bait holders from soft latex tubing, 3/8 inch outside diameter and 1/4 inch inside diameter, available at home improvement stores. Pinch the tubing and cut out semicircles to make round holes, or make two straight cuts for diamond-shaped holes.

"I use the Owner #1 Mutu Light Circle hook. My overall experience in small Wisconsin rivers is catching as many 14- to 26-inch channel cats with the circle hook as I used to with trebles on the back end of the rig. I also catch fewer catfish less than 14 inches than before. Catfish are rarely gut-hooked. Aside from the satisfaction of catch-and-release fishing, you also get fewer snags."

McKay's Dipworm

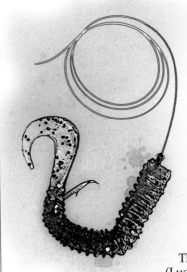

Kirk McKay, Winnetka, California, a contributor to In-Fisherman publications, says he's tried just about every kind of dipbait rigging out there. "I've had great success on a homemade dipbait rig for channel catfish. I save torn up worms from bass fishing to make it. Ribbed soft-plastic worms tend to work best to hold dipbaits. I've found that channel catfish like baits soft and chewy.

"I often use Phenix worms for bass, and they work well on the dipbait rig," he says. "The worms are soft and salt-impregnated. Threaded on a circle hook as shown (I use a 4/0 Owner Mutu Circle hook), fished on a 3-way rig, and dipped in a nice warm tub of Hog Wild or Bowker's, it's the most consistent thing I've found for channel cats. A rod in a holder catches just as many cats as when I'm holding the rod."

are big pellets containing a number of ingredients including alfalfa and cottonseed meal. A 50-pound bag of 20-percent range cubes, available at many feed stores, costs about $6.

Cottonseed cakes and range cubes aren't offensively odiferous, and that appeals to anglers who find spending a day afloat with a 5-gallon bucket of rank soybeans to be a miserable ordeal. Yet, to devotees of foul-smelling chum, it's the redolence of the fermented grains that attracts channel catfish and stimulates them to feed. These anglers gladly endure the smell to reap the benefits it renders.

RESERVOIRS, RIVERS, RECIPES

On a map of the U.S., draw a line from slightly north of Topeka, Kansas, southward to Laredo, Texas. There lies the axis of the chumming world for channel catfish anglers.

Reservoirs have been the domain of channel catfish chummers, and the roots of this can be traced back at least four decades. But some folks recall that as long ago as the late 1940s and early 1950s, anglers at the Lake of the Ozarks in Missouri used cottonseed cakes and grains as chum around their boat docks to attract crappies, carp, and channel cats.

Until 1993, most anglers thought that chumming a riffle or a hole in a river wouldn't work because the current would swiftly wash the chum downstream, limiting its effectiveness. But after the Great Flood of 1993, Wayne Smith and

Catdaddy Shumway, both of Topeka, Kansas, successfully chummed holes and riffles and some runs in the rapidly flowing Kansas River. Their chum was created by mixing chicken or turkey blood with woodchips, allowing it to stew in a 30-gallon barrel until it generated a massive population of maggots.

They deposited several gallons of their chum upstream from lairs that they wanted to ply. As the chum coursed downstream through a spot such as a logjam it activated the channel catfish and an occasional blue. They caught catfish on treble hooks encased in bloodbait presented upstream from the chummed logjam.

Nowadays, Shumway, a catfish guide and tournament angler, uses a chum that he concocts out of ground shad. The fish he catches with it are bigger than those he and Smith caught by using the blood-woodchips-and-maggot mixture. At a hole he chums with ground shad on the Kansas River, for example, Shumway has caught three In-Fisherman Master Angler Award flathead catfish. He's also caught and released from this same hole blues and flatheads weighing from 30 to 88 pounds, belying the notion that chumming only works for small channel cats.

Across Texas, catfish anglers chum streams by placing a fish basket or tow sack partially filled with range cubes in the lair they're fishing. Because the cubes stay intact for up to 3 days, anglers can move them and fish from spot to spot.

Not every chumming site is created by design. At the marinas around Lake Texoma on the Texas-Oklahoma border, for instance, anglers fillet scads of striped and white bass nearly every day. Filleted-out carcasses are tossed into the water, forming a pile of unintentional chum, which attracts Texoma's blue cats. Some blues consistently gambol about the vicinity of the chum heaps, where anglers can tangle with some titans and numbers of smaller fish.

Likewise, channel catfish are caught around docks at Grand Lake, Oklahoma, where anglers dispose of carcasses of filleted crappies and white bass. Shumway's use of ground shad on the Kansas River is a clever way to duplicate Lake Texoma's and Grand Lake's accidental and effective chum sites.

Clyde Holscher, a multispecies guide from Topeka, Kansas, finds that the gizzard shad populations in northeastern Kansas are often meager, making it an arduous task to collect a supply of shad to grind into chum. So, he and the bulk of skillful chummers across northeastern Kansas who pursue channels and small blues in reservoirs employ soybean and milo mixes.

He makes his soybean chum in 5-gallon plastic buckets, each having a lid with a narrow slit cut partway across the top. The slit allows the fermentation gases to escape but also keeps flies out, preventing maggots from developing. Anglers who want maggots in their chum should drill holes in the lids to allow flies to enter the bucket and lay their eggs in the moist, rotting soybeans; maggots develop in 8 to 20 hours during the heat of the summer.

Holscher prefers unadulterated soybean chum, however, a mix that exhibits a golden hue and has a mild aroma. He fills one-third of a bucket with soybeans then fills it with water and secures the lid. He normally begins to chum after it's fermented for just 48 hours, and uses it until the bean color changes from gold to gray. Like many other chummers, Holscher finds that gray soybeans are too rank and not as effective as gold ones. He says that in August, a milo-soybean chum (you can test various mixes) is more effective than one made from pure soybeans, and he makes it the same way as his soybean chum.

WORKING A CHUM SITE

During the summer at Kansas reservoirs, Holscher fishes vertically in deeper water, at times down to 50 feet, pointing out that Dave Schmidtlein of Topeka is the master of the vertical presentation.

Most Kansas chummers use two anchors, one off the bow and another off the transom, but Schmidtlein shuns anchors except when the wind howls. Instead, he works with a bow-mounted electric trolling motor on his Ranger bass boat. Even when the wind roars, he uses only one anchor set off the bow. This one anchor helps tame the wind and waves, keeping his boat on top of the channel catfish covert while he uses his trolling motor to slowly move around and across the spot. He says that the two-anchor system prevents anglers from probing the entire perimeter of a lair, inhibiting them from presenting baits from a variety of angles, which often can be a critical factor.

Schmidtlein prefers 8- to 9-foot light-action rods, similar to 7-weight flyrods, and spools medium-size spinning reels with yellow or chartreuse braided line from 10- to 50-pound test, opting for the heaviest line when he's fishing brushpiles. He's caught significantly more channel catfish since he switched from mono to braided line, he says, adding that the prepared bait he uses elicits soft bites—at times, almost phantom bites. A long, soft-tipped rod makes a good strike indicator when catfish aren't phantom biters, and a good number of soft strikes wouldn't have been detected if he hadn't used braided line, he notes.

Strikes are identified by holding the rod tip several inches above the reel. He routes the line across his forefinger and then runs it between his hand and the rod, and feels 75 percent of the strikes on the braided

line before he detects them on the rod. That scenario seldom occurred, he says, when he used less sensitive monofilament, especially when probing depths of 30 feet or more and battling a pesky wind.

With the long rod, Schmidtlein can slowly lift his bait several feet off the bottom, a deadly way to generate a bite. He says that channel cats regularly bite as the bait rises. Despite the light rod, he has enough leverage for a solid hook-set. In addition to his slow-lift presentation, he finds that deepwater channel cats often suspend, he says, and a longer rod allows him to more easily cover a 10-foot depth zone off bottom. After a major feeding frenzy in summertime, schooling channel cats often suspend 4 to 10 feet off bottom and at times up to 25 feet above it.

Precise depth control and braided line are critical elements of his vertical presentation for suspended fish. He marks his line at 5-foot intervals with a black permanent-ink marker and at 10-foot intervals with a red marker. Yellow and chartreuse hold the marks well, allowing him to determine depth as the bait descends. When he finds how deep fish are biting, he counts the marks on his line to lower baits to that same depth.

To some anglers, bright line scares off fish, he says; but he believes the opposite—that it attracts their attention to the bait. If an angler thinks the bright line is a detriment, a black permanent marker can be used to camouflage the bottom portions of the line.

For terminal tackle, Schmidtlein prefers a #6 heavy-duty treble hook, choosing a #4 if he's catching some catfish that weigh more than 4 pounds. Immediately above the hook, he uses a slipsinker ranging from 1/8 ounce in shallow water to 5/8 ounce in 50 feet of water. At times, however, he finds that the catfish strike better on a sliprig consisting of a slipsinker, a small barrel swivel, and 18 inches of leader, rather than with the sinker resting on the eye of the hook.

When the fish are tentative, he switches to light line without a sinker and a #10 hook. But if there's wind and the fish are deeper than 20 feet, his weightless tactic becomes problematic. It also tends to hook catfish deep in their throats, severely injuring some fish and jeopardizing catch-and-release.

BAITS AND SEASONAL LOCATION

Schmidtlein uses two baits at his chum sites. The first is a punchbait made mostly from fermented cheese, a bait that's soft and contains fibers, with a binding element that helps it adhere to a treble hook. The hook is baited by grasping its

One Chum Recipe

Schmidtlein:

- Wash and rinse soybeans or milo about seven times until the water runs clear.
- Leave the lid slightly ajar on one corner of the bucket, letting the chum ferment for 2 or 3 days in the sun.
- When the water becomes cloudy and the chum emits a bad-beer odor, drain off the liquid, seal the bucket completely or transfer it to an airtight container. Or enclose the bucket inside a couple of heavy trash bags, tying the bags until they're airtight.

Catdaddy Shumway mixing up a batch.

After storing the chum for a year, it has a strong, yeasty, stale-beer odor. The two keys to keeping it for extended periods are getting it clean so it doesn't compost, and removing any sources of oxygen.

shank with a pair of needlenose pliers and sweeping it in a figure-8 motion through a container of bait. In the water, it has a smoky hue, creating a cloud around its periphery that he says is attractive to channel catfish. Moreover, some of the fiber suspends in the water, creating another chumming ingredient. His punchbait is durable, allowing him to garner three bites before he has to rebait. One of the keys to catching a lot of channel catfish, he says, is being able to rebait quickly, which he can do in about 6 seconds with this bait.

The second bait he uses is a doughbait that he makes out of fermented soybeans and other savory ingredients. Some of his colleagues call it Cat Candy and find it offers several advantages: It works for casting and retrieving, especially in current situations; it can make a treble hook snagless when probing brushpiles; and when catfish prefer a weightless presentation, it's often more effective than punchbait. The disadvantage is that channel cats tend to nibble at it.

Schmidtlein says that, overall, his punchbait is more effective than his doughbait. Holscher uses a punchbait called J Pigg Stink Bait and he finds it works better than a doughbait, too. Both anglers chum only during the summer, the best time being from about July 4 until Labor Day. Before that, many of the

Say Yes to chum!

channel catfish in northeastern Kansas reservoirs are scattered, recovering from the rigors of the spawning season. Around July 4, large concentrations of channel cats gather in deep water along the edges of humps, points, and creek channels. As Labor Day approaches, the massive schools begin to disperse.

Early in the summer, Holscher chums points and drop-offs in 15 to 20 feet of water in the vicinity of the best spawning grounds. In August, he and Schmidtlein ply deep midlake humps and channel bends, where Schmidtlein occasionally ventures into depths of 50 feet or more. Then as the Labor Day dispersal takes place, Holscher returns to the points and drop-offs that he fished in early summer.

During a typical day of chumming, Schmidtlein catches about 150 channels. His best outing occurred in the summer of 2005, when he and his two sons caught and released 403 channel catfish. On that day, his sonar revealed a band of channel catfish 18 feet thick along a drop-off that plunged into 35 feet of water.

Holscher doesn't tangle with as many channel catfish as Schmidtlein does, he says, because most of his own clients are novices who don't have Schmidtlein's touch at detecting a bite or setting the hook. Still, he says, it's a rare four-hour outing when two of his clients don't catch and release 100 catfish.

Holscher's found that chumming is a great way to introduce people to the joys of catching catfish. And Holscher agrees with Schmidtlein and Shumway: Chumming expands knowledge of their quarry, even for veteran catfish anglers.

But to Shumway's chagrin, until last year he hadn't been able to chum on the tournament circuits because it was prohibited by event organizers, who proclaimed it to be an unsportsmanlike tactic. Shumway, Schmidtlein, Holscher, and scores of enlightened anglers disagree. To their delight, on August 11, 2007, Ken Freeman's Outdoor Promotions' Big Cat Quest Tournament at Lake Texoma allowed anglers to chum, and in 2008 chumming is allowed at all of the Big Cat Quest events. Perhaps in years to come, Freeman's innovation will also spawn an interest in chumming outside of its traditional domain in Kansas, Oklahoma, and Texas.

BLOODMEN OF THE HIGH PLAINS

Good bait can be difficult to acquire. During midsummer in Kansas reservoirs, for example, gizzard shad can be difficult to catch in a net. Other baits, such as hunks of sour shad or the green worms of the Wakarusa River in Kansas, are so redolent that cat anglers risk being ostracized. And some baits are just plain messy and tricky to use, which probably is an apt description of bloodbait. Moreover, certain governmental health departments have warned that bait made from chicken blood might be a threat to public health, and the U.S. Department of Agriculture even became persnickety about packing plants selling it to baitmakers.

Despite their bait woes, diehard catmen remain undaunted. Not even the federal bureaucracy can put a crimp in their tactics—the good ones always find a way to catch their quarry. And when times become the most trying, catmen who resort to bloodbait usually have the advantage.

Bloodman: Charles France—Starting in 1954 and for 25 years thereafter, Charles France of Wyandotte, Oklahoma, didn't know that Grand Lake channel cats could be caught on anything but congealed chicken blood during the mid-summer drifting season. Back then, France found that blood was more effective than shiners, worms, and chicken livers. Thus, chicken blood was the only bait he used.

Nowadays, bloodbait isn't such an integral part of France's angling repertoire. In 1974 he discovered that a fresh gizzard shad proved a highly effective critter for waylaying Grand Lake channel cats. What's more, shad aren't as difficult or as messy to use as bloodbait.

So, France usually prefers to drift across the gravel flats of Grand Lake with a gizzard shad or two impaled on a 4/0 Eagle Claw #84 hook tied on 12-pound monofilament and weighted with a #7 lead shot. If the shad are 4 or 5 inches long or larger, he uses only one shad. If they're only 2 or 3 inches long, he uses two.

When the water is relatively clear and the gravel flats aren't littered with silt, he can be spied drifting with the wind from early June into November. His favorite flats are 8 to 15 feet deep, but he's caught numbers of channel cats from flats only 6 to 10 feet. And he occasionally probes several shallow main-lake humps. Every day before France begins drifting, he spends an hour or so looking for schools of shad to toss his cast net across. Once he garners enough for a day's fishing, he merely turns his boat sideways to the wind and drifts across the flats. On days when fresh gizzard shad are difficult to obtain, he buys a bucket of congealed blood. He encases a hunk of blood around a #4 treble hook, which is tied to 12-pound line and weighted with a #7 lead shot. Then he begins drifting, reliving the good old days when bloodbait was king.

France says that bloodbait still is as effective as it was in the 1950s and '60s—that, in fact, blood at times catches more cats than any other bait. And France knows he'd catch more cats if he drifted with blood every day; but it's such a grungy and fragile bait he uses gizzard shad instead, when he can find them.

Bloodman: John Thompson—Like France, John Thompson of Ottawa, Kansas, has pursued cats with bloodbait for decades, starting in the 1940s on the Neosho and Cottonwood rivers in Kansas. To this day, he regularly takes a bucket of bloodbait to those rivers, where he tangles with numbers of channel cats including some big ones. Years before his first outing on those waterways, his father was there floating a wad of blood through a riffle and into a cat's lair, and from his family's perspective, bloodbait is the best manmade bait for enticing channel and blue cats, especially in rivers and streams.

Thompson makes his own bait, unlike France, purchasing 55 gallons of raw chicken blood from a packing plant in Oklahoma. Lately, he says, he hasn't been hassled by the Department of Agriculture or other governmental agencies, and over the past 40 years, he's experimented with turkey, pork, and beef blood but has found chicken blood best. Some folks add brown sugar, anise, and other spices to their bloodbait, Thompson notes, but he thinks these additives are unnecessary.

The more the blood is drained and frozen, the tougher it becomes.

To process the chicken blood, he pours it on a screen and allows the plasma to drain through. Once most of the liquid has seeped out of the congealing blood, he freezes it. After the blood is frozen, he allows it to thaw on the screen, letting more of the liquid drain. When no more seepage occurs, he freezes it again. The more the blood is drained and frozen, the tougher it becomes. He prefers to freeze it only twice, because he likes the blood to be tender as it drifts downstream with the current into a river cat's lair. By the time he finishes processing 55 gallons of chicken blood, Thompson has about 28 gallons of bait.

For chasing cats at a reservoir by casting or drifting across mudflats, Thompson makes the blood tougher by processing it four times. Bloodbait is such a fragile commodity that it quickly disintegrates, leaving only a bare hook as it bumps into stumps, boulders, logs, and brushpiles. The problem with tougher bloodbait, he says, is that it becomes spongelike, the blood quickly washing out of it, diminishing its potency. So, like France, he prefers to use fresh shad rather than tough bloodbait when he drifts across reservoir flats. But he quickly reverts to blood when shad are unavailable.

Upon the streams and small rivers that meander across the savannas of eastern Kansas, Thompson is often called the king of finesse bloodbaiters. He shuns such terminal tackle as weights, swivels, snaps, and treble hooks, instead opting for a light-action 7-foot fiberglass spinning outfit, 10-pound monofilament, and an Eagle Claw #84 hook. If the current is running at a torrid pace, he adds a #3 lead shot to his line.

With this outfit, Thompson can float a hunk of blood on a #1 hook from the upstream side of a logjam, through the center of a snag, and past the downstream portion of the jam. Of course, he loses a number of fish, trying to coax them out of a maze of limbs and root wads; but he says if you can't entice a cat to bite, you'll never maneuver it out of its snag-infested abode, anyway. And the best place to entice a cat is in a logjam.

A theory among some catmen says a potent bloodbait will draw cats several yards out of their lairs, provoking them to engulf that bloody morsel;

but Thompson disagrees. Even if true, he says, he doesn't like waiting for the cats to come to him. That's why he floats his bloodbait into the cat's lair, and he's remarkably dextrous at floating a chunk of blood downcurrent. In fact, he's been known to float his bait more than a hundred yards down a riffle, a monumental feat. After every float, be it short or long, he rebaits his hook with a fresh portion of blood.

John Jamison, of Springhill, Kansas—an accomplished tournament angler—calls Thompson the guru of Kansas catmen. He says Thompson has taught scores of young catmen the ropes. One of Thompson's greatest revelations is that the hotter the weather and water, the better it is for floating hunks of blood down a riffle or into a snag. Hence, from 9 p.m. to 3 a.m., Thompson and his cadre of young anglers usually can be found probing a riffle, especially in the heat of the summer.

Bloodman: Catdaddy Shumway—Renee "Catdaddy" Shumway of Topeka, Kansas, agrees with Thompson's contention that bloodbait works best during the hottest days of the year. Consequently, Shumway doesn't start using blood until water temperatures reach around 50°F. Yet during fall on the Kansas River, he's enjoyed some fine cool-weather fishing with bloodbait, and caught numbers of nice-sized blues and channel cats during a November snowstorm.

For years, Shumway and Wayne Smith of Topeka traveled the country, from Kansas to the Red River of the North to Santee-Cooper, South Carolina, in search of channel and blue cats. Of course, they always carried gallons of Cat Busters bloodbait and chum, which Smith himself made.

During the winter of 1998-99, Shumway bought Smith's bloodbait and chum business and is now the proprietor of Catdaddy's Cat Busters Blood Bait, which he sells to bait shops within about a 100-mile radius of Topeka. He also manufactures a new chum made with garlic, anise, crushed soybeans, turkey blood, and brown sugar, and is launching a mail-order business to supply catmen across the nation with bloodbait and chum.

For years, Smith and Shumway bought chicken blood from a Tyson Foods plant in Missouri, but federal red tape put an end to that. Now Shumway buys

Catdaddy Shumway says chumming often increases the effectiveness of blood bait during summer.

turkey blood from a packing plant at Carthage, Missouri, then laces it with brown sugar and anise. Shumway says he can't tell the difference between chicken blood and turkey blood in their ability to lure channel and blue cats.

The way Shumway fishes bloodbait is as easy and effective to employ on a reservoir as on a river or stream. On a reservoir, however, he doesn't drift, but instead anchors his boat at a cat hideaway and uses chum. He contends that his chum not only stimulates cats to feed but also attracts them to his anchorage, and suspects that reservoir cats will travel at least 25 yards to investigate his aromatic mix.

> *The way Shumway fishes bloodbait is as easy and effective to employ on a reservoir as on a river or stream.*

In the swift waters of the Kansas River, a good chum is even more effective than in the relatively still waters of a reservoir. For instance, Shumway says, a good chum might be powerful enough to lure Kansas River blue and channel cats from more than 25 yards, drawing them several yards outside a massive logjam. Properly placed, chum steers the cats right to the bloodbait lying in the swift current in about 3 feet of water, some 10 feet in front of a logjam.

Shumway likes to fish some of the swiftest sections of the Kansas River, areas littered with massive logjams. To do this, he anchors his boat broadside with the current, using two heavy anchors with large flukes and two long pieces of rope, which he attaches to grippers on the bow and stern of the boat's starboard side. He always anchors about 40 to 50 yards upstream from a snag, and immediately tosses a half gallon of chum into the current, which runs into a logjam. Then he gingerly casts his bloodbait toward the logs, allowing it to drift to within 10 feet of them. He uses a 1/2- to 5/8-ounce sinker to keep the bait near bottom in the swift current.

Except for the weights, he uses identical tackle on a river and reservoir: a salmon-action 8-foot spinning rod, 30-pound Ande line, a #3 snap-swivel, and a #1 nickel treble hook. Reservoir rigs usually are weighted with a 1/4-ounce sinker. He anchors his boat then tosses chum around it, affixes a large gob of blood to the hook, and carefully drops the bait to bottom of the area he's just chummed.

If the water is deep enough, he often fishes vertically, adjusting the depth of the bait to the depth of the cats, which he monitors on a sonar unit. The cats can be either suspended several feet off the bottom, cruising near the surface, or belly to the bottom. When chumming shallower spots, he makes a gentle lob cast to the covert and allows the bait to settle into or near the chum.

Although Shumway prefers pursuing reservoir cats with anchors, chum, and bloodbait, some catfish tournaments prohibit chumming. When this occurs, he puts away his anchors and chum and merely uses a wad of blood. He adds two more 1/4-ounce egg sinkers, turns his boat sideways with the wind, and drifts across the flats. During the course of the drift, he guides the boat so the bait floats and bounces through humps, ditches, foundations, roadbeds, drop-offs, and brushpiles.

To prevent the blood from constantly falling to pieces as it bounces off the obstacles that clutter the reservoir bottom, he concocts a tougher batch. His drifting bloodbait is made more durable by adding a touch of salt and exposing it to a day or two of Kansas sunshine.

Shumway doubts that bloodbait ever will be popular with run-of-the-mill fishermen, so a lot of bait shops don't stock it. He suspects, however, that newcomers eventually will appreciate the power of a fine bloodbait.

Chapter 6

Lures for Catfish

SPINNER RIGS, CRANKS, SOFTBAITS AND FLIES

According to *In-Fisherman* Editor In Chief Doug Stange, the spinner rig is one of the finest lures for catfish. The combination of lure and livebait simply makes sense and has long been catching catfish in certain areas of the country.

"Catfish are extremely vibration-sensitive," Stange says, "and the essence of spinner rigging is to attract fish via vibration, along with visual cues, or flash. Add a crawler or a leech, and powerful scent and taste are added to an already potent visual and vibratory package."

Stange says that during summer and early fall, the same style of spinner rigging popular for walleyes is one of the better baits available for channel catfish, in many waters. "I'm referring to a crawler-harness-style rigging with 2 or 3 hooks in tandem following the spinner, which developed as an adjunct to the popular 1960s Red Devil spinner style, composed of a spinner and a single hook.

"I first used a coarse version of the tandem rigging after finding them in Red's Tackle Shop at Big Bend Dam, South Dakota, during the mid-1960s," he recalls. "Then, during the early '70s or so, when this rig was beginning to catch on, I fished with a version of it, the Bena Rig, made by Greg Bena of Sutherland, Iowa. The Bena Rig even at that early date was tied fine enough to compare with the best commercial spinner rigs we have on the market today.

"I offer dates relative to this issue because already back then, anglers fishing on Lake Sharpe and Lake Francis Case in South Dakota were routinely bagging combo stringers of walleyes and channel catfish as they drifted spinner rigs and crawlers behind early-day bottom bouncers," he says. "So lures and channel cats are no recent deal. Also, one of the finest stringers of big channel cats and big walleyes I've ever witnessed was caught in the mid-1970s by Iowa's fishing professor, Jim McDonald, using the Bena Rig and crawlers on Storm Lake, one of Iowa's shallow, fertile natural waters.

"This rigging and an almost endless variety of modified rigs produce catfish for those who apply them in the right situations," Stange says. "It's a superb rig, for example, for walleyes and channel cats in portions of the Great Lakes during summer and early fall. Use a larger blade—#5 or larger—in this instance, though. More thump to call fish roaming vast portions of open water.

"On large rivers like the Mississippi and Ohio, the rigging works for cats holding on or near wing dams. When things get difficult along wing and

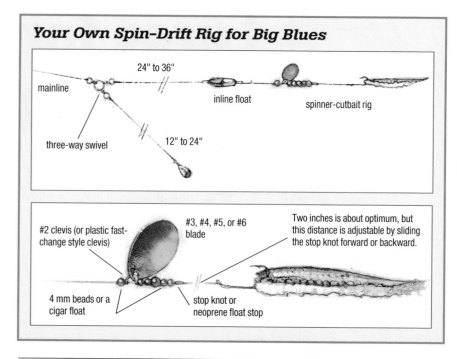

Your Own Spin-Drift Rig for Big Blues

mainline

24" to 36"

inline float

spinner-cutbait rig

three-way swivel

12" to 24"

#2 clevis (or plastic fast-change style clevis)

#3, #4, #5, or #6 blade

Two inches is about optimum, but this distance is adjustable by sliding the stop knot forward or backward.

4 mm beads or a cigar float

stop knot or neoprene float stop

The Classic Spinner Rig for Cats

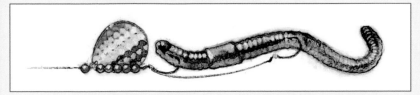

The classic tandem-hook spinner rig (or harness) tipped with a crawler or leech. Typical blade sizes: #2 or #3. But #4, #5, or #6 blades often are an option for cats in warm water, especially the open-water portions of large lakes and reservoirs.

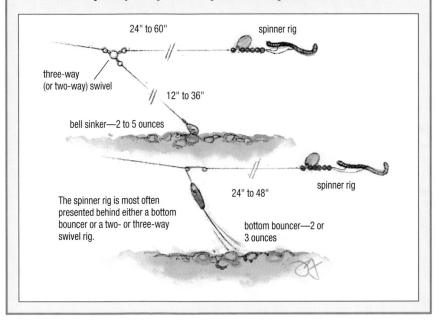

24" to 60"

spinner rig

three-way
(or two-way) swivel

12" to 36"

bell sinker—2 to 5 ounces

spinner rig

The spinner rig is most often
presented behind either a bottom
bouncer or a two- or three-way
swivel rig.

24" to 48"

bottom bouncer—2 or
3 ounces

closing dams, don't forget to try leeches. Catfish love leeches. And they can find your leech presentation more easily when it's trailing behind a spinner.

"During summer, I've also caught channel cats with a spinner-crawler combo, using a controlled boat drift while bottom-bouncing the combo along the deep channel lip in pools #3 and #4 on the Mississippi River," Stange explains. "It's also been a productive rig fished on a static line behind a boat anchored just off riprap banks buffeted by heavy current on the Missouri River near Sioux City, Iowa.

"Use crawlers in conjunction with the spinner rig to catch channel cats," he suggests. "Fish a dead chub or a strip of cutbait, and flatheads also happen along. And, again, when things get tough, don't forget leeches. Hold the rod so the tip is at a right angle to the main current, occasionally lifting the tip in order to keep the spinner spinning and attracting cats."

Stange says that some semblance of this spinner rigging should work almost anywhere cats swim, whether trolled, cast, or drifted in natural lakes, reservoirs, or large rivers across North America—as an addition to the drift rigs used

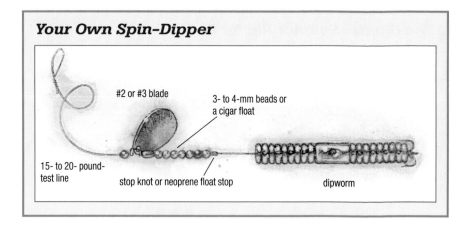

Your Own Spin-Dipper

#2 or #3 blade

3- to 4-mm beads or
a cigar float

15- to 20- pound-
test line

stop knot or neoprene float stop

dipworm

by Santee-Cooper, North Carolina, catfish guides. "Instead of a crawler, try a strip of cutbait behind a big spinner to call big blue cats and an occasional fat flathead. Again, spinners call cats and the addition of bait intensifies and focuses catfish reaction," he says.

How about a spinner in conjunction with dipbait? "I received a tip from a Wisconsin guide to use a spinner ahead of a dipbait worm during summer," Stange says. "He anchors in current above a snag or above a hole. Then he dunks the dipworm portion of the combo into his favorite dipbait and flips the rig out so it holds in place just in front of the snag or at the head of a hole—calling all cats with vibration, scent, and taste. The opportunities with spinner combos are limited only by your imagination."

JIGS

Leadhead jigs can be fished as classic lures for catfish, as when a bucktail jig (tipped with bait or fished without bait) is cast into a tailwater area teeming with catfish. Or they can be used as a tool (a sinker) to anchor livebait or deadbait in position so a catfish can eat it.

One of the most prominent jig options was written about by *In-Fisherman* contributor Ned Kehde, who described how some Kansas anglers flip jig-and-crawler combos for flatheads spawning in holes in riprap habitat along cause-ways and at the face of dams. This tactic is a potent option anywhere cats hole up during spawntime, not just in reservoirs but in rivers, once cats move into holes in snags or into holes in cutbanks.

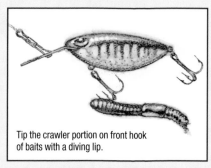

One Hot Combo for Cats?

Tip the crawler portion on front hook
of baits with a diving lip.

A combination of crankbait tipped with a portion of crawler, a common choice for walleyes during the 1950s and 1960s, has enjoyed a recent rebirth of popularity in some areas. Doug Stange suggests that this combo should be a fine option for cats.

A jig also can be coupled with a slip of cutbait or a livebait. Doug Stange sometimes uses a 2-, 3-, or 4-ounce saltwater jighead to anchor a big baitfish (hooked in the tail) right below the boat when he's anchored near a snag that holds flatheads. This rig also provides good control when you're flipping and dipping a big bait right into a snag for flatheads, a tactic that sometimes works even during the day when flatheads are really cranked during prespawn, once water temperatures have shot up into the 70°F range for the first time in the year.

CRANKBAITS

No surprise, given how sound- and vibration-sensitive catfish are, that they crunch their share of crankbaits all across the country—crankbaits of various styles in lakes, rivers, and reservoirs, mainly during summer and into fall, but also throughout late spring on some waters.

In Wisconsin, guide John Kolbeck keys on a crankbait pattern for channel cats on the Wisconsin River. He flatlines Rebel Crawdads and Storm Wiggle Warts as he trolls along and over rock lips and humps where

Leadhead Jig Options

Classic bucktail jig tipped with a slip of cutbait, an option for cats feeding on shad, minnows, or other baitfish.

A 3-inch strip of cut baitfish fillet—one of the best all-around options for channel and blue cats in almost any situation, whether the fish are on bottom or suspended.

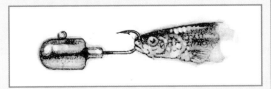

Livebait fished head forward—a good drift-pattern option.

A livebait anchored by its tail, so it struggles away from the weight of the jig.

channels are searching for crayfish. Lipped baits with an intense wiggle carom off rocks and get hung up less often than baits with shorter lips. Not surprisingly, he likes crab-colored lures, with brown and orange his favorite combo.

The best areas are those with mild current and plenty of rocks. Watching his sonar, Kolbeck keeps lures running shallower than about 8 feet. Let out only enough line, he advises (usually 50 to 75 feet of 10-pound test) to keep lures barely ticking bottom. No need to worry about keeping lures away from the boat. Cats aren't boat-shy. An occasional snap of the rod tip in crack-the-whip fashion often helps to trigger them.

Trolling Crankbaits for Channel Cats in Smaller Rivers

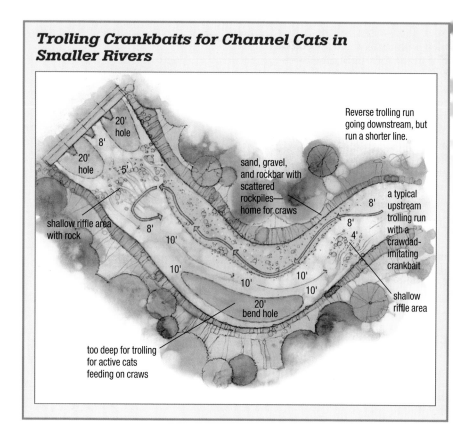

Reverse trolling run going downstream, but run a shorter line.

20' hole

8'

20' hole

5'

shallow riffle area with rock

sand, gravel, and rockbar with scattered rockpiles—home for craws

8'

8'

a typical upstream trolling run with a crawdad-imitating crankbait

8'

4'

10'

10'

10'

10'

10'

10'

shallow riffle area

20' bend hole

too deep for trolling for active cats feeding on craws

Meanwhile, in Missouri, Virgil Tagtmeyer since the early 1980s has been using cranks to catch cats from the waters of the Osage River. At first, he used Natural Ikes and Bombers, weighted to get into river holes lying 20 to 30 feet deep. Today, he relies on the Manns 20+ to troll deep in the waters below Truman Dam, at the headwaters of Lake of the Ozarks. One day during May several years ago, Tagtmeyer boated a 77-pound blue cat that had engulfed a Mann's 20+. Then, as the day progressed, a friend added three 40-pound-class flatheads to their bag. Channel cats are even more likely to take crankbaits.

He suspects that the catfish leave deep holes at night and spread over shallow flats as they search for food. During the day, they concentrate in holes, particularly holes at bends in the old Osage River channel. The drop-off can be from 4 into 30 feet of water. On sunny days, though, the cats usually lie from 20 to 26 feet deep. If Tagtmeyer marks a big fish on sonar, he fishes at that depth. And if baitfish schools are running at a given depth, he trolls lures in that zone.

When current in the Osage is too brisk to work lures into good spots, he fishes the big water of Truman Lake, where he trolls over expansive mudflats mostly devoid of timber. During both 1993 and 1995, he caught flatheads and blue cats weighing up to 30 pounds, but in most waters channel cats are the more typical catch.

Tagtmeyer prefers to troll with a superline in the 30-pound-test range, but he uses a wire leader to protect this thin line near the lure. It takes about 90 feet of line to take the Manns Stretch 20+ into 20 feet of water.

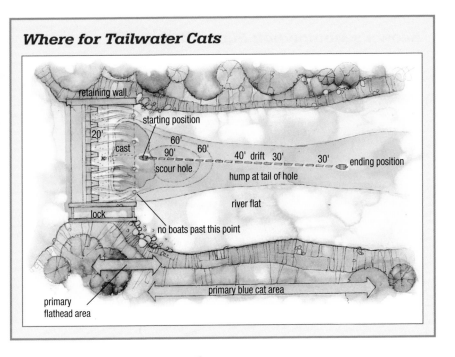

Where for Tailwater Cats

retaining wall

starting position

20'

cast

60'

90'

60'

40' drift

30'

30'

ending position

scour hole

hump at tail of hole

river flat

lock

no boats past this point

primary blue cat area

primary flathead area

And then during summer, in Kentucky, guide Jerry Keown catches flatheads and blue cats in the 40-pound class, along with lots of stripers, as he drifts minnowbaits below the Cannelton Dam on the Ohio River. This same tactic works for channel cats in most waters. He prefers floating baits like the Smithwick Rattlin' Rogue because of its erratic action in current. He uses a Carolina rig to keep this bait on or near bottom—a 2-ounce egg sinker above a #5 barrel swivel, an 18-inch leader with a snap, and the minnowbait.

Regulations prohibit boats from entering the 100-foot zone below the dam, so Keown uses a flippin' stick and 20-pound line to fire long casts at the face of the dam. Letting the lure drop to the bottom, he then slips his outboard into neutral and lets the current carry the boat downstream. As the boat drifts, he snaps the bait forward a few feet, then lets it work on its own in the current before he snaps again. After drifting 200 or 300 yards down the river channel, he motors back to the dam and repeats the process.

Most fish are caught in the first 100 yards of the tailrace—from the face of the dam to the tail of the scour hole, where relatively slack water builds along the bottom before boiling downstream. When the first dam gate is open and the current's ripping along the retaining wall, some of the biggest flatheads also hold tight to the wall in water almost too fast to fish. Meanwhile, most of the blue cats hold in faster water along the channel ledge downstream from the first hump below the scour hole.

According to Keown, you can throw out the book on location when striped bass are rampaging on the surface—a half-acre mass of 7- to 15-pound stripers smashing into massive schools of gizzard shad. The bait's flying, the stripers are slashing, and the cats are gorging on the dead and dying baitfish that drift down. The only drawback is trying to decide whether to cast unweighted baits for stripers or weighted baits for cats.

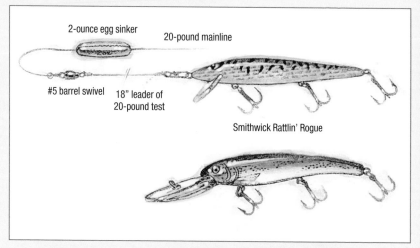

Keown's Minnowbait Rig

2-ounce egg sinker

20-pound mainline

#5 barrel swivel

18" leader of 20-pound test

Smithwick Rattlin' Rogue

The Mann's Stretch 20+, Virgil Tagtmeyer's preferred crankbait for bumping bottom for giant cats in the headwaters of Lake of the Ozarks and Truman Reservoir.

SOFTBAIT SURPRISE

Years ago, most of us believed that softbaits weren't a legitimate alternative to cut or live baitfish, or even attractor baits like dipbaits. Recent developments, however, have redefined the softbait lure category. In the bass and saltwater arenas, some of the hottest softbaits no longer contain synthetic plastisol, for one thing. Rather, these third-generation baits, including select products from the Berkley Gulp! line, FoodSource Lures, and Fishbites, are formulated with ingredients that begin dissolving the instant they're submersed, and eventually they biodegrade completely. Some of them even provide nutritional value to fish.

Third-generation softbaits are proving effective on catfish because they offer an appealing balance of taste, scent, shape, and texture. They likely won't replace natural cutbait—arguably the best all-around bait ever. Yet, the more we experiment with softbaits and identify situations in which they excel, and as bait formulas for enticing cats continue to improve, softbaits have earned a legitimate spot your catfishing arsenal.

PRESENTATIONS AND BAIT OPTIONS

Softbaits excel when coupled with a jighead or beneath the same float riggings you'd use with traditional baits. They could be effective alternatives to cutbait while drift-fishing reservoirs, too. In many ways, these baits are the most efficient options for catfish, and when you're actively casting and retrieving them—a fairly exotic approach for catfish anglers—softbaits also are a lot of fun to fish.

Even though some of them, such as those labeled as "cutbait alternatives," were designed to be fished stationary on bottom or under a float, most work better when you add action, particularly the case with channel cats. Choose baits that resemble something alive and provide some action when you pull them through the water. Thin, flat baits work better than thick, rigid ones. A thinner bait worked on a jig imparts a swimming, undulating action that appeals to catfish. Under a float or on bottom, current provides a subtle waving action.

Berkley Gulp!—Gulp! baits reportedly have 400 times more scent dispersion than regular soft plastic baits. They're 100 percent biodegradable and composed of all-natural ingredients. When kept out of water for extended periods, however, it's vital to return Gulp! baits to their ziplocked package, or they harden and become unfishable.

Several varieties and sizes of Gulp! have proven appealing to channel cats, chief among them the curlytail varieties like the Minnow Grub and the Jigging Grub (a Cabela's Gulp! exclusive). The Jigging Grub has the traditional curlytail grub shape, while the Minnow Grub has a fatter body. Rig grubs on a 1/8- to 1/4-ounce jighead and deadstick or retrieve them slowly over bottom. Ultra-slow crawls with 20- to 30-second pauses can be effective. When catfish strike a jig-and-grub combo, you're reminded that they really are hunters.

Some of the Gulp! Saltwater products, including the Shrimp and Peeler Crab, have produced nice catches of channel cats, as well. We've caught some good fish on these baits drifted under slipfloats in rivers. Catfish should also find Gulp! Cut Bait appealing. It comes in precut strips that mimic cut fish, something to try on drift rigs.

Trolling Tactics

For decades, Virgil Tagtmeyer of Sedalia, Missouri, has trolled Mann's 15+ and 25+ crankbaits through and around the deep holes in the upper reaches of the Lake of the Ozarks, where he's caught a large number of big flatheads. For two days in May of 2000, *In-Fisherman* Publisher Steve Hoffman and Field Editor Ned Kehde tested Tagtmeyer's trolling tactics at Lake of the Ozarks. Even though the weather and water conditions were far from ideal during our many hours and miles of trolling, they caught and released 24- and 70-pound flatheads, convincing them that trolling crankbaits is another method that flathead anglers could use and refine.

Robby Robinson of Marion, Ohio, finds that rocky terrains in Ohio reservoirs harbor primarily pint-sized flatheads, anglers elsewhere who troll riprap areas with crankbaits have tangled with some hefty specimens. Kansas biologist Leonard Jirak notes that the size of the flatheads in the rocks in Kansas reservoirs is related to the size of the rocks and crevices. Recently some anglers at highland reservoirs have begun thinking about trolling deep-diving crankbaits along bluffs.

Strikes while trolling are sporadic, which tries an angler's patience. But because proper trolling tactics necessitate attention to details, such as consistently monitoring boat speed, depths, and GPS coordinates, some anglers find that their patience quotient expands when trolling for flatheads, allowing them to fish longer and more efficiently.

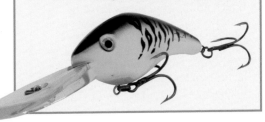

Crankin' the Flats for Flathead Cats

Richard Kurtzeborn, St. Louis, Missouri, sent us this tip, originally printed in a past issue of In-Fisherman's *Catfish In-Sider*:

Since landing a 21-pound flathead on a crankbait below a dam on the Mississippi River, I've returned many times to develop a pattern. Most of the fish I've caught were on 2- to 5-foot flats, where they cruise in search of shad and other baitfish; or they were off the edge of the flat, particularly on the downstream side.

This situation normally calls for a shallow-running crankbait, but a normal retrieve speed proved too fast for flatheads. Instead, I use a deep-running crankbait retrieved at about half the normal speed. This gets lures bumping along the bottom in shallow water at a speed the cats quickly can overtake.

I've experimented with several crankbaits and eventually lost most of them to snags. Losing a lot of high-dollar cranks can become expensive, but many companies offer a range of less costly baits that work well at slower speeds.

White and natural crayfish colors are best, and rattles may help fish locate the bait in stained waters. If the lure snags, I usually lock the drag tight and pull back sharply, snapping the line. Many times the lure returns to the surface, where it can be snagged with a topwater lure on a light spinning outfit.

There's no such thing as a typical fishing session, though. Some days I catch 2 or 3 fish, while other days I catch nothing but snags. Livebait definitely is more consistent, but average size usually is much higher as crankbait fish typically weigh 20 to 50 pounds. This technique might not be the best for numbers but it's one of the most exciting.

The newest addition to the Gulp! line of softbaits is Gulp! Alive!, packaged in livebait-style tubs filled with Gulp! Alive! attractant. Reported to absorb 20 percent more Gulp! scent and yield a more natural swimming action, Alive! baits can be recharged by placing them back into the tub of attractant. In limited trials on a small river this summer, Gulp! Alive! Squids produced several channel cats fished beneath slipfloats. Berkley's new Gulp! Alive! Swimming Mullet looks like another catfish catcher.

FoodSource Lures—Developed through a 3-year cooperative partnership between Auburn University fishery researchers and food scientists, FoodSource says their lures are the only ones made of 100 percent real food. In laboratory trials, fish not only ate these baits, but also grew and thrived on them.

Also unique to FoodSource is that even after baits are left out of water, they can be re-softened and recharged. Simply place them in water or a water-based solution for a few minutes and return them to a bag of unused baits.

Of interest to catfish anglers are the 3-inch Saltwater Shrimp Tail, Catfish Bites, Big Cat Meal, and the Goliath Grub. Fish the Shrimp Tail on a classic set rig or drift one below a float. Rigid, non-action baits, such as the Big Cat Meal, reportedly work well during summer, particularly when dipbaits and other prepared baits are producing catfish. Chunk-style baits might work fine in pay lakes or other settings where cats frequently encounter a wide variety of discarded baits, such as doughbait or cheese.

The FoodSource Goliath Grub, a giant 9-inch curlytail, can be productive, but you need to modify

Softbait Selections

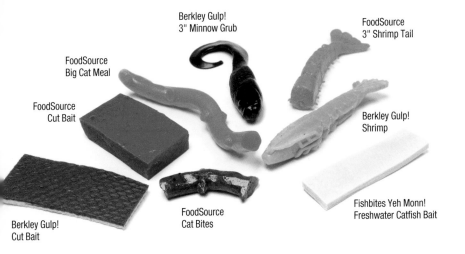

FoodSource
Big Cat Meal

Berkley Gulp!
3" Minnow Grub

FoodSource
3" Shrimp Tail

FoodSource
Cut Bait

Berkley Gulp!
Shrimp

Berkley Gulp!
Cut Bait

FoodSource
Cat Bites

Fishbites Yeh Monn!
Freshwater Catfish Bait

it to get it working right. Tear the flat tail section from the tube-shaped body. The tail from this bait is as close to an ideal piece of imitation cutbait as it gets. Hooked once through the base (torn-off side) of the tail with a 1/0 Eagle Claw 84, this little flap of scent and taste waves and flutters in current.

There's something catfish find attractive about these thin, flat strips. Scent and taste remain fundamental attractors, but in many instances, the elements of visual appearance and natural action in the water make a positive difference. Catfish not only detect minute movements and vibrations, but in many environments they can visually discern familiar cues in their natural food. When set-rigged on bottom, interspersed drags or short rod-tip sweeps activate these "flappy" softbaits to trigger cats.

The cube-shaped chunks of cut baitfish that we often use sprout thin, fleshy strips of skin that subtly flutter and flap in current. This is a trigger but an easy one to overlook because built into natural baits, so we don't often think about it. Still, catfish likely respond to this as part of the overall food package. Even if they can't always see it, they can feel it.

Fishbites—Developed through decades of study by marine researcher and University of Florida professor Dr. William Carr, Fishbites are a synthetic alternative to natural cutbait. Carr's research has led him to conclude that, when it comes to the chemical stimulants fish use to detect and track prey, what humans smell in the air and what fish detect in the water are very different, because fish sense and react only to chemicals that are dissolved in water. Moreover, even strong, airborne odors (strong to us) do not necessarily dissolve in water so they may not attract fish.

Fishbites baits consist of nearly odorless (to us), highly water-soluble

Berkley Gulp!
3" Minnow Grub
on jighead

Comparing Bait Characteristics

Starting Samples (equal parts)	**Berkley Gulp!** ▮ Minnow Grub, Peeler Crab **FoodSource** ▮ Big Cat Meal (blood), Cutbait (blood) **Fishbites** ▮ Yeh Monn! Catfish Bait (Shad and Bloodworm)
Original Texture	**Gulp!** ▮ soft and spongy **FoodSource** ▮ soft, but less pliable **Fishbites** ▮ very soft, very pliable
Original Scent (in air before submersion)	**Gulp!** ▮ highly fragrant, fishlike **FoodSource** ▮ somewhat fragrant, more of a sweet smell **Fishbites** ▮ fragrant, slightly fishlike, slightly sweet smell
Visual Blood Trail (in water)	**Gulp!** ▮ Turned water slightly cloudy after 1 week; minimal visual dye trail. **FoodSource** ▮ Immediately turned water red color; by far the most visual dye trail. **Fishbites** ▮ Bloodworm turned water immediately surrounding the bait slightly red; exuded the least overall visual dye trail.
Scent in Water	**Gulp!** ▮ Water powerfully laced with scent after 1 week **FoodSource** ▮ Water very powerfully laced with scent after 1 week **Fishbites** ▮ Scent barely detectable after 1 week
Degradation	**Gulp!** ▮ Very little physical breakdown after 8 weeks. Baits appear slimy and slightly softer than original, but otherwise completely intact. **FoodSource** ▮ Baits swelled in size within one week. Water stained almost entirely red. All color leached out into water after 4 weeks. Very soft and delicate after 4 weeks, but otherwise wholly intact. Still intact after 8 weeks, but bait falls apart in hands. **Fishbites** ▮ Completely dissolved within 1 week, leaving only a light cloud of gelatimous ooze hovering around the bait's mesh backing

To gauge the degradation and other characteristics of Berkley Gulp!, FoodSource Lures, and Fishbites over time, equal-sized samples of each bait type were placed into identical half-gallon tubs filled with non-chlorinated well water. Daily observations occurred over an 8-week period at room temperature. Samples also were checked daily for odor and water coloration. While certainly a crude test in terms of measuring scent dispersion, the trial nonetheless provides anglers with an idea of the relative characteristics of each brand.

ingredients. This is a radical idea in the catfishing realm that might represent one the biggest advancements in catfish baits in decades. Originally designed as an alternative to live- and deadbaits for saltwater applications, Fishbites now offers Yeh Monn! Freshwater Catfish Bait, a 13-inch long by 5/8-inch wide ribbon of bait that anglers cut into desired lengths and shapes.

Yeh Monn! flavors include crayfish, liver, shad, and worm, and Saltwater Fishbites products contain additional flavors such as shrimp, clam, and crab. Fishbites are "physically right" for cats, too. Strips come in thin slices, so they offer a natural flapping motion underwater, particularly in current. The bait is attached to a fine, light mesh backing, so the strips stay on the hook well and are durable. These biodegradable baits hold good potential as cutbait alternatives.

In addition to being biodegradable, these third-generation softbaits are highly appealing to catfish on both an olfactory and a visual level. So long as development dollars continue to support further research into the realm of natural lure alternatives, the potential for newer, even more desirable catfish softbaits is high.

FoodSource Lures Big Cat Meal

CATS ON THE FLY

"Fly-fishing for catfish!? Yeah, right. Who you tryin' to kid? I didn't just fall off the pumpkin truck, Bubba." Don Wirth, a longtime contributor to In-Fisherman publications, says that this was his initial response when he read his assignment letter directing him to report on this topic for In-Fisherman's *Catfish In-Sider* in 1999. "I figured any sane catman would agree—going after catfish with a flyrod just sounds too wacky to be true.

Fishbites Yeh Monn! Freshwater Catfish Bait on float rig

"Imagine my surprise when, after delving into the subject, I found that the flyrod approach is anything but wacky. Quite the contrary, it's intriguing, productive, and exciting," he says. Wirth spoke with two legendary anglers—the late catfish great Ed Davis, of Fayetteville, North Carolina, and Dan Gapen of Becker, Minnesota—about their catfish fly-fishing experiences. Here's what Wirth reported in his original article:

Ed Davis' Approach—Ed Davis is one of those guys you could talk to for hours about fishing. A skilled multispecies angler who's held over 50 International Game Fish Association (IGFA) and National Fresh Water Fishing Hall of Fame line-class world records for various species, he has recently started flyrodding for cats big-time, and he currently holds 7 flyrod catfish records. "This approach is truly in its infancy," Davis admits. "Every trip is a learning experience. If you think of fly-fishing as a gentle pastime, then tying into a 40-pound blue on a flyrod will turn your head around."

Of course, the biggest surprise to most catmen is that catfish take a fly at all. A look through Davis' photo album should quell any doubts. "I've caught channels, flatheads, and blues on streamer flies," he says. "My specialty is fly-fishing for blues; they readily eat a fly when they're feeding on live baitfish. At times, channels are so easy to catch on a fly that they're a nuisance." Flatheads? "Yeah, they take a fly, too, but they're hard to hook. They usually spit it out immediately."

Davis frequents the Cape Fear River and finds fall an ideal time for flyrodding. "During fall, big blues gorge on schools of threadfin shad near the surface," he explains. "Blue cats intercept schools of baitfish moving downstream, rolling on the surface to engulf mouthfuls of shad. Seeing a 50- to 75-pound blue cat rolling on the surface like Flipper is an awesome sight.

"This scenario makes for exciting flyrodding," he claims. "Not much finesse involved here—just lay a streamer fly in the school of bait, strip it a time or two, and hang on. Often you see the cat swim right up and eat your fly." Davis' biggest flyrod blue, caught in July 1997, weighed 42 pounds, but he's hooked much larger fish. "I've had blues on my flyrod that easily weighed 70 pounds but I didn't boat them. It's possible, though, to land a 100-pound-plus blue on a flyrod. Heck, tarpon fishermen boat 150-pounders on flyrods. If you play the game right, you can whip a really big fish with this rod.

"When blues are feeding on baitfish near the surface, they stake out a short stretch of river, work the bait school as it moves downstream, then swim back upstream for another shot at an easy meal," Davis says. "I've also found that they prefer to feed on the side of the river with the most intense current. On the Cape Fear, this often puts them in relatively open water, near sandbars and ledges. This is great for flyrodding, because they have less chance of breaking you off in heavy cover."

Davis uses a basic outfit for cats. His rod is an 8-foot 8-weight Shakespeare; he removed the stock guides and tip and replaced them with Fuji components. "One thing you quickly discover when fly-fishing for cats is that line abrasion is a major problem, whether from underwater obstructions, the catfishes' sandpaperlike teeth, or rough line guides. Using the Fuji guides and tip helps reduce abrasion and allows for longer casts."

Davis mates the rod to a Martin 72 flyreel, spooled with 50 yards of 20-pound Dacron backing and an 8-weight, weight-forward floating flyline. An 0X tapered leader is attached to the end of the flyline with a nail knot, followed by an 18-inch length of 18-pound Sevenstrand Wire or 20-pound Ande Premium. "The Steelon leaders are super abrasion-resistant and flexible enough for flycasting," Davis notes.

He has found that catfish aren't finicky about fly patterns or presentations. "Lefty's Deceiver, a streamer pattern popular with saltwater fishermen, is a good all-around choice. Red and white works fine under most conditions, but blue cats seem to like a bit of tinsel tied in. In off-colored water, chartreuse and other bright colors sometimes produce better. I caught my 42-pound blue on a yellow perch pattern.

"A stout hook is mandatory for catfish," he says. "The hooks on most freshwater flies are too small and the wire's too thin. A big blue cat can easily straighten a #2 or #4 freshwater hook. Stick to saltwater flies, which have bigger, stouter hooks—streamers with 1/0 to 3/0 hooks."

After his fly hits the water, Davis lets it sink a bit and then begins a slow hop and twitch retrieve. When a fish takes, he sets the hook hard and prepares for a long battle. "Landing a big blue on a flyrod may take 30 minutes," he says. "Get impatient and they break off every time."

Dan Gapen's Method—Legendary multispecies angler Dan Gapen also has recently succumbed to the flyrodding-for-cats bug. His addiction was jump-started during a recent trip to the Red River of the North in Manitoba. "Big channel cats were feeding on goldeyes below the dam," he says. "The baitfish were packed into little current breaks, cuts, and eddies. I moved in close enough to

cast a big streamer fly into these spots and immediately began hooking big channel cats. In one morning, I caught channels weighing 19½, 27, and 24 pounds, plus many smaller fish."

Gapen wasn't surprised that catfish responded so eagerly to this unorthodox approach. "Hardly a fish swims that won't take a fly," he claims. "It's the most natural presentation imaginable, especially in current."

Gapen uses a custom flyrod crafted by Chicago rodmeister Jim Grandt. This 9-weight stick is 9 feet long and designed for heavy, hard-pulling fish. He pairs it with a single-action Alcock flyreel from England. The combination has served Gapen well when dealing with big fish like channel cats and northern pike.

Gapen says he avoids weighted (sinking) fly-lines, especially when fishing below dams. "They create far too much drag in heavy current, pulling the fly off its mark and causing you to miss light takes. I use a 10-weight, weight-forward floating line, the first 3 feet of the tip cut off for longer casts with bulky flies." To this, he ties a 25-inch leader of 30-pound mono using a nail knot. He then tapers the leader down to 12-pound mono by adding sections of 25-, 20-, and 15-pound line. "You shouldn't go below a 12-pound tippet when gunning for catfish," he recommends. "A lighter tippet folds back during the cast and won't lay out a big fly properly.

For catfish, he favors the Tantalizer and Danny's Fancy patterns tied by his business, the Gapen Company. In heavy current, he recommends pinching a 3/0 lead shot on the nose of the fly.

Flies for Cats

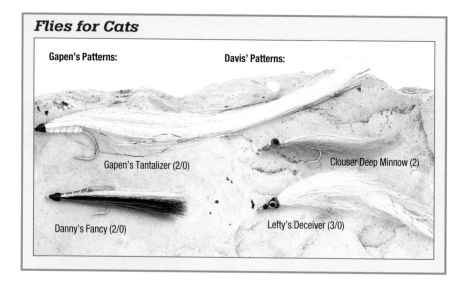

Gapen's Patterns:

Davis' Patterns:

Gapen's Tantalizer (2/0)

Clouser Deep Minnow (2)

Danny's Fancy (2/0)

Lefty's Deceiver (3/0)

"A big cat hooked in the swift current of a tailrace puts up an awesome fight," he says. "Channels typically make one long run, then start rolling until they head for the bottom. Often you think you're hung up because the cat won't budge. If you rap the rod handle several times, however, the fish usually starts moving again."

Gapen has experimented with flyrodding for cats on slow-moving rivers, too. "On a recent trip to the Kankakee River in Indiana, channel cats were holding beneath overhanging mulberry trees, feeding on ripe berries dropping into the water. I took a small Woolly Bugger fly, tipped it with a piece of green catalpa worm, and caught a bunch of channels in the 4- to 5-pound class."

"Bring a flyrod along on your next catfishing expedition," Gapen says. "You'll be amazed how well cats respond to a fly."

Thus the allure of lures for cats. Evidence from anglers North, South, East, and West, using combo systems that couple bait with lures. Anglers using jigging spoons, rattlebaits, traditional crankbaits, streamer flies, leadhead jigs—even surface baits. Catching catfish not just by accident, but by design.

Small Waters, Big Opportunities

FINDING AND CATCHING STREAM CATFISH

Some anglers perceive the river sections they fish as isolated entities, encapsulated between shorelines on both sides, with the upper and lower ends bounded by limits on their willingness to travel. But to envision smaller streams as spots for channel catfish, you have to consider such streams as part of a larger, open-drainage network. Bigger rivers are pipelines fed by smaller tributaries, with tributaries born of even smaller tributaries, which originate in the joining of the smallest rivulets at the uppermost reaches of the capillary-like system of watercourses. Getting personal with potential waters also can take a fair amount of legwork and a sense of exploration, to discover an overlooked hotspot you might come to call your own.

The connectedness of streams and rivers and the channel catfishes' remarkable ability to move long distances are what make some streams, often far separated from a larger river, good spots in which to find catfish. *In-Fisherman* Editor In Chief Doug Stange has written about his spring-through-summer catfish exploits in small Iowa streams, with some prime spots far up a watershed, 100 miles or more from a river the size most anglers would call good catfish water. One of his most productive streams was just 8 to 10 feet across and no deeper than 3 feet.

One Man's Creek is Another Man's River

A friend from west Texas was disconcerted at his first encounter with a midwestern "creek" that was 20 feet wide, with holes up to 4 feet deep. "Wal, dang," he drawled. "Down home we'd call this a river. In west Texas, anything that's deep enough to get yer boots wet and has a current is a river." He paused. "But as long as there are catfish in it, I don't care what you call it. Let's fish."

Small rivers and streams can support self-sustaining populations of channel catfish, if the right habitat exists for the fish's year-round needs—food, cover, suitable flows, good water quality, and overwintering sites. Other streams provide a seasonal home to catfish from spring into summer. Catfish in some populations migrate long distances from larger rivers to smaller tributaries to reach ideal spawning habitat, which is often more available in tributaries than in larger rivers. Some catfish continue to hole up in smaller waters to feed until water levels drop too low in mid- to late summer, or until dropping water temperatures in fall send them downstream to more comfortable environments.

STREAM CATFISH SCIENCE

Greg Gelwicks, Interior Rivers and Streams Research Biologist for the Iowa Department of Natural Resources, has studied channel catfish in small rivers and streams extensively. He evaluated smaller flowing waters as habitats for several gamefish including channel catfish, which involved pinpointing movements using radiotelemetry. His findings on two small rivers in northeastern Iowa, the Turkey and the Wapsipinicon, reveal that habitat plays a key role in the seasonal use of these systems by channel catfish.

Turkey River: The Turkey River study focused on the lower reach of this system, between its confluence with the Mississippi and a dam 40 miles upstream. All of the catfish tagged in the Turkey moved 28 to 35 miles to the Mississippi each fall from September to November, where they stayed throughout the winter. Catfish returned to the smaller river each spring to spawn and remained in positions near their initial tagging locations throughout summer.

Spring movement into the Turkey coincided with warming periods. "Catfish returned…when water temperatures warmed from about the mid-40°F to the 60°F range," Gelwicks says. "One year it warmed up early and catfish began moving up the Turkey in March. Then a cold snap hit and they moved back out to the Mississippi. In early to mid-April there was a sharp warming trend into the mid-50°F range, and catfish went up the Turkey again and stayed there."

The Turkey River is an example of a stream in which catfishing can be good from spring through summer, but residence year-round is limited by the lack

Anatomy of a Catfish Stream

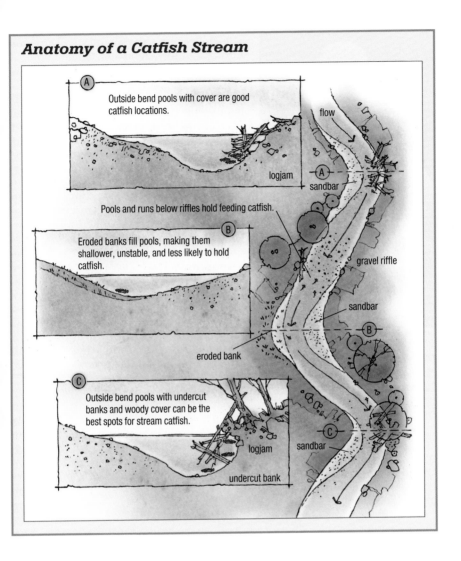

(A) Outside bend pools with cover are good catfish locations.

flow

logjam

(A) sandbar

Pools and runs below riffles hold feeding catfish.

(B) Eroded banks fill pools, making them shallower, unstable, and less likely to hold catfish.

gravel riffle

sandbar

(B)

eroded bank

(C) Outside bend pools with undercut banks and woody cover can be the best spots for stream catfish.

logjam

sandbar

(C)

undercut bank

of overwintering habitat. "All depths recorded in the Turkey River study were less than 6 feet. A few deeper pools were found in the lowermost areas of the study reach, but the primary wintering location was the Mississippi River," Gelwicks says.

Wapsipinicon River: Gelwicks also tracked catfish in the Wapsipinicon within a 15-mile stretch bounded by lowhead dams. These findings show that whether or not a stream section sustains channel catfish year-round—especially those isolated from a larger river—depends on the availability of wintering habitat. "In the Wapsi, all catfish overwintered in a single hole about 20 feet in depth. It's an old sandpit that provides the only suitable wintering habitat in that stretch. In spring, catfish left that hole and spread throughout the 15-mile stretch," he says. Gelwicks describes a good hole as being at least 10 feet deep, with enough current to keep the water oxygenated.

Professional angler and world traveler, Kim Bain-Moore, formerly of Queensland, Australia, with a nice small-stream catfish taken while fishing with the In-Fisherman staff.

Gelwicks says that many small streams throughout Iowa hold substantial numbers of good-sized catfish in summer, an observation he based on electrofishing surveys. Many of these wadeable tributaries have maximum depths in pools of just a few feet. "Some streams, especially in the southern Iowa Drift Plain, contain a high density of catfish," he says. "Where we see high densities, they're typically slow-growing and run a bit smaller, likely because of competition."

Gelwicks notes that, without barriers to fish passage, channel catfish in spring move up into smaller streams, where anglers can tangle with numbers of them through midsummer. "Typically by the end of July, flows decline, water levels start dropping, and the largest catfish vacate these areas," he says. "These streams continue as good nursery areas for young-of-the-year catfish, because of good forage and lack of predators. We've sampled young-of-the-year flatheads in these streams, too, indicating that some adult flatheads use upper reaches of streams, as well."

In Missouri, adult channel catfish have been found to inhabit smaller tributaries into early fall, suggesting that these environments provide suitable habitat throughout the growing season. While at the University of Missouri, Dr. Jason Vokoun sampled catfish with hoopnets in northeastern Missouri's Grand River—a tributary of the Missouri River—as well as in two smaller tributaries of the Grand, Big Creek, and Yellow Creek rivers, with Yellow Creek about 15 feet wide and Big Creek about 30.

Adult channel catfish dispersed throughout the mainstem Grand and its tributaries in June. Samples showed adult catfish remaining in tributaries into October, after which they moved downstream again to overwinter in the mainstem Grand, primarily in scour holes that form around bridge support structures.

IDENTIFYING POTENTIAL SPOTS

Good maps can help narrow the search for streams that have potential for good catfishing. Starting at the main river, you can track streams up the drainage from the primary tributaries off a main river, then into secondary tributaries, and so on up the drainage.

Maps don't replace on-the-ground reconnaissance or word-of-mouth from reliable sources, but they can provide clues as to which locations are accessible and likely worth a visit. U.S.G.S. topographic maps, moreover, are a great resource, showing streams and rivers, unimproved roads, dams, elevation, and more—things you might not find on a typical roadmap.

In the search for small-stream catfish, Gelwicks highlights the importance of connectivity. If there are no barriers to catfish movement and enough water,

Potential Catfish Streams

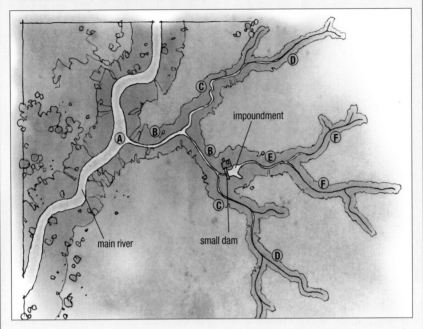

In this sample drainage system, channel catfish are likely to be found in the **main river (A)** year-round, although in spring a large contingent is likely to move into the **primary tributary river (B)** during early Prespawn. The primary tributary may support a year-round population of resident catfish if it contains suitable overwintering habitat. Lacking wintering habitat, catfish vacate streams and spend winter in the main river.

Channel catfish are likely to move into **secondary tributaries (C)** in search of spawning areas and can remain there through summer if suitable flows persist. If flow and spawning habitat are adequate, catfish may move into upper sections of secondary and perhaps **tertiary tributaries (D)**. These smallest tributaries often suffer intermittent flow or low water in mid- to late summer, forcing catfish to vacate.

A dam blocks movement of catfish from the lower river into the upper sections of the drainage system. Catfish may be present in **streams above the dam (E and F)** if the impoundment or the primary stream feeding it provides year-round habitat needs. The area immediately downstream of the dam is a good spot to find congregating catfish during their upstream migration in spring.

channel cats can continue up the tributaries in search of spawning sites and later for summer habitats. In some systems they may travel only as far as the lower reaches of primary tributaries; but where connectivity and habitat allow, or where a source population exists farther up in the drainage, catfish may be found well up into these systems.

Just as important as connectivity is habitat, particularly at the scale of a stream "reach"—the dominant characteristics over a longer stretch of stream. You might identify a potentially productive reach on a map, but a visit reveals poor habitat and far less chance for good catfishing. In a study of catfish populations in Iowa rivers and streams, biologist Vaughn Paragamian noted that catfish abundance was keyed to habitat quality. He found the best stream reaches for both numbers and sizes of catfish offered a variety of depths, sufficient cover, and variations in current.

In Paragamian's study, woody cover in the form of brushpiles, fallen trees, rootwads, and logjams were most important in streams that lacked rocky substrates, but woody cover was beneficial in all catfish streams. Catfish abundance was lower in channelized reaches, which lack habitat diversity and cover. Search instead for reaches that contain a good mix of deeper pools and riffles, which provide a broad spectrum of habitats and variations in current.

COVER WATER

Whether you're floating a navigable stream or wading, plan on fishing a fairly lengthy reach to find the best spots. You might get the urge to park yourself in a lawn chair under a shady bridge where you'll likely catch a couple of cats, but more could be had elsewhere.

Cover a mile or two of water and fish from spot to spot, as you evaluate the different kinds of habitats the stream reach provides. If it's not panning out, you might retreat to another stream or continue fishing another mile, perhaps at another access point. Sooner or later you develop a sense of a stream's overall potential.

Pools that contain woody cover are good spots to find stream cats in summer. Current deflects against outside bends and scours sediments, especially when flow is high in spring, creating some of the best spots to find catfish. As flows recede in summer, these pools are quiet spots that attract both resting and feeding catfish. Pools can also form below riffles or around bridge pilings, and some exist as former sandpits.

Deeper pools that hold cats in winter might not necessarily be best in summer, but they often do hold fish and are worth scouting. A productive summer pool might be of only moderate depth. In the Turkey River that Gelwicks studied, channel cats were found most frequently in 2 to 4 feet of water in summer, areas substantially shallower than wintering spots. So, in many smaller catfish streams, a good pool might be only waist-deep.

Certain types of woody cover can be better than others, as can the amount and location of wood. Snags made up of several large logs are generally

Keep Moving, Keep Searching, Keep Learning

Walk a mile and compare the riffle-hole-run series that occurs there. Try fishing in each area. You'll soon see, and certainly your catch will indicate, that some of these series are much better than others. Deeper holes with extensive cover often hold the most catfish. Eventually, it becomes obvious that staying long in marginal areas isn't productive. Might even be better to walk right on by until you reach something that's really worth fishing.

Now walk (or float) another mile. And another. And another. Say, over the course of a summer, you eventually cover 20 or 30 miles of river. Now we're really getting somewhere. This is when you begin to realize that some 5- or 10-mile sections of river aren't nearly so productive as other sections. You might even look at a map and realize that a lot of the best sections have narrower, more winding river portions. Eureka. Sometimes you can even narrow the search by looking at a map.

And then, if you stay at it long enough, you'll also begin to view all 50 or 100 miles of river as an entity, where the catfish population shifts during certain seasons. Most of the catfish population might, for example, shift into the upstream third during spring, the downstream third during fall and winter. Then again, in high-water years, the preponderance of fish might stay upstream all year long.

That's looking at river catfishing on a grand scale. At its most basic level, once you determine on a grand scale where the fish should be, it's still a matter of going to a river section, finding the best portion of that section, and then fishing the cover edges of the riffle-hole-run sections in that area.

An old Iowa farmer once said, "Got a hog farm to the east, a chicken ranch to the west, and that feller up north has himself a big feedlot full of cattle. I never have to wonder which way the wind's blowing."

Honestly, river catfishing is a lot like that. Once you understand what to look for, once you've spent time looking and fishing and evaluating, and doing it more and more over the course of a good many years, you can almost sniff the wind—or at least read the current—and just know that fish live there.

Creek Catfish

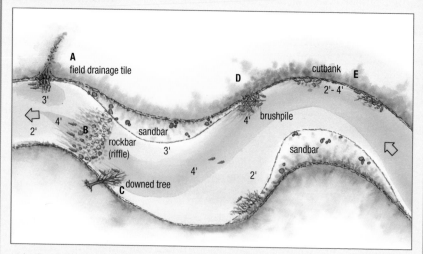

A) Cool, fresh water from field drainage tiles attracts catfish on hot summer days.

B) Rockbars (riffles) oxygenate water and hold invertebrates that attract forage fish and cats.

C) A single small tree in deeper water will hold cats—so will a brushy bank in only 2 feet of water.

D) A big brushpile will hold catfish at its top, along its sides, and on its downstream side.

E) Look for catfish lurking around rocks and debris at the base of cutbanks.

preferred over a single log or treetop with a few wispy branches. Cover in the faster current near the head of a hole is typically a good place to find feeding cats, while cover in quiet water at the lower end of a hole is mostly resting territory. Cover spots located at the heads and cores of holes are often the best places to fish.

Although channel catfish can live in areas of zero current, the best pools tend to have some flow. Catfish tend to avoid more isolated and stagnant pools, which can suffer localized dissolved-oxygen deficits.

Because outside bends bear the brunt of current in high water, they're also zones of high erosion, often leading to sloughing, where banks aren't stabilized by terrestrial vegetation. Erosion is more prominent around areas with bank disturbance, such as where livestock can access streams or where banks have been cleared. Holes in these areas tend to be less defined with more unstable sediments. Although logjams can accumulate along these bends, they typically don't hold as many catfish as logjams found on an outside bend with a healthy bank.

Root systems of trees, brush, and other forms of vegetation help bind soils on stream banks and can lead to the formation of undercut areas. Water scours soil underneath root systems, carving out secluded habitats with overhead cover. Cutbanks that house log complexes can be some of the best catfish spots of all.

RIGGING UP

Small-water catfishing is a simple operation, requiring minimal tackle and just a few supplies. Most stream cat duty can be accomplished with a 6- to 7-foot light- to medium-action spinning rod and a medium spinning reel spooled with 8- to 12-pound-test monofilament. When wading, a small shoulder bag is helpful for carrying supplies: extra hooks, floats, weights, pliers, sunscreen, a bait knife, bug repellent, bait, a stringer, and maybe lunch. Because of briars, ticks, and poison ivy, long pants are a good idea for trailblazing on stream banks.

A splitshot rig (see Chapter 3 on making rigs), with one or two shot pinched onto the line about a foot above the hook, is great for slowly drifting baits along and under snags and cutbanks. A sliprig with a slightly larger bell sinker holds baits on bottom—a good choice when you want to keep your bait pinned to likely catfish locations.

Streams are dandy places to fish float rigs, too, where you can slowly drift baits off bottom along logjams, cutbanks, through runs and mid-channel pools. For baits, you usually can't go wrong with small chunks of cutbait or small, freshly killed baitfish. The same goes for a gob of worms. Crickets, grasshoppers, and frogs are other good options, particularly when they're seasonally abundant.

In the end, there's something therapeutic about getting up close and personal with small rivers and streams. Most times you're fortunate to have the solitude—watching, listening, and feeling these waters as they roll by, sand and gravel shifting underfoot, all the while figuring out the intricacies of flow. A twig floats along, ever so often twisting in a micro-eddy then gliding on its way, turning again before it lands. Could be a catfish there.

ABOUT RIVER ACCESS

Anglers fishing on small rivers are more likely to deal with matters of access than are those fishing larger waters. One thing's clear: If you need to cross private property, always get landowner permission—you'll be glad you did, when you catch a bunch of fish and want to return to fish another day. However, it's not that simple: Water access rules can be inconsistent and confusing between jurisdictions.

Riparian rights, a fancy name for the convoluted laws and regulations related to ownership of lakes and river systems, vary widely from state to state. Federal law confirms the general principle that the public has a right to fish and boat on rivers, but a number of state and local governments dispute whether those principles apply in their jurisdictions, especially on smaller rivers.

The result is a hodgepodge of regulations that keeps anglers befuddled and property rights attorneys driving BMWs. The extremes range from rules that provide Kansas anglers public access to only three rivers in the state, to those in Wisconsin that allow use of any waterway deep enough to float a kayak at some time during a normal year.

Elsewhere, it gets more complicated. In Iowa, for instance, fishermen in boats can legally float down any river or stream that "supports a vessel capable of carrying one person for a total of a 6 months' period in one out of every ten years," but must have permission from adjoining landowners to wade all but specified segments of rivers in that state. And in Oregon, a court case is pending against a

duck hunter who legally floated his duck boat on a portion of the Klamath River adjacent to a private hunting club, but allowed his decoy anchors to contact the river's bottom, constituting "trespass" of the club's property.

PUBLIC WATERS—IN THEORY

There's a thread of sanity and logic that can be traced through the varying approaches that some states take toward riparian rights, however. Legal historians have tracked these rights back to Roman law, to the Magna Carta in England, and to Public Trust Doctrine in the U.S. This doctrine maintains that the government, state or federal, holds in trust for the public all fish and wildlife, as well as the waters in rivers, streams, and lakes. When landowners purchase property with a waterway running through it, whether they own the land beneath the waterway depends on local property laws. But the government always holds in trust for the public all the fish and wildlife on that property, as well as the water in any navigable waterway.

The ongoing challenge has been to define "navigable." At first glance, navigable would seem to apply to waters large enough to support a commercial boat, possibly a steamboat. But numerous court cases, including in the U.S. Supreme Court, have ruled that navigability is defined by whether or not the waterway could support "commerce." Since fur trading and logging were both major sources of commerce in the 1700s and 1800s, navigability was commonly decided by whether or not canoes (used for fur-trading) or logs could be floated downstream at some time during a year.

In recent years the popularity of canoes and kayaks has led some state courts to reaffirm the longstanding rule that navigability includes canoes and small craft. Wisconsin courts formally reaffirmed navigability to include "any stream that can float the lightest recreational craft in common use," says Mary Ellen Vollbrecht, Wisconsin's Chief of Waterways Protection. "With the small kayaks now in use, that means some very small streams are legally navigable in Wisconsin, and the public has the right to use them for recreational purposes."

Vollbrecht noted that, in Wisconsin, "recreational purposes" include floating, wading, fishing, portaging, and general access to that portion of streambeds and riverbeds below the ordinary high water mark. Landowners in Wisconsin who own land adjacent to waterways may own the land beneath the water, but courts have ruled that the public has a right to use the water as well as the land below the ordinary high water mark.

"We call it the "Wet Foot Law," says Vollbrecht. "As long as your feet are wet, you have the right to be on, in, or along any lake or river in Wisconsin."

In Kansas, the legal interpretations of the Public Trust Doctrine, navigability, and public use of waterways are far different from Wisconsin's. "Agricultural and private property rights are a big issue in Kansas," says Doug Nygren, Fisheries Chief for the Kansas Department of Wildlife and Parks. "Our courts have tended to defend landowners' rights to control waterways that cross their lands. The issue is our legal definition of navigability. According to the definition used by our courts, only three rivers in Kansas are navigable—the Missouri, the Kansas, and the Arkansas.

"Those are the only rivers that the public has free access to, other than where rivers and streams pass through government parks or wildlife areas. All the other rivers and streams in Kansas are defined as non-navigable and therefore are the private property of landowners who own the land adjacent to them. The public can't boat on them without permission from the landowner, even if they don't touch the bottom or the shoreline."

Pennsylvania, like Kansas, specifies which of its waterways are navigable and therefore available for public use. "The problem is that nowhere in our regulations or rules is there a list of all the [navigable] streams and rivers," says Dan Tredinnic, Press Secretary for the Pennsylvania Fish and Boat Commission. "You've either got to be an expert on the legal history of rivers and streams in your area or know somebody who is. There have been repeated situations where the Commonwealth believed a waterway was navigable and therefore public, but the adjacent landowner said it wasn't and it had to go to court to be decided."

Tredinnic noted a situation in northeastern Pennsylvania in which a fishing club leased land adjacent to a popular trout stream then declared the stream and streambed its private property. A local angler asserted that the stream was legally navigable so the public had a right to access it and took the fishing club to court.

"It took the better part of four years, but ultimately the angler won the case and that stretch of the stream was added to our list of navigable public waterways," says Tredinnic. "But the courts made no effort to expand the definition to the entire stream or to similar rivers, so navigability and public access are still on a mile-by-mile, stream-by-stream, river-by-river basis, in Pennsylvania."

CAN'T WE ALL JUST GET ALONG?

There's hope for anglers, boaters, and others who use rivers and streams for recreational purposes. According to Eric Leaper, Executive Director for the National Organization for Rivers (*nationalrivers.org*), all navigable rivers and streams in the U.S. are theoretically open to the public. "There are numerous U.S. Supreme Court decisions regarding public use of rivers," says Leaper. "The Court has repeatedly ruled that the public has the right to use navigable rivers, and favors the view that navigable rivers are those that meet the old guidelines of being able to float a canoe or logs at some time during a year. The National Organization for Rivers doesn't deny that a landowner can own the bed and banks of a navigable waterway, but we believe that the public has an easement, a legal right, to use the waterway and its bed for recreational purposes."

The Debate Continues

In 2006, a Louisiana District Court ruled that the public does not necessarily have the right to hunt or fish on the waters of the Mississippi River within Louisiana.

This alarming court ruling had its genesis in 1996, when several anglers were arrested for fishing while floating in a boat on an oxbow of the flooded Mississippi River a mile or more from the river's main channel. The oxbow was normally cut off from the river except during flooding, but well below the ordinary and high water mark of the Mississippi River in the area. Later that year, the Louisiana Attorney General issued an opinion that stated, "The public has a perfect right to use the water and water bottoms [of naturally navigable water bodies] for all traditional purposes related to navigation and to include both recreational and commercial activities, such as fishing. "

Despite that opinion, the East Carroll Parish District Court continued its injunction against public access to Mississippi waters. The defendants, with support from numerous bass fishing clubs as well as commercial crawfish producers, appealed the decision all the way to the Louisiana Supreme Court, which in June of 2005 declined to review the case. In April 2006 Federal Magistrate Judge James Kirk ruled that the arrests were illegal, and that the waters between the ordinary low-water and high-water marks are subject to public use, including "boating, sailing, and fishing and hunting from boats."

In late August of 2006, however, Louisiana District Court Judge Robert James added an unusual twist to the legal saga. He ruled that while the public has a right to use the river's waters regardless of the river's level, those activities are limited to "activities that are incidental to the navigable character of the Mississippi River and its enjoyment as an avenue of commerce. The Court finds that fishing and hunting are not included in these rights."

Local observers expect the case will be appealed to higher courts, possibly to the U.S. Supreme Court, because of its potential to influence hunting and angling rights elsewhere.

Leaper acknowledges that many states, especially in the western U.S., apply restrictive definitions of navigability to protect water rights in areas where irrigation, livestock watering, and other private enterprises hinge on control of rivers

Our Forefathers Understood

The public's right to use waterways was a significant issue in the early days of the U.S. Rivers were the interstate highways of the time, and early American courts repeatedly ruled in favor of the public's right to travel rivers that could be used, as noted in one court case, "as highways for commerce, over which trade and travel are or may be conducted in the customary modes of trade and travel on water."

Congress supported the theme of public access to navigable waterways when it enacted the Northwest Ordinance of 1787, to govern the original survey and later development of lands west of the Appalachian Mountains. The Ordinance stated that "navigable waters…shall be common highways and forever free, as well to the inhabitants of the state as to the citizens of the United States, without any tax, impost or duty therefore."

Since that Ordinance has never been repealed or overruled, the implication is that as long as a waterway is navigable, the public has the right to use it for commerce and recreation.

and streams. He believes that if those restrictive definitions of navigability and public access were contested through the court system and ultimately brought before the U.S. Supreme Court, the public's right to use those waterways would favor the traditional test.

"But we tell people it's better to inform and educate than to litigate," he says. "We believe the public has the legal right, a public easement, to boat, canoe, wade, or fish in most of the streams or rivers in the U.S. Where local laws seem to disagree, we recommend that people work within the system to reconfirm public rights on rivers, in keeping with the Public Trust Doctrine and other legal precedents.

"If a landowner confronts people or refuses the public's right to travel on a waterway passing through his property, we recommend that boaters or anglers avoid a confrontation, politely move downstream, and later have their attorney contact the landowner to ask him to stop bothering boaters and anglers. Or, they could contact government agencies and elected officials and ask them to contact the landowner. If one government agency or official doesn't cooperate, there are others to work through."

Leaper emphasizes that there are numerous legal precedents set by the U.S. Supreme Court that support the public's rights to fish and boat even on small rivers, as long as they're navigable in small craft. The problem is that property ownership rights are often decided at the state level, and some states, in an effort to protect landowner's rights, pass laws or uphold local court rulings that deny public access to these waters or tightly define navigability. Litigating or having new laws passed that uphold the public's right may be difficult, he notes, and may not be feasible.

The good news is that anglers and boaters in many cases have been able to work through an attorney or various government agencies to reconfirm the public's right to access these waterways. For specific information about riparian law in your state, contact your state game and fish department or a local game and fish law enforcement officer.

Chapter 8

Channel Cats

**A SYSTEMATIC
APPROACH TO
SUCCESS**

Knowing the behavior of the fish you target is a key first step to developing a systematic approach to angling. Each species goes through seasonal periods of response, which guide fish location and feeding patterns. Channel catfish, in particular, display routine seasonal movements and habitat selection in rivers, making location fairly predictable for enlightened anglers. Once you understand what to look for and spend time evaluating spots, you'll find fish. Then it's simply a game of working with the best presentation strategy.

CLASSIC RIVER EDGES, CLASSIC CATFISH

In one *All In The Family* episode, Archie Bunker stood, cigar in hand, next to his favorite living room chair, lecturing his wife, Edith, on his difficulty in getting her to understand the obvious logic of his ways. "The problem," he told her, "is that I explain in English and you listen in Dingbat."

So, too, does the easy logic of the ways of catfish in rivers often pass by the casual river angler. Like Edith, most anglers really haven't a clue. They find a bridge, park their vehicle, and walk down and plant a lawn chair—and never move. Or they get permission to drive down to the river through a farm, park at the point of easiest access—and never move. Catfishing can be so much more, particularly if you actually like to catch them.

Catfish location is all about identifying river edges, but the game must be played in a larger context than "find a river edge, find cover, find catfish." Every edge, every piece of cover won't attract catfish during each season—yet edges still ultimately key fish location and, thus, catfishing success.

Wading wet is one of the most compelling ways to probe portions of a small river when the water's down during summer. It's also one of the finest ways to view close up the river components upon which successful fishing depends. This form of fishing, though, given an angler's limited ability to cover water, works best when key river areas have been discovered via a more mobile method.

The larger context in question has everything to do with the natural physical layout of rivers as they proceed from beginning to end, in continuous series of riffles, holes, and runs. This is by now an idea often expressed in In-Fisherman publications, including in our catfish book, *Channel Catfish Fever*, published in 1989. We first began to write about river layout in the mid-1970s. We still contend that it's just about the most important basic idea in river fishing. Letters from hundreds of you over the years suggest that this kind of fishing success can be learned, though it takes time.

In any case, it's remarkable how an angler's fishing success can improve once he begins to see river structure for what it is and how it so naturally affects catfish location each season. Catfishing, after all, like most fishing, remains first a matter of finding fish.

The process is much easier to learn if you start looking at small rivers, where the catfish's world is compressed into a smaller area. In a large river, major holes may be half a mile apart. On a small stream, half a mile might have 10 holes. You can move and see

Typical Big River Pool

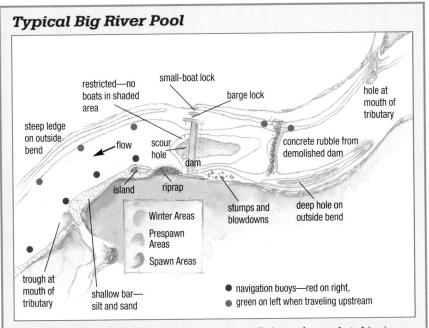

restricted—no boats in shaded area

small-boat lock

barge lock

hole at mouth of tributary

steep ledge on outside bend

flow

scour hole

dam

concrete rubble from demolished dam

island

riprap

stumps and blowdowns

deep hole on outside bend

Winter Areas

Prespawn Areas

Spawn Areas

trough at mouth of tributary

shallow bar— silt and sand

navigation buoys—red on right,
green on left when traveling upstream

The same principles that guide location in small rivers also apply to big rivers. While not as obvious on a large river, various structural and cover elements and current breaks that attract catfish across the seasons can be found throughout a river reach.

lots of water. More importantly, the continuing combination of riffle, hole, and run, and the cover (or edge) elements that often exist there, also are obvious.

Catfishing on small streams relates directly to catfishing on larger rivers. Yet the anatomy of larger rivers is more subtle and confusing. If larger rivers are all that's available, learning to find catfish may take longer.

As river water meanders downhill, it flows over bottoms of varying hardness. Riffles form over hard-bottomed areas and are shallower, because current doesn't wash away hard bottom. Riffles form natural dams that obstruct moving water. A pool of water builds at the head of a riffle and eventually flows over it, quickening over the constricted area. In most small rivers in farm country, riffles rarely run for more than 30 or 40 feet.

The force of water flowing over and down a riffle scours the softer substrate at its bottom, forming a hole or a wider and deeper river section. Depth of a hole varies according to the steepness of the riffle, subsequent current patterns, and the size of the river. In a small stream, a typical hole might be 30 feet long, 20 feet wide, and about 4 feet deep. The biggest and deepest holes might be only twice those dimensions.

Holes gradually become shallower at their downstream end as suspended materials sink when the current slows. The tail end of a hole becomes a run, which is a river flat, an area with minimal change in depth. The bottom usually is sand and silt with some gravel, plus plenty of debris like wood and brush. And, you guessed it, at some point the river flat winds and finds its way to another hard-bottomed area, a riffle forms, and begins another series of riffle, hole, run.

Flooding helps to distribute timber, brush, and other debris throughout a river. Fallen timber most likely occurs in conjunction with a river hole because of the increased scouring action of current there. Once a tree falls and is held by its roots to the bank, it becomes a prime obstacle gathering floating debris. The biggest snags form in conjunction with riverbend holes. The most extensive of these become prime holding areas for catfish, usually the best areas in a river.

Free-floating timber and brush also settle easily at the margins of a hole, or at least at its tail end, as the current slows and a run forms. Boulders that serve as cover also (again because of the scouring action of current) more likely occur in conjunction with a hole. Cover on river flats (runs) is, by comparison, haphazardly placed and, of course, rests in shallower water and therefore tends to draw smaller catfish. Cover in conjunction with a riffle usually doesn't draw catfish unless they're feeding and have moved up from the hole.

Holes, then, are the primary home (or holding area) for catfish most of the time. Catfish tend to spend a major portion of their time holding in or near the

In larger rivers, particularly rocky sections often indicate a riffle, followed by a hole and a run. Because river components are easier to see in small rivers, beginning anglers should start there. Once learned on small rivers, knowledge of river structure and catfish location more easily transfers to larger rivers.

cover elements in and around holes. When feeding actively, they often move upcurrent into and through riffle areas. At times, they also spread downriver into runs. This is the essence of understanding catfish location in rivers.

But don't stop there. Walk a mile and compare the riffle-hole-run series that occur there. Go ahead and try fishing in each successive area. You'll soon see, and certainly your catch will indicate, that some of these series are much better than others. Deeper holes with extensive cover often hold the most catfish. Eventually, it becomes obvious that staying long in marginal areas isn't productive. It might even be better to walk right on by until you reach something that's really worth fishing.

Now travel another mile. And another. And another. Say, over the course of a summer, you eventually cover 20 or 30 miles of river: Now we're really getting somewhere. This is when you begin to realize that some 5- or 10-mile sections of river aren't nearly so productive as other sections. You might even realize that a lot of the best sections have narrower, more winding river portions.

And then, if you stay at it long enough, you'll also begin to view all 50 or 100 miles of river as an entity, where the catfish population shifts throughout certain

Riffle-Hole-Run

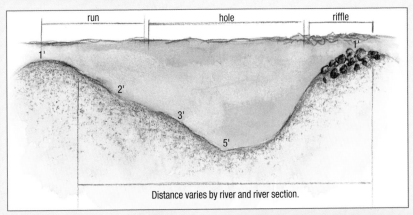

run | hole | riffle

1' · 2' · 3' · 5' · 1'

Distance varies by river and river section.

HOLE

RIFFLE

RUN

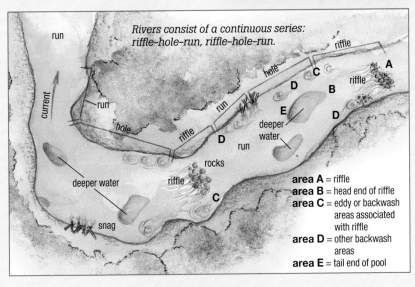

Rivers consist of a continuous series: riffle-hole-run, riffle-hole-run.

run

current

run

hole

bole

riffle

deeper water

snag

rocks

riffle

C

D

riffle

hole

D

C

A

riffle

B

E

deeper water

D

run

area A = riffle
area B = head end of riffle
area C = eddy or backwash areas associated with riffle
area D = other backwash areas
area E = tail end of pool

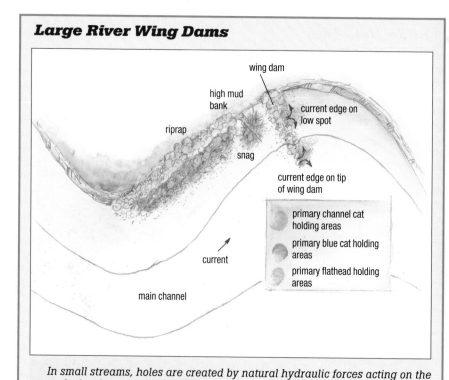

Large River Wing Dams

wing dam

high mud
bank

current edge on
low spot

riprap

snag

current edge on tip
of wing dam

current

main channel

primary channel cat
holding areas

primary blue cat holding
areas

primary flathead holding
areas

In small streams, holes are created by natural hydraulic forces acting on the streambed or through modifications by humans. In big rivers, current also carves scour holes, which often form near artificial structures that deflect current as well, such as wing dams.

seasons. Most of the catfish population might, for example, shift into the upstream third during spring, the downstream third in fall and winter. Then again, in high-water years, the preponderance of fish might stay upstream all year long.

That's looking at river catfishing on a grand scale. At its most basic level, once you determine on a larger scale where the fish should be, it's still a matter of going to a river section, finding the best portion of that section, and fishing the cover edges in the riffle-hole-run sections of that area.

Larger rivers also contain classic edges, many associated with holes and structural and cover elements that attract catfish. Current edges in tailwaters, eddies, current seams, and scour holes around wing dams, midriver holes, barge moorings, and logjams are spots in big rivers that function fundamentally the same to attract cats as they do in small rivers.

PRIMETIME BONANZA

Many anglers consider the Prespawn Period as the best time of year to fish for channel cats. It begins soon after river levels stabilize from the high water caused by melting snow and spring rains. Unlike pike and walleyes, which move toward spawning areas before the ice fully melts, channel cats are in no hurry to reproduce. They're much more concerned with finding food.

The Prespawn Period lasts for several weeks or even a couple of months, in many parts of the country. This is an extended period when the overall mood of the fish is aggressive, providing the most consistent action of the year, both for size and numbers of fish.

Prespawn patterns, in terms of location and presentation, generally carry right through summer. Fishing is often more challenging during the spawn, but catfish don't all spawn at the same time, so you'll find fish in mixed moods with some always catchable. Once the spawn is complete, they settle into summertime habits, which isn't much different from the Prespawn Period in terms of location. Put the right bait in the right place at the right time. When you do, fishing can be phenomenal.

SCOUTING TOP LOCATIONS

Tracking studies in the North reveal that the best wintering holes are the deepest ones available in a long stretch of river. In some cases, channel cats swim down smaller streams to the confluence with a larger river. They hold in the core of deep, slack holes until the water level begins to rise and temperatures warm in late winter or early spring.

This begins a tumultuous period of rising water and catfish movement—usually upstream—toward productive feeding grounds. Wintering holes offer protection from current but inadequate food for large numbers of fish, so the fish move toward areas that concentrate food. Those on small rivers might move only a short distance before settling into middepth holes with downed trees or other cover. Cats in larger rivers might move many miles before a dam or other impassable barrier blocks further migration.

Identifying top catfish locations during the Prespawn Period depends largely on the size, depth, and current speed of the river you're fishing. The nature of a river often changes from one stretch to another, making this process more

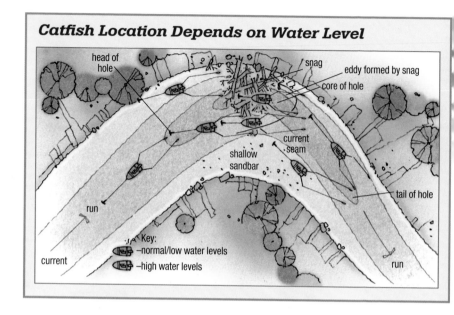

Catfish Location Depends on Water Level

head of hole
snag
eddy formed by snag
core of hole
current seam
shallow sandbar
tail of hole
run
current
run

Key:
—normal/low water levels
—high water levels

complex. We've always advised learning to find cats on small to midsized streams before tackling larger rivers, but that's not an absolute rule.

Holes often are the basic holding areas for catfish during the Prespawn Period—not the deep, slack holes they occupied during winter, but middepth depressions with cover such as snags, boulders, and around wing dams. The size and depth of the hole matters, but the amount and quality of the cover seem to be more important. The fish might not hold near a logjam in the middle of a shallow run, but neither are they usually found in a large, deep hole that's void of cover.

You need to fish a lot of water in order to identify top locations. If you try the bend hole immediately downstream from the boat ramp, you're probably overlooking a much better hole around the next bend. You're also fishing the same area that most other anglers fish. To catch more and bigger cats than the average angler, move more often and cover more water.

THE SPOT ON THE SPOT

Once you've identified a good hole—or better, a few good holes, preferably a few miles from a boat ramp or popular shorefishing access—how do you proceed? If you're like most catmen, you probably anchor upstream from the cover element, cast your baits to the front or side of it, and wait for a bite. If you don't get bit in 20 minutes or so, you pull anchor and move to the next spot.

That's not a bad strategy when the fish are really cranked and the action's fast, but that's the exception. In most small rivers, truly great spots don't exist every mile. Use a run-and-gun tactic when you're exploring a river stretch for the first time, or when you're fishing streams with lots of good holes and an above-average catfish population.

Several factors determine how channel cats set up in a hole, none more important than water level and current velocity. High water usually means faster flows, so if we limit ourselves here to high, normal, and low water levels, we'll have covered most of the conditions you'll encounter.

Tackle & Rigging Refinements

Understanding how channel cats relate to changing water conditions is one key to finding and catching them in rivers. Novice anglers too often look for a shortcut—a secret bait or terminal rig or rod-and-reel combination—to help them catch more fish. Bait and tackle don't matter if you're not fishing in the right spot.

If you've chosen a good spot, though, after carefully evaluating river conditions, then tackle and rigging refinements can improve your catch. During the early season, for example, channel cats often bite tentatively, sampling rather than engulfing baits. Standard J-hooks are a better option than circle hooks in this situation, because they allow you to set the hook as soon as a fish grabs the bait.

More tackle and rigging tips:

■ Use a softer rod for circle hooks than you would for standard J-hooks. A bass-style flipping stick is a fine choice for many catfishing situations, but the tip is too stiff for circle hooks. A softer tip allows cats to move with a bait without feeling resistance.

■ With circle hooks, keep the reel engaged—but use a freespool clicker with J-hooks. Increasing line tension causes a circle hook to rotate in a fish's jaw until the point catches the soft flesh in the corner of the mouth. With a standard hook, though, it's necessary to mini-mize tension and manually set the hook.

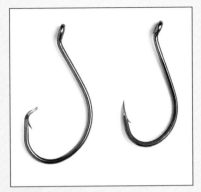

■ Leader length makes a difference. In current, long leaders result in more snags. A 12- to 18-inch leader is fine for clean-bottom areas in slow to moderate current, but a 3- to 6-inch snell is better suited to faster flows.

■ Many anglers have been taught to use the lightest possible jigs and sinkers, but this rule has little application in catfishing. The main line slides freely through the sinker to minimize resistance, and a heavier sinker is less likely to roll, keeping baits in position and minimizing snags. So don't be stingy with the weight.

■ We usually use monofilament line in low water. In heavy current, on the other hand, we use braids. Monofilament offers better abrasion resistance when fishing close to wood and other cover, but the thinner diameter of a braided or fused-filament superline offers less water resistance. Low-stretch superlines also are superior for detecting light bites in heavy current.

During normal water levels, active channel cats hold in areas that provide the best opportunity for a meal. Current is the purveyor of those meals, so it's easy to see why current seams are such high-percentage fishing spots. These areas allow cats to hold out of the main force of the current, positioned to easily intercept morsels carried by the faster water.

In a small river hole, the most active cats might hold in the tail of the riffle at the head of the hole. This is a where the fast water pouring over the shallow riffle slows, dumping its load of insects, baitfish, and carrion—all the stuff channel cats crave. Active catfish get first crack at the food that washes into the hole.

Another top spot is the area

in front of a snag pinned along an outside bend. Inactive fish hold in or behind the snag to escape the current, and then move in front of the timber when they're ready for a meal, thus patrolling another edge along which food is delivered by current.

These same spots are productive during low-water levels, but the sweet spot tends to be more concentrated. Instead of holding in the tail of the upstream riffle, active cats may move right into it (usually a late prespawn and summer tactic), or fall back into the core of the hole. Increased depth in this area offers better overhead protection from predators. Active cats also continue to hold around cover objects, spending the most time along the deeper outside edge, rather than near the bank.

A SYSTEMATIC APPROACH TO HOLES

Low or Normal Water—Once you get a feel for the water level and current speed, and the layout of the hole and available cover, put together a presentation strategy. During low or normal water levels, when active fish are likely near the head of the hole or in front of cover objects, don't motor in and drop an anchor in the core of the hole. Begin by 'nibbling' on the edges.

Your first move might be to anchor in the riffle, which itself can be a productive spot during summer when the water's low and warm but probably holds few cats early in the season. Your target now is the head of the hole. Drop a sliprig into the shallow water at the tail of the riffle during normal levels, or use a split-shot rig to drift a bait into the head of the hole during low-water levels.

The bait itself isn't so important this time of year. Fresh-cut sucker is easy to get and cats love it. But nightcrawlers and even chicken livers also produce, though sometimes they attract smaller cats than cutbait. It's not the best time for dipbaits

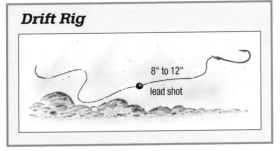

Drift Rig

8" to 12"

lead shot

or other commercial options, although often they work. The effectiveness of dipbaits tends to peak in mid- to late summer.

Let the bait sit for 5 minutes. No bites? Reel in and cast again, into slightly deeper water this time, perhaps at a slight angle toward the deeper outside bend. Sometimes a small area holds several good-sized channel cats. If you're still not on the board, it's time to move toward cover.

Move the boat quietly into position, a comfortable casting distance above the cover. Space often is compressed on small rivers, so you might not have to move far from your initial anchor position. During normal flows, stick with the sliprig, casting the bait toward the center of the snag and about 10 feet upstream. If you don't catch fish in 5 to 10 minutes, reposition your bait in the current seam along the outside edge of the snag. That usually works, but if it doesn't and the snag looks particularly promising, try one more spot, along the inside edge of the wood right up against the bank.

In low-water conditions, the shallow area near the bank seldom produces, unless it's a cutbank with deep water pushing up against shore. You would normally focus on the outside edge of the snag. A sliprig's not a bad option but a slipfloat rig works, too. Set the float stop high enough so that the bait just ticks and drags occasionally on bottom. Let the float drift by releasing line, then check the drift when the bait enters a high-percentage zone such as near the tip of the snag. Hold the bait stationary a few seconds to a few minutes to give cats time to react.

High Water—It's during high water that catfish location really changes. The same spots that afforded current protection during low and normal flows are too fast during high-water periods. In this situation, active cats more likely hold in the eddy that forms behind the snag, or near the tail of the

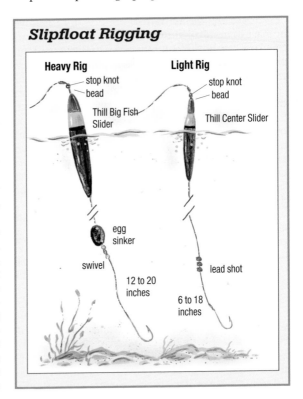

Slipfloat Rigging

Heavy Rig

stop knot
bead
Thill Big Fish Slider

egg sinker
swivel
12 to 20 inches

Light Rig

stop knot
bead
Thill Center Slider

lead shot
6 to 18 inches

hole. They may also vacate the main river by moving into areas flooded by high water, spots that would otherwise be dry.

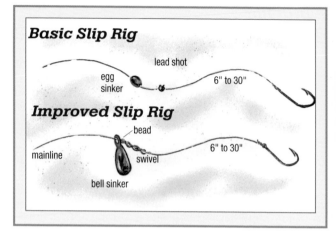

If the water's high, don't bother with a float rig or split-shot rig unless you're fishing a backwater area. Generally, stick with an old reliable sliprig. Anchor first behind the snag, either even with the outside edge of the wood or directly behind the center of the snag. The former position usually is a better choice in moderate current. Drop the anchor in line with the outside edge of the snag but several yards upstream, and let out the rope until the boat's in position. Baits deployed directly downstream should hit the outside edge of the eddy formed by the snag.

If the current's running hard, move in behind the snag. Depending on the depth of the hole and the amount of underwater cover, you should be able to push the boat right up against the wood. Throw the anchor on top of the snag and cinch the rope to a bow cleat. In some situations, a second anchor deployed from the stern makes a more stable fishing platform. A sideways position also allows you to cover the edge and core of the eddy simultaneously .

Your initial casts should be short, covering the area just behind the snag. If you don't get bit in 10 minutes, reel in and position your baits farther back in the hole. Sometimes, the area immediately behind the snag holds the most fish, especially in extremely high water. In this case, drop your bait directly over the side of the boat and hold the rod (instead of using a rod holder) to minimize snags and better detect light bites.

Once you've thoroughly fished the area behind the snag, move to the tail of the hole. In moderately high water you might anchor toward the outside bend of the tailout area. But when the water's high and the current's ripping, the slacker water running on the inside of the bend usually holds more fish—particularly on sharper bends with a large sand- or gravel bar that functions like a wing dam, pushing the brunt of the current toward the main channel.

Whichever side of the river you fish, drop the anchor far upstream from the spot you intend to fish. In most situations, run the boat against shore, especially when you're fishing the inside bend. On the high-bank (outside bend) side , you can run right against the bank and toss the anchor on shore.

In either situation, your target is the area where the bottom starts to rise up—where the back end of the hole transitions into a run. Evidence of this transition usually is visible on the surface: The fairly slack water moving through the hole picks up speed as it's constricted into the shallower, often narrower run. This visible current change usually is several yards downstream from the actual physical transition. You can also use a sonar unit to pinpoint the area you intend to fish.

Tailwaters

Tailwater areas below dams get better and better as spring progresses into early summer. By the time water temperature cracks into the 70°F range, cats are going crazy—and most of the party is taking place in tailwaters. Depending on the tailrace area, you might find channel cats, blues, or flatheads, or some combination thereof.

If there's a problem with fishing tailwaters, it's that sometimes reaching the fish holding in fast-water areas right below the dam can be difficult. However, much of the feeding takes place there, as cats push into current breaks formed by obstructions on the bottom or by the way the water gathers as it's released from the dam.

Even just downriver from the dam, to be successful you must read current, watching in particular how different currents meet to form an edge or eddy. Most of the cats hold along these current edges or roam through eddy areas. Some also move up onto shallow shoreline flats, which often are swept by large eddy areas, where the current isn't very swift . These are prime flats for presenting a bait below a float.

If you've never fished tailwaters and the process sounds puzzling, don't be put off, just go and have at it. Usually late spring into early summer, so many fish are there that you're bound to catch some. You'll soon see to where other folks are fishing and begin to understand what makes them successful. Most cat anglers are generous with their advice and willing to explain what they're doing to catch fish—especially the channel cat anglers. The flathead crowd tend to be more taciturn.

The whole topic of tailwaters is a special case in river catfishing, so we've devoted an entire chapter in this book to providing some tips on how to fish these areas.

Kansas Fluffing

John Thompson of Ottawa, Kansas, perfected his method for "walking" baits down the riffles of the Marais des Cygne and Neosho rivers, revealing them in time to Royce Stiffler of Eudora, Kansas, and several other eastern Kansas catmen. In the late 1970s, Thompson showed John Jamison of Spring Hill how to entice channel catfish by walking bloodbait on the Neosho.

These anglers call bait-walking "fluffing." Jamison finds that it works not only on the Neosho and Marais des Cygne, both relatively small streams, but also on the Missouri, Kansas, Ohio, Tennessee, and Mississippi rivers. The only difference is that heavier tackle is needed on bigger rivers.

The key to Thompson's method is knowing when a bait has settled or found a dead spot in the current. This might be a rock, log, or even a slightly deeper area into which baitfish naturally settle, and where catfish seek shelter from the current.

When Thompson, Stiffler, and Jamison fish smaller rivers like the Neosho, they like 8-foot light-power fiberglass rods and spincast reels spooled with 8-pound-test monofilament. They prefer not to use sinkers, but if necessary, they use a small split shot. When they work with bloodbait, they wrap a thin strip in layers around a #2 Eagle Claw Lazer Sharp wide-bend hook—wrapped tightly, it's durable. With other bait, they opt for #2 Eagle Claw 84 hooks.

For the Kansas River, they choose 8-foot medium-power fiberglass rods and spincast reels spooled with 17-pound-test mono. They choose the same hooks as on smaller rivers, but a larger split-shot is needed in the stronger current of the Kansas River.

They admit that fluffing isn't an easy technique to learn. The mistake that most beginners make, Jamison says, is using a sinker that's too heavy, which doesn't let the current carry the bait downstream. Instead, the sinker and bait stay on bottom, just the line flowing downstream—misread by the angler as the bait properly fluffing.

Bait-walking is an effective method for delivering baits to catfish holding in specific spots, whether it's the tight quarters of a logjam or a snag-free hole. It's also a good way to cover more ground to seek out catfish over larger areas.

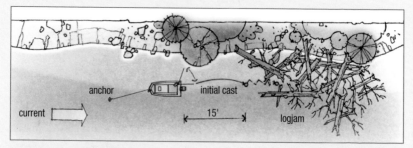

Once the bait settles to bottom, raise your rod so sinker and bait lift off bottom. As current carries the bait, slowly drop your rod until your sinker hits bottom, strip two feet of line off the reel, and repeat lift-drops until the bait settles. Probe front, sides, and interior of the logjam.

This system also applies to larger rivers, but instead of fishing 10 or 15 holes a day, you might only have time to fish two or three holes, on a navigable river like the Upper Mississippi. Instead of that, you might try a dozen spots in each hole and locate several channel cat concentrations. Keep moving—keep to this proven game plan—and you'll catch your share of prespawn channel cats.

BOJANGLES, CAMPFIRES, AND THE NITE BITE FOR BIG CHANNEL CATS

Doug Stange, In-Fisherman Editor In Chief: A small fire is the center of the universe as darkness falls and anglers like you and me sit silently, patiently, on a sandbar opposite a big riverbend hole, listening for a reel clicker to call out evidence of a whiskered intruder. Some nights the action begins at dark and continues for hours. Occasionally, the action peaks late at night, while at other times it never begins and the night is tempered by no more than a fish here and there. A final short round of action is typical, if not guaranteed, during those hours before sunrise, the increasing light apparently signaling a last chance to feed before another day dawns bright and hot.

Lots of you have asked, so I thought I'd take time to answer: Fishing at night has for me never been a consistent connection to larger channel cats, even during the hottest portion of summer. Occasionally, yes. Most times, no. So after more than 30 years of spending hundreds of nights on the prowl, I believe that no overwhelming big-fish pattern prevails. A minor pattern here. A minor pattern there. Just depends. Fishing at night is, however, good enough to be worthy of note. And even if it weren't, I'd still do it just for the excitement and the chance to share a campfire with friends.

Lock-and-Dam Pools: Mississippi River

Before the dams were built, the upper Mississippi River was a braided river," notes Mike Steuck, Iowa Department of Natural Resources research biologist. "Those old, braided channels are still there, submerged in the lower pools, and they're great spots for channel catfish. Catfish hold along the upper edge of the old channels in the main pool. The average depth of a pool might be 10 feet, but the old channels drop into 15 feet or more.

"Finding catfish along the edges on a particular day takes some experimentation," he says. "Sharp drop-offs are good, and any curves or bends in the drop seem to attract cats. I just work up or down the edge of an old channel drop-off, move 100 or 200 yards along that edge, and usually find channel cats within one or two moves.

"I look for a firm bottom—no shifting sand or muck. In the summer when mayfly larvae are hatching from areas of firm mud bottom, catfish gorge themselves on those larvae. Even 5- or 10-pound catfish suck up a bellyful of larvae when they get a chance."

Stumpfields, the submerged remnants of tree-groves in the pools above dams on the Mississippi, are another prime openwater hangout for channel catfish. Steuck says that current dictates where he fishes in stumpfields.

"In summer, I fish the upper ends or the sides, depending on where the current is coming into the stumpfield," he says. "Channel cats like to lie on the edge of the stumps, where the current washes food to them. But during the spawn in June, I'll move to the middle of the stumpfields, because for spawning they're more interested in the cavities and holes in the old

Now, I know a few of you like a little story with your catfishin', particularly if it includes my old buddies Zacker and Toad. Well, one night we'd had ourselves a big ol' midnight feast of cold Kentucky Fried, and the bone piles built up pretty good here and there around our campsite on a sandbar. Feeling fat and sassy, we all settled in for a snooze before morning light broke.

Round about first light I heard rustling in camp, peeked out of my sleeping bag, and there was a big ol' raccoon, butt toward me, tail waving high in the air, not 10 feet away, digging in one of the bone piles. A big dominant male he was, with a set of bojangles like an old Hereford bull; so it wasn't any surprise that when I tried to shush him out of camp, he would have none of it—would just turn, bare his teeth and hiss. He was diggin' those chicken bones, doing the breakfast shuffle, counting his blessings, such as they were.

Soon enough everyone was awake and watching this old boy chewing bones. Funny thing was he'd get grease on his paws—even his feet—and sand would

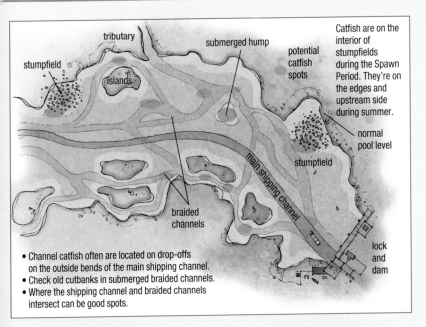

tributary

stumpfield

islands

submerged hump

potential catfish spots

Catfish are on the interior of stumpfields during the Spawn Period. They're on the edges and upstream side during summer.

normal pool level

stumpfield

main shipping channel

braided channels

lock and dam

- Channel catfish often are located on drop-offs on the outside bends of the main shipping channel.
- Check old cutbanks in submerged braided channels.
- Where the shipping channel and braided channels intersect can be good spots.

stumps and rootballs than they are in what food the current brings them."Navigation maps are excellent references when trying to pinpoint the location of channel drop-offs and stumpfields in Mississippi River pools. Army Corps of Engineers offices and local bait shops have these maps, and they also can be downloaded from *mvd.usace.army.mil*.

Steuck notes that side cuts and shoreline channels associated with lock-and-dam pools on the Mississippi are generally silted, shallow, and slow-moving. "That means if you find current, there's generally a little deeper water, and that's a good place to find channel cats. Lots of guys fish the downed timber along the sides of those cuts; but if you find a drop-off out in the middle, you're probably going to find channel cats along its top edge."

stick to them when he walked. Annoyed, he'd stop and then stick way out and up, toes pointing straight as arrows, first one back leg, then the other, and would try to kick off the sand by doing a pathetic three-legged dance—all the while his tail, big butt, and those old bojangles shaking left-right, up-down. Well, we all got to laughing so hard Zacker finally had to get up and water the bushes, or else.

We fished the next day and didn't think much about our buddy Bojangles until we set camp on the same sandbar that night. Now Zacker always carried a pint XXX bottle with him for his arthritis. So just after midnight, Zacker sets this trap—three big yummy-looking chocolate brownies, frosting and all, laced with two sturdy shots of his Russian XXX, mixed neatly in a coffee can set 30 feet away on the sandbar.

Well, it didn't take two hours for that old beggar Bojangles to hit camp. We all awoke to a ruckus and a mournful *whoOOO-chip-chip-chip, whoOOOoo-chip-chip*, which I guess is coon talk for, "How dry I am," or maybe, "The last word in lonesome is me." As we peeked out from our bags, Zacker shined a flashlight toward the ruckus. Bojangles was sitting flat on his butt, tail sticking out at an odd angle between his legs, fur all messed up with chocolate frosting along one side of his face, the can held tight between his paws and legs. His eyes shining in the light, his head would nod a little left and then nod back a little right. *WhooOOOooo-chip-chip-chip.* Have you ever seen a raccoon grin?

Finally, ol' Bojangles stumbled down to the water, intent on swimming the river. He started, then hit the first part of the current, which turned him, and he swam in a circle, hitting the shoreline just about where he started. He stood there for a moment, a little wobbly, considering this odd turn of events: *"But I just left here a moment ago."* After two more tries, exhausted by his circuitous activities, he just flopped himself down on the sandbar and went to sleep. Ever heard a raccoon snore?

Now, I know a few of you like a little story with your catfishin', particularly if it includes my old buddies Zacker and Toad.

Raccoon critters aside, I was about to make observations about the night bite for big channel cats. Typical were our early experiments on the Red River below the Lockport Dam just north of Winnipeg, Manitoba, now the most famous channel catfishery in the world. Toad Smith and I first saw this portion of the river on a June day in the early 1980s. We'd heard tales of the fishery and went to check it on our return from a trip for pike.

We walked down to the bank to a small group of people set up just below what was then Lilly Ann's and now is catman Stu McKay's Cats On The Red—no one else fishing. There on a stringer made of 25 feet of 1/4-inch chain were 15 of the biggest channel cats we'd ever seen. Manitoba had no limit on cats at the time, and the stringer didn't hold a fish under 20 pounds. Nearby a sort of commercial cat-cleaning operation was in progress, with three men cleaning fish and three women canning the fish over several camp stoves.

That was sort of the beginning of the new age of catfishing on the Red in Manitoba. A few articles alerted anglers to the fishery, and the rest is history, including Manitoba's proactive plan to protect the unique fishery, beginning about 1990, with restrictive harvest regulations.

By about 1986, having caught hundreds of 15- to 24-pound channel cats from this fishery during many day trips, Toad, Manitoba friend Ted Jowett, and I began to wonder if we weren't missing the big fish. We resolved to spend a few August nights fishing, to check out a nocturnal bite for big cats.

We fished eddy areas below the dam, as well as the head of prominent holes up- and downriver. One night we caught 28 fish. Toad always counted. Couple small fish and 24 fish from 14 to 23 pounds. Never saw another angler after midnight. Never scratched a fish larger than we would have caught during the day. Seemed the fish never stopped feeding, no matter the time of day, until most of those holding in an area had been caught. That is, if you fished an eddy area below the dam one night, the catch would be drastically reduced the next night. Same thing for fishing the head of a major hole two nights in a row.

The fish in this portion of the Red have gotten larger over the years, but it has everything to do with harvest protection and little to do with time of day. I haven't conducted the same sort of experiment in recent times, but today I'd expect to catch a fair number of 15- to 26-pound fish, as well as a few pushing beyond 30, especially during September—the same sort of fish you'd catch during the day.

We did, however, learn interesting things about fishing at night. The Red has a good flow (at least a consistent flow) most of the year, even when the water's down during summer. Once you move downriver from the tailwaters, the river probably averages 150 yards from bank to bank. Some of those shorelines have a distinct lip connected to shallow flats that connect to midriver holes. So say a shoreline has a lip that drops immediately into a foot or two of water, connected to a flat that runs 3 to 8 to 11 feet deep, which then drops into a hole maybe 15 to 20 feet deep.

If Toad Smith has a legacy in catfishing, something he introduced to the sport beyond his huge personality, it is float-fishing.

If Toad Smith has a legacy in catfishing, something he introduced to the sport beyond his huge personality, it is float-fishing. Toad was using floats when I first heard of him in the early 1970s. Today, drifting cutbaits below a float is popular on the Red and in a few other areas of the country, but it was entirely unheard of back then.

We anchored at the head (upstream end) of major shallow flats and used the current to drift baits over those flats. No need for a lighted float. Just keep your reel in freespool and monitor the drifting float with your fingers as it moves downriver. You can easily feel a fish take the bait. We could easily drift baits for more than 100 yards downriver before reeling in and beginning again. Set the bait below the float so it just bumps bottom most of the time. If the depth changes and the bait drags or floats a foot or so above bottom, cats will still take it. The float not only keeps the bait moving but also keeps it from snagging.

Those flats held a lot of fish at night, and they still do. The surprise was how many pushed right up against lipped shorelines. It seemed like the action peaked in the hours before sunrise, although we also caught fish along those edges during the day. Twenty-pound fish in just a foot or two of water. About 1988, we shot TV shows on consecutive early mornings by fishing from shore on spots like this. I shot one show with Toad, the other with Englishman Duncan Kay. The portion of the filming where Toad and I stood in hip boots drifting baits downriver along those lipped shorelines was never shown, although the other action eventually made it into some of our early videos.

You know, that style of fishing isn't unlike the fishing that transpires this time of year on major river systems like the Mississippi, where falling water levels make it possible to anchor or wade and drift floats over the shallow portions of sand- and gravel bars on or near wing dams. Cats push up onto these flats to feed at night, and it isn't unusual to catch 50 fish a night, though rare to get a fish surpassing 10 pounds. The best wing dams seem to be on inside riverbends, although that isn't a hard rule. The most popular baits are grasshoppers, nightcrawlers, and dipbaits. Most of this is close-range fishing and anglers seem to prefer lighted floats, though the times I've fished this pattern, I didn't find them necessary.

If there's a class of water where an angler has a fair shot at bigger channel cats at night, it's on bodies of water that have a good population of flathead cats in conjunction with channel cats, just the situation we were fishing the night old Bojangles The Bandit wandered into camp. Because of their aggressive predatory nature, flatheads rule these waters, moving all but the biggest channel cats out of primary feeding areas. So, when flatheads feed in daytime during prespawn in May and early June, they hold near large snags and move channel cats into snags on river flats.

Reasons for fishing at night go well beyond the slightly improved chances it provides for taking larger channel cats.

Once summer arrives, flatheads feed mainly after dark, prowling areas with large snags in deeper river holes. Most average-sized channel cats do much of their feeding during the morning, after flatheads stop feeding and hole up for the day. Because only the largest channel cats aren't intimidated by flatheads, only the largest prowl right along with the flatheads after sundown.

After dark on these waters, I target large channel cats by fishing with deadbait, which flatheads tend to ignore in favor of live-bait, the livelier the better. Actually, big channel cats will take either livebait or deadbait, but in my estimation, they tend to prefer fresh cutbait. A typical good set would be with a freshly killed shad or, on the rivers I usually fish, a freshly killed sucker about 8 inches long. I cut off the head and snip off the tail (so the bait casts well and lays well in current) and make a series of cuts to the backbone on one side of the bait.

Using a hook like a 3/0 Mustad 92671 or Eagle Claw 84, I slip the hook through the tail-end of the bait, leaving the hook point exposed. I typically use a simple set rig consisting of a bell sinker (sliding on my mainline) slid right up to the bait. No need for a leader between the hook and sinker. Then I set the reel on freespool with the clicker on and put the rod in a rod holder. Of course, you can get by with a forked stick.

The main mistake anglers make at night is to let cutbait sit too long without tending it. You know how it goes. You set several lines as the sun goes down. Nothing happens for a half hour—so you let the lines sit. After all, they haven't been hit. The key is to fish cutbaits aggressively. Let a bait sit for 20 minutes, then reel it in and freshen it up.

Cutbaits work because they exude juices (blood and oil) that attract cats. Freshen the bait (reactivate it) by making a series of cuts on the other side of the bait, then cast to a different spot. Twenty minutes later, reel in the bait and step on it to squash it a bit, reactivating it again. Then make another cast. It's unusual to go an hour in early evening without getting bit. By then it's time to flip that old bait into the woods for the coons, and put on a fresh bait.

As I've said, when you're set up on a good hole that hasn't been heavily fished, it's unusual not to get action during the first hour after dark. That usually is a hot time for flatheads, too, so I usually also have a livebait such as a lively bullhead set out for flatheads. If nothing's happening during the first hour into the second, chances are it's going to be a long night. Sometimes I just take a three-hour snooze by the fire through the middle of the night, in order to be ready for the peak period that usually begins about the time light begins to crack the eastern horizon.

By this time, your baits having been set for several hours, it's time to freshen them, then stir the fire and make coffee. I've often gone an entire night without any serious fish, only to get into a few nice ones just before dawn. If they don't bite then, chances are you're on a real bummer of a hole, at least until the water rises again and cats have a chance to move back in. This pattern continues into early October in the North Country, and well into early November in parts farther south.

Fishing after dark, in my estimation, only modestly increases the odds of catching larger channel cats, and then only in a few predictable situations. Still, those situations are an important part of the game, especially if you have access to rivers and perhaps reservoirs where flatheads dominate. Don't expect to catch many channel cats in those waters, but the ones you catch likely will be good ones.

Reasons for fishing at night go well beyond the slightly improved chances it provides for taking larger channel cats. Our ancient ancestors ended each day sitting around a campfire. You can almost feel the vibrations across the ages as you consider the stars, the night sounds, the catfish, and have a chance to cross paths with critters the likes of old Bojangles, and characters the likes of Zacker and Toad Smith.

Bojangles, I have to tell you, was the next morning looking the worse for wear. The old boy was still snoozing sprawled on his side, tail pointed south, legs headed east, as I began to poke the fire. "Maybe he's dead?" Toad wondered, as he looked out from his bag. Then a leg twitched, his head raised, and the old boy righted himself. "Just hung over," Zacker said. Such a sad-looking raccoon. Face still matted with chocolate and sand, he began a long slow shaky walk down the sandbar, tail no longer raised jauntily, but dragging in the sand.

"Probably never eat another piece of chocolate cake," Toad said.

"Been there, done that, lesson learned," Zacker said.

Only on a sandbar in the wilderness with these guys, I said to myself. Oh my, it was always hard to tell what another day would bring.

LATE-SEASON PATTERNS

Experiences of top catmen along with results of scientific studies have tightened our grip on the seasonal response of catfish, from small rivers to the largest of watercourses. Myths about notoriously tight-lipped catfish late in the year have been dispelled—in fact, autumn catfishing can be fruitful when conditions are right. At other times, channel catfish can be anything but aggressive, especially after a bout of a miserably cold October or November rain (or worse). But when the cold steel of the hammer drops and the going gets tough at traditional summer spots, the tough get going—right down to the places channel cats ride out Old Man Winter.

"My understanding of seasonal patterns for channel catfish evolved when I regularly fished the Big Sioux River and its smaller tributaries in Iowa," Stange explains. "Lots of channel catfish were in shallow feeder tributaries well upstream from the Sioux in spring. We're talking miles and miles off the main tributary, some no wider than a few yards with water not much deeper than 3 feet. Deeper pools in those same areas held smaller catfish through summer and early fall.

"By late September or early October, catfish vacated summer locations and moved downstream. Catches were better in deep sections of the Sioux, as well as in the deepest holes in lower reaches of the tributaries. Understanding movement patterns to wintering habitat, and knowing what makes a good overwintering area, are keys to catching late-season catfish," says Stange.

SCIENCE REVEALS MOVEMENT DETAILS

Findings of tagging and tracking studies verify traditional ways of thinking about late-season catfish, while results of other studies go against the flow. It hasn't been easy going, since collecting large samples can be difficult and channel catfish have been known to expel internally implanted transmitters, requiring some industrious solutions. Diligence pays off, as these studies provide some of the most detailed information on fall and winter movements.

Late-season movements of channel catfish were investigated in the Lower Wisconsin River system. Biologists implanted radio transmitters into 187 channel catfish and followed them some 85 miles on the Lower Wisconsin River and 65 miles of the adjoining Mississippi.

The fall migration of catfish began in mid-October, with most fish arriving at overwintering sites by early December, reports biologist Don Fago. The Mississippi River was an important overwintering area, especially for fish tagged there and in the lower reaches of the Wisconsin River. Of the catfish tagged in the Wisconsin, 64 percent moved downstream to the Mississippi to overwinter.

But not all catfish moved downstream. A substantial proportion (23 percent) of the fish tagged in the Wisconsin overwintered at Prairie du Sac Dam, the most upstream point of the study site. Many fish tagged at the dam remained there for the remainder of the winter.

The farther downstream a fish was tagged in the Wisconsin, the more likely it was to move to the Mississippi to overwinter. Most of the fish tagged in the Wisconsin 28 to 44 miles upstream of the mouth moved to the Mississippi, while only 21 percent tagged at Prairie du Sac Dam, about 85 miles upstream from the mouth, overwintered in the Mississippi.

The study suggests that in this large tributary of the Mississippi and others like it, finding late-season catfish isn't just a matter of looking downstream, but also upstream if suitable wintering habitat is within reach of the fish. In this case, both the Mississippi and deeper scour holes below an upstream dam provided winter refuge for catfish in this relatively wide and shallow river.

Transitions of catfish downstream in fall have been documented in a number of studies. In smaller tributaries to big rivers like the Missouri or Mississippi, or even good-sized rivers like the Wisconsin, whether or not most catfish leave the tributary in winter likely depends on the availability of suitable wintering habitat in the tributary.

Take the Platte River in Nebraska, for example, a wide and shallow tributary to the Missouri. University of Nebraska-Lincoln researchers implanted 45 channel catfish with transmitters in the lower Platte between 1988 and 1990 to document movement patterns.

Dr. Ed Peters reports 67 percent of movements were downstream in fall, and all movements were downstream in winter, most likely to escape the cold water and current in the shallow Platte, where overwintering habitat was limited. Channel cats moved to deep scour holes in the Missouri, then back up the Platte to spawn in spring.

A study in Perche Creek in Missouri, a tributary to the Missouri River, showed that some channel catfish resided in this tributary year-round, while another group was transient, moving between Perche and the Missouri. Researchers at the University of Missouri and the state's Department of Conservation tagged channel catfish in lower Perche and in an adjacent section of the Missouri to document these movements.

Most catfish tagged in Perche Creek were considered year-round residents, while most Missouri River catfish were transient, moving into Perche at some point. A general pattern of movement downstream in fall was observed, regardless of whether catfish were resident or transient. All the transient fish in Perche

Creek moved to the Missouri River to overwinter. The percentage of transient fish increased farther downstream in Perche, with 72 percent of transient fish using the lower 5 miles.

LATE-SEASON PATTERNS REFINED

Small Rivers—In early fall, catfish are likely to inhabit the same holes where they spend the summer. But once water cools to around 60°F, most evidence points to movement downstream to deeper wintering holes with slow current. Downstream transitions likely dominate movement now because these areas contain relatively deeper water. Don't overlook suitable wintering habitat that may be upstream or in the general river stretches where catfish spend warmer months. They congregate at these wintering spots, particularly once the water temperature drops below the 45°F to 50°F range, and there they remain from late fall throughout the winter.

In early fall, traveling catfish gather where shallow water or other obstructions block movement. Many catfish anglers enjoy success by fishing riffle and run areas upstream of deeper holes. Eventually, the biggest, deepest holes concentrate catfish.

No hard evidence exists to suggest what the minimum depth of a suitable wintering site is in smaller rivers. It appears to be relative to what depths are available—a deep pool in a big river is generally deeper than a deep pool in a small river, and the shallowest rivers are likely to be vacated. Fish the deepest holes, especially those with some form of cover, and the cats should be there or at least on their way. If they're not, keep moving. The most successful anglers are those who fish as many

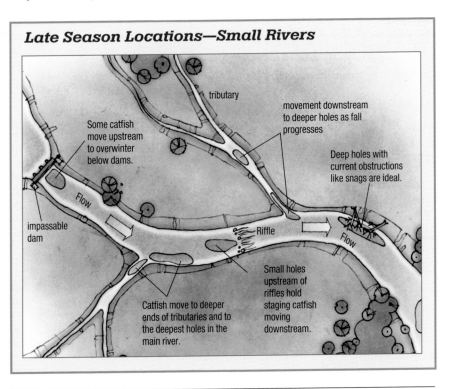

Late Season Locations—Small Rivers

tributary

movement downstream to deeper holes as fall progresses

Some catfish move upstream to overwinter below dams.

Deep holes with current obstructions like snags are ideal.

Flow

impassable dam

Riffle

Flow

Small holes upstream of riffles hold staging catfish moving downstream.

Catfish move to deeper ends of tributaries and to the deepest holes in the main river.

holes as possible. If a river-run reservoir is within reach, Stange suggests the best late-season strategy is to fish deeper areas of a reservoir from a boat.

"There's no doubt weather influences catfish in fall, so watching weather patterns is critical," he says. "October has been a consistent bite month in the smaller rivers I fish in the Upper Midwest. Then the weather gets colder and the nasty late October and November rains and snow slow the bite. I've found that a bout of warm, moderate weather for several days gets fish active again, sometimes even into early winter."

According to Stange, temperature isn't the only factor. "High water can be a disaster. The best bet is if stable mild temperatures are accompanied by stable flows, especially on the moderate to low end of the spectrum. High water and cold weather stimulate movement of channel catfish to wintering areas. If you get a week of moderate weather afterward, fish those wintering holes catfish likely moved to.

"In the South, opportunities for channel catfish are more flexible, even through winter. Fairly mild temperatures won't confine them to winter locations typical of more northern rivers. You can catch channel catfish all year down there but, in winter, the best bets might be in reservoirs," he says.

Large Rivers—Studies indicate that big-river catfish emulate their small-river counterparts late in the season, moving mostly downstream to deeper winter quarters protected from heavy flows. Deep holes near the mouths of tributaries attract catfish that migrated out of tributaries, as well as river residents. Scour-holes associated with wing dams also congregate catfish.

Iowa DNR researchers exmained late-season habitat use by channel catfish that were radiotagged in Pool 13 of the Mississippi River: Catfish during the

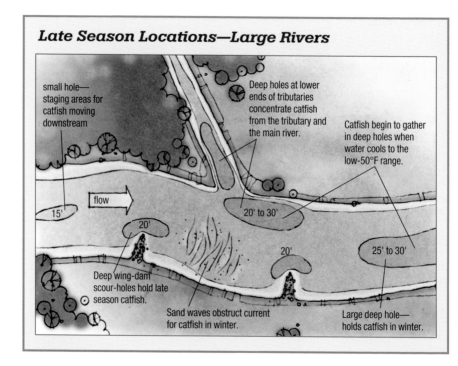

Late Season Locations—Large Rivers

small hole— staging areas for catfish moving downstream

Deep holes at lower ends of tributaries concentrate catfish from the tributary and the main river.

Catfish begin to gather in deep holes when water cools to the low-50°F range.

flow

15'

20'

20' to 30'

20'

25' to 30'

Deep wing-dam scour-holes hold late season catfish.

Sand waves obstruct current for catfish in winter.

Large deep hole— holds catfish in winter.

Missouri River Wing Dams

Channel catfish use of wing dams in winter was studied by the Nebraska Game and Parks Commission. Deep-water electrofishing was used to sample catfish from wing dam habitats in sections of the Missouri River bordering Nebraska.

Deep scour-holes around wing dams with eddy currents are valuable winter habitat, reports biologist Brad Newcomb. The deepest scour-holes held the most catfish, with no catfish at depths less than 12 feet or in currents more than about 1 foot per second. Notched dams provided more suitable winter habitat compared to regular dikes, and catfish appeared more attracted to scour-holes with rock substrates.

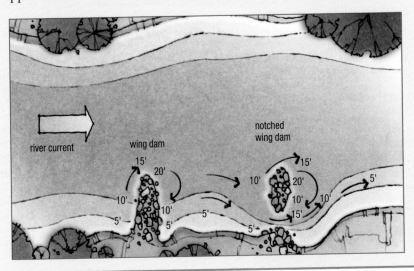

fall-winter period were primarily found in main-channel border areas. Bottom areas that contained sand waves were also used frequently, likely providing current breaks near bottom. Scour-holes near wing dams were an important late-season habitat, as well. As river flows changed, current modified the location of sand waves; catfish responded by moving to new sand waves and different wing dams. Average depths of fish locations increased from about 8 feet during the spring-summer period to about 14 feet in fall and winter, but catfish were found in water as deep as 40 feet.

The winter habitats of channel catfish in the Missouri River were examined by the Missouri Department of Conservation in 1982 and 1983. Eighteen channel cats were outfitted with radio transmitters in a central Missouri stretch of the river. Biologist Tim Grace noted that some catfish moved short distances up tributaries and wintered in 10- to 20-foot holes, while others stayed in deep holes at the mouths of tributaries. Channel catfish selected the deepest available—25 to 30 feet—in the Missouri.

Knowing the river well helps fine-tune location. Red River of the North Guide Stu McKay notes that from September through mid-October, locating channel catfish is challenging because they're spread over many miles. He reports that in early fall, they're often caught from shallow flats, where they're likely feeding on frogs or juvenile white bass. When the water temperature drops to the low-50°F range in late September, they return to the main river channel. When water cools below 45°F, the catfish become increasingly sluggish, falling back to Lake Winnipeg. But some remain in the river and can be caught through the ice, he says.

COLD CATFISH COMFORT FOOD

"Late season is time for bottom-oriented presentations like sliprigs and split-shot rigs," says Stange. "I use a single hook like the Eagle Claw 84 or Mustad 92671, or a beaked design like the Eagle Claw L7226. A jig tipped with a minnow or cutbait is another good option, especially for more vertical presentations from a boat. Float rigs aren't really good anymore.

"I'd rank cutbait at the top for late-season channels—and it needs to be fresh. I've had good success fishing live minnows well into November, and they're also a good bait option for river walleyes this time of year. Freshly killed larger minnows like suckers, with a few slits cut into the side, also produce well. Keep replacing baits regularly to be sure they're oozing substances attractive to catfish."

A fresh chunk of sucker fillet is Stange's favorite bait. "It's important that the fillet isn't too thick. Cut a thin strip about 3/4 of an inch wide and 1 to 1½ inches long. If suckers aren't available and you use coarser-scaled fish as bait, remove the scales—they don't like scaley baits right now."

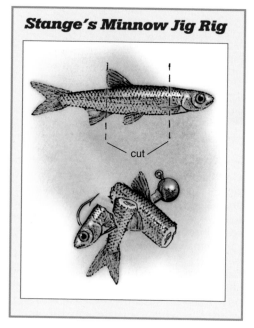

Stange's Minnow Jig Rig

cut

Another of his favorites is a minnow cut into thirds and stuffed onto a jig—tail, midsection, and head. The midsection is added first so the long axis is perpendicular to the hook. The tail section is added next, followed by the head, which holds the package together.

"We used to write about channel catfish as if there was an end to fishing as cold weather set in," says Stange. "But the truth is, there really is no end to catching catfish—even ice fishing, if you're so inclined. Fall offers up the chunkiest channel catfish a water body has. The growing season is wrapping up, eggs are starting to develop in females, and body condition is at its peak. Finding them means understanding what triggers movement and identifying wintering habitats. For year-round catmen, there is no bitter end."

Chapter 9

Species Specifics

The Means to Mighty Blues

**BIG RIVER
BLUE CATS**

Giant blue catfish present one of America's most exciting but overlooked angling opportunities. If you haven't gone gunning for these monsters, get yourself properly geared up with a safe boat and the right tackle, and head for the nearest big river.

Rivers like the Mississippi, Missouri, Ohio, Tennessee, and Cumberland are some of the best venues for big blues. In this chapter, top catmen fishing some of these waterways share their methods. But if you fish other rivers not covered here for blue cats, the same principles for success apply.

Jim Moyer of Clarksville, Tennessee, is a living legend among catfishermen. Over the last 30 years, the retired military officer has spent thousands of hours fishing for big blue cats in the nation's best trophy waters. His largest, from the Mississippi River near Alton, Illinois, weighed 87 pounds 3 ounces; he's caught hundreds over 50 pounds. Moyer knows that major rivers, with their swift current, snaggy cover, and relatively light fishing pressure, offer the best potential for world-class blues. Here he offers a primer on fishing these great waterways for the mightiest of freshwater gamefish.

MOYER ON BLUE-CAT FISHING

The major rivers of the central U.S. have always been premium venues for giant blue catfish. Waterways including the Mississippi, the lower Missouri, the mid-to lower Ohio, and the Cumberland, where I went to school on the haunts and habits of this great species, rank among the best bets for trophy blues—fish over 50 pounds.

Blue cats can be found in slackwater reservoirs, but big rivers have what it takes to grow these fish to giant size: the right temperature regime, plenty of dissolved oxygen, deep swift channels, structure like cascading ledges, snaggy bottom cover, and an ample supply of baitfish. Compared to reservoirs, bigger rivers receive

Legendary Guide Jim Moyer targets big rivers for big blues.

relatively light fishing pressure, most of which is concentrated within 5 miles of a boat launch.

There's no telling how large blue cats can get in the rivers mentioned—I wouldn't be surprised to see a 130- to 140-pounder caught in my lifetime. Historical records mention blues weighing over 200 pounds in the days before dams were constructed along these waterways.

Boats for Big Rivers—If you're serious about scoring a mega-blue, you need a big, safe boat. Major rivers are sub-

Moyer's riverboat features a custom-designed, removable rod rack.

ject to heavy commercial traffic, and it's no fun bucking a barge wake in a 14-foot jonboat. I use a 20-foot Lund 2025 deep-V with a wide 102-inch beam; this is a safe, roomy, stable craft that can take plenty of rough water. It's powered by a 225 hp Mercury OptiMax outboard, powerful and fuel-efficient. I mention this because in a big river, you're going to do a lot of running. Boat ramps are usually few and far between—50 miles apart on some rivers—and you invariably find the best trophy water far from an access point. You can't get by with a couple of 6-gallon gas tanks. My boat's fuel tank holds 58 gallons.

Most of my fishing is done while anchored, but a strong, quiet trolling motor is important for boat positioning and for other tasks like retrieving hung lines. I use a 36-volt MotorGuide powered by Optima batteries. Reliable batteries are a must. The last thing you want to do is spend the night on the river because your big motor wouldn't crank, especially in winter, which is prime time for big blues.

Your boat should be outfitted with several rod holders. I have a removable rod rack. It holds several Santee rod holders, the strongest I've found, and attaches to my boat with downrigger mounts. As for electronics, a graph with GPS capability is a big help for getting you back to offshore ledges in a jiffy and is especially useful when night-fishing.

I use two anchors. One is a unit of my own design that weighs 14½ pounds and is good in rocks. The other is a standard 9-pound naval fluke anchor for use on slick mud bottoms. Three to 5 feet of chain is installed between the anchor and the rope, helping to wedge the anchor into the bottom and reduce rope abrasion.

Frequently, you have to retrieve your anchor to avoid a passing barge or a big tree drifting downriver. A buoy ball attached to the boat end of your anchor rope floats the rope, allowing you to untie and move the boat without hoisting the anchor. Once the barge or obstruction passes, just grab the buoy ball, unhook it, and tie the rope back to a boat cleat. I carry 150 feet of 1/2-inch poly rope per anchor. It usually takes 3 feet of anchor line for every foot of water you're fishing.

Current Events—The flow in rivers I fish is controlled by dams. Big blues thrive in current, and when an upstream dam starts generating, current kicks in, sweeping algae and organic matter off bottom, activating the food chain by triggering baitfish to feed, which in turn lights up predator fish.

Prime Cuts

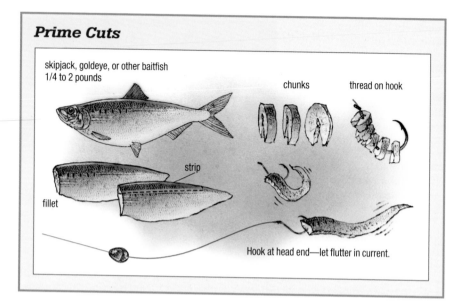

skipjack, goldeye, or other baitfish
1/4 to 2 pounds

chunks

thread on hook

strip

fillet

Hook at head end—let flutter in current.

Current also infuses the water with life-giving oxygen and moderates its temperature, preventing the river from getting as hot as nearby lakes in summer. The tumbling action of current distributes oxygen from top to bottom, so there's less chance of a thermocline forming, common in slackwater reservoirs.

I'm often asked what level of current generation is most conducive to catching big blues. From my experience, a flow of 35,000 to 55,000 cubic feet per second (cfs) is about right, but then, it depends on where you're fishing. If the river's only 100 yards wide, 55,000 cfs would put it above flood stage. As long as you notice a good swirl behind your boat when you're anchored, you should do all right.

Current can get too fast to fish, though I doubt this bothers the blue cats. I use up to 16 ounces of lead on my bait rigs if I have to. Safety becomes the primary concern when the current's really smokin'—it's possible for the bow of an anchored boat to get sucked under, and floating debris can make bottom presentations impossible. Never anchor close to a dam. And always wear your life-jacket when river fishing.

Gearing Up—Heavy-duty tackle is a necessity. I'm now marketing rods of my own design, the Jim Moyer Boss series: 7½-foot one-piece bait-casting sticks in light, medium, heavy, and extra-heavy powers. These strong E-Glass rods are perfect for river catfishing. For big blues I recommend the heavy- and extra-heavy-power rods.

I'm a longtime fan of Abu Garcia Ambassadeur wide-spool baitcasting reels like the 6500 and 7000 series. These have the line capacity, line-out feature, winching power, and reliability required

Fresh bait—can't beat it for big river blues. Here, Moyer doubles up on skipjack herring.

Moyer's Bottom Rigs

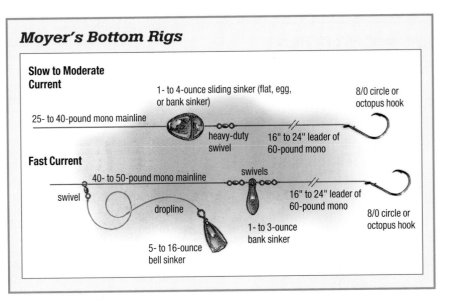

Slow to Moderate Current

25- to 40-pound mono mainline

1- to 4-ounce sliding sinker (flat, egg, or bank sinker)

heavy-duty swivel

16" to 24" leader of 60-pound mono

8/0 circle or octopus hook

Fast Current

40- to 50-pound mono mainline

swivel

dropline

swivels

16" to 24" leader of 60-pound mono

1- to 3-ounce bank sinker

8/0 circle or octopus hook

5- to 16-ounce bell sinker

for tackling big catfish. I usually spool my reels with 40-pound-test Berkley Trilene Big Game mono and use up to 60-pound test for leaders.

Baits and Rigs—Deadbaits rule for big blues and my favorite is skipjack herring. These big baitfish (up to 2 pounds) are abundant in rivers in my region and can be caught below dams on hook and line, using a spinning outfit with a couple of crappie tube jigs tied onto the line. Other regional bait favorites include goldeye, white suckers, chubs, and gizzard shad.

I used to insist on catching bait the morning of the trip, but I've discovered that if it's refrigerated for 3 to 5 days, it consistently out-performs fresh bait. This storage time draws blood and oils toward its outer surfaces, enhancing the aroma and taste for catfish. I also keep frozen bait on hand in case I run out of fresh or refrigerated bait, preserving it in vacuum-sealed bags.

I use Gamakatsu circle and octopus hooks (mostly 8/0) on my rigs. Patience is required with circle hooks; don't set the hook as soon as you detect a bite and expect many hookups. Instead, hold off a few seconds until the rod loads then give the rod a steady, sweeping set. Circle hooks catch 95 percent of the blues that bite—fish are usually hooked in the corner of the mouth or center of the lip, making for clean releases.

Keep plenty of spare line, hooks, swivels, and sinkers on hand, because hangups are just part of the game. And don't try to break 40-pound line with your hands—wrap it around a boat cleat and move the boat to break it, instead.

MOYER'S CUMBERLAND RIVER CALENDAR

Dead of winter (water temperature: 35°F to 40°F)—This is the best time of year to catch giant blue cats, because they remain active and feed heavily in cold water. Target the midsection of the river, keying on ledges from 30 to 40 feet deep—spots that drop off quickly into deep water. If you're unsure where to locate ledges, position your boat near the bank and idle slowly toward the middle of the river, watching on your graph to find where bottom cascades into deep water. Steeper ledges are better than areas with gradual depth changes.

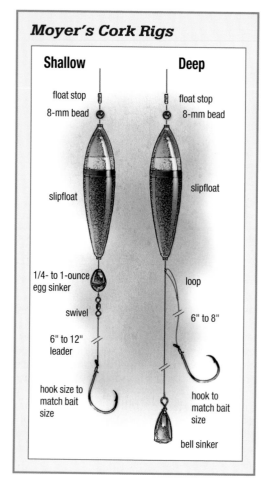

Moyer's Cork Rigs

Shallow

float stop
8-mm bead
slipfloat
1/4- to 1-ounce egg sinker
swivel
6" to 12" leader
hook size to match bait size

Deep

float stop
8-mm bead
slipfloat
loop
6" to 8"
hook to match bait size
bell sinker

Cover in the form of submerged trees, stumps, and logs is a big drawing card. Anchor upstream of the ledge with your boat's bow facing into the current, then gradually let out enough rope to get into position. Make long casts parallel to the ledge, placing your baits between 30 and 40 feet deep. One of your rods typically gets the most bites, so once the productive depth has been determined, cast one or more rigs to the same contour, staggering them 10 to 15 yards apart.

Early spring (water temperature: 45°F to 55°F)—Blue catfish and most other river species generally make upriver moves as the water warms. I often find them within 5 or 6 miles upstream of where I was catching them in winter. Continue to fish steep, deep ledges, with most of your rigs in 30 to 40 feet of water. If it's an unseasonably mild day and overcast, I often cast a rig on top of the drop, maybe 15 feet deep, to catch a roaming blue or a big flathead or two.

Spring (water temperature: 55°F to 65°F)—I find blue catfish located 2 to 3 miles below an upstream dam during this period. Seasonal rains have the water high, murky, and oxygenated. Male blues are nosing around for spawning sites, while big females continue to feed along the edges of steep drops before nesting. Blue cats can be found shallower now, so I fish mostly 12 to 20 feet deep. Keep at least one rig 25 to 30 feet deep, unless the shallow bite is strong.

Spawn Period (water temperature: 70°F to 75°F)—I usually fish for spawners at night because it's too hot for comfortable fishing during the day. Blues spawn around rocks and scattered woodcover in water 5 to 15 feet deep, on sloping banks with deep-water access. Cork fishing is fun and effective during the spawn; be sure to cast to visible cover like rockpiles and laydown logs.

Summer (water temperature: 80°F+)—Big-river blues sulk in deep, dark water and don't eat as often. Fish the coolest, most heavily oxygenated water you can find. The biggest and fastest-flowing rivers like the Mississippi are best for blues in hot weather. Fishermen on nearby Kentucky Lake catch them by vertical-jigging minnows along 60-foot channel drops, but this ain't for me. It's usually too hot, with humidity to match, so I don't bother fishing for blues in the summer.

Ledge Fishing

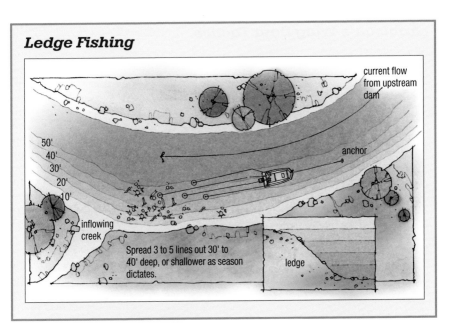

Fall (water temperature: 55°F to 60°F)—It seems to take forever to cool down some rivers to the point where you can fish them again successfully, but once they're down to that 60°F mark, it's time to get back out there. My area rivers can get pretty low this time of year, which pulls predator and prey alike off the banks and sends them to deeper haunts. While the river is falling, try slipfloat rigs around steep banks. Once the river stabilizes, 30 to 40 feet becomes the magic depth again, so hunt up those ledges and start soaking those bottom rigs.

WINTER INTO THE SPAWN PERIOD ON THE MISSOURI

John Jamison of Spring Hill, Kansas, has racked up many catfishing honors, including as 2007 National Points Champion on the Cabela's King Kat Tournament Trail, also placing second in the 2006 Cabela's King Kat Classic. In winter, he primarily fishes the Missouri River from the Nebraska line to Columbia, Missouri. "I cover such a large area because every year is different from the previous, depending on winter migration, which is directly influenced by the amount of water we receive each year," he says. "In low-water years, I don't see a lot of fish far upriver."

Jamison fishes for winter cats in water down into the 30°F range but says winter patterns begin earlier, when temperatures fall to about 52°F and lower. "That's when blues make a big shift, from swifter outside bends to deeper water with less current. The best spots are scour holes around wing dams. The Missouri has a lot of dikes and scour holes but few concentrate blue cats, so you have to search to find fish.

"Current in scour holes runs at about 2 mph compared to 3 to 5 mph in outside bend areas. Depth is important but not the only factor. I normally prefer scour

Jamison's Wing Dam Tactics

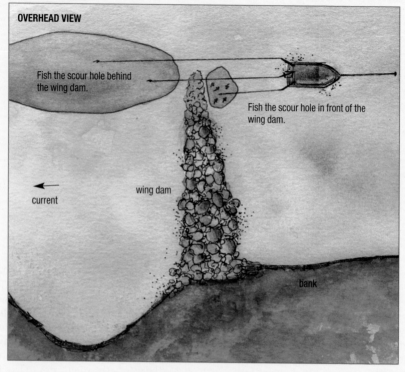

OVERHEAD VIEW

Fish the scour hole behind the wing dam.

Fish the scour hole in front of the wing dam.

current

wing dam

bank

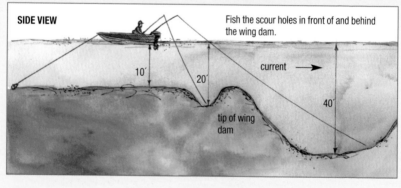

SIDE VIEW

Fish the scour holes in front of and behind the wing dam.

10′

20′

current

40′

tip of wing dam

holes that are 30 to 45 feet deep and seldom fish any that are shallower. A scour hole that's immediately above a good summertime outside bend or channel swing holds more fish than one in a straight stretch of river."

In winter on the Missouri, Jamison primarily fishes from an anchored position, because he hasn't been able to slow a drift enough to be effective in cold water. "I start by placing two rods at the front of a scour hole and two a little farther into it," he says. "I continue to move baits towards the back of the hole until I locate fish. When they're aggressive they tend to be toward the front side of the hole, but I also catch a lot of fish in the back or tailout. Fish in the core of the hole tend to be the least active."

Downsized presentations are key to Jamison's approach. "I believe that smaller is better in winter," he says. "I use a 7/0 to 10/0 Daiichi Circle Wide hook (DZ85) in warm water, but down through the mid-30°F range, I switch to a 5/0 size to better match the smaller baits I use then. My primary winter bait is shad. I cut the head off and use only that. The whole bait is about the size of a quarter to a 50-cent piece, compared to the rest of the year when I'm baiting with 6- to 8-inch sections of cut skipjack herring, shad, or carp."

Blues become particularly sluggish during midwinter cold fronts, he notes. "When there's a combination of a south wind and mild temperatures, blues tend to hit more aggressively. When the wind blows from the north and air temperatures are down in the 30s or lower, the fish bite more gingerly, even big fish, and the smaller hook-and-bait combo has the advantage."

He doesn't fish with the same piece of bait for longer than 20 minutes, noting that changing baits often is key to developing a stronger scent trail. "I think that a small bait emits more scent in cold water than it does in warm water; or maybe the scent dispersion lasts longer when it's cold. Blues still eat big baits, but the smaller baits seem to have the advantage in winter."

Freshly caught bait is often preferred among blue cat anglers. But Jamison offers a theory to the possible benefits of using previously frozen bait. "A common thought in winter is that most of the forage base is winterkill, not fresh livebait," he says. Gizzard shad and other baitfish often experience pulses of mortality in winter, when dead carcasses provide a source of food for catfish." I find that bait stored frozen and then thawed is a better option than fresh. Thawed baits develop a stronger and more distinctive odor, more closely mimicking a winterkilled baitfish. It might be just enough of a difference to attract more cats, at times.

"I learned another trick from a fisherman who's fished the Missouri for years," Jamison says. It's called a stink bucket. Put a bunch of carp fillets in a bucket and throw in a couple of whole shad for flavoring. Refrigerate the bucket for a month

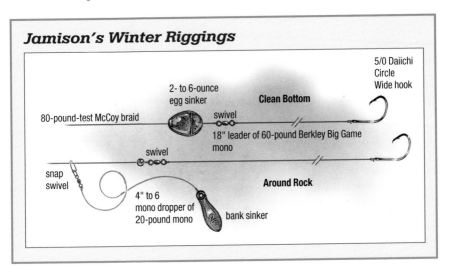

Jamison's Winter Riggings

80-pound-test McCoy braid

2- to 6-ounce egg sinker

Clean Bottom

swivel

18" leader of 60-pound Berkley Big Game mono

5/0 Daiichi Circle Wide hook

swivel

snap swivel

4" to 6 mono dropper of 20-pound mono

bank sinker

Around Rock

or so, and use chunks of cut carp for bait. It works so well I hesitate to mention it." The formula he's referring to is a milder version of a true sourbait, which can be a top option for channel cats feeding on winterkilled shad in early spring.

To present baits, he uses a sliprig. He threads a 4- to 6-ounce egg sinker on 80-pound-test McCoy braided line that's tied to a barrel swivel, followed by an 18-inch leader of 60-pound Berkley Big Game monofilament and then the hook. He hooks the shad through the eyes or, if the current's fast, under the mouth and through the snout to keep the mouth from catching too much water.

If he's fishing around a lot of rock, Jamison ditches the egg sinker and opts for a dropper—a bank sinker tied to a 4- to 6-inch section of 20-pound mono. The dropper's hung on the mainline using the snap end of a snap swivel. If the sinker gets snagged, the dropper breaks, saving the rest of the rig. He uses braid exclusively for a mainline, noting that since he's made the switch, his hooking percentage has risen to above 90 percent.

Through trial and error, he arrived at a leader length of around 18 inches for his coldwater setup. "In the slower currents in the scour holes, you can get away with a longer leader. It allows the bait to waft around in the current without flapping too wildly. When leaders get too long, though, you lose control over the bait. I sometimes walk baits downriver through spots, lifting the rig off bottom and letting it move downstream in increments, and that gets difficult when a leader's too long."

To match the lighter-style fishing in winter, he downsizes rod weight, using the Blue Cat Number 2, the lightest of his three signature series E-Glass models available from The Rod Shop (816/454-6740) in Kansas City, Missouri. The Number 2 is an 8-footer and has the softest tip in the series. This helps to detect lighter bites that often occur when midwinter fronts move through.

SPRING

In March and early April, blues forage frequently and ravenously, says Jamison. And as the water begins to slowly warm during the transition from winter to spring, the fish become so gluttonous that even a harsh cold front won't completely stymie their wolfish nature. In fact, he caught and released a 77-pounder as a brutal cold front and north wind sashayed across central Missouri in the early spring of 2003. But day in and day out, he says, the best fishing occurs after several consecutive days of balmy weather, with warm breezes from the south.

Missouri River catmen continue to ply wing dams in March and early April. But Jamison says that most anglers probe only the current seam that courses off the tip of the dam and the scour hole below. They usually don't fish the scour hole above the dam, which is where he tangled with the 77-pounder and half of the other blues he caught during the early spring of 2003.

Before he fishes a wing dam, he examines it with sonar, beginning his exploration by motoring upstream in the seam of the current below the wing dam and slowly moving above it, searching for a scour hole along the face of the dam. Not all wing dams have a scour hole above them, but the best ones do, he notes.

While searching for the contours of a scour hole, he also monitors his sonar, and, when it reveals a gaggle of big fish milling about near the bottom, they're usually blue catfish. A large congregation of suspended big fish, meanwhile, normally indicates carp, although sometimes, he says, those suspended fish are blues rather then carp, and the only way to positively identify them is to catch one.

Fishing the Tip of the Wing Dam

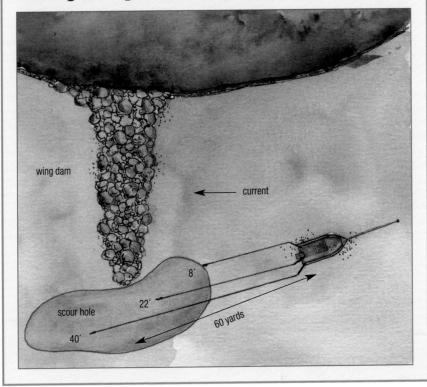

Jamison's favorite bait is either a fresh gizzard shad or goldeye. But since a substantial amount of winterkill moves downriver in March, blues will also inhale a freshly frozen shad or goldeye impaled on a 10/0 hook.

If the river rises more than 6 inches above its normal flow, the location of the blue cats that gather along the current seam at the tip of a wing dam will change. Jamison says they move into the scour hole immediately below the dam, a move that gets them away from the debris flowing downstream and shelters them from the current.

In the locales he fishes on the Missouri River, the channel depth during normal water levels ranges from 12 to 15 feet, while the depth along the outside bends of the river ranges from 20 to 25 feet. He avoids fishing portions of the river that are devoid of bends, he says, as one of the verities of Missouri River blue-cat fishing is that those parts of the river with a multitude of bends are also graced with a multitude of blues cats.

The water temperature for his late-winter and early-spring pattern ranges from 34°F to nearly 50°F, but as it rises and eventually broaches 45°F, the massive congregations of blues begin to disperse, and individuals scatter far and wide throughout the river system. Consequently, the number of blues Jamison catches diminishes: Instead of tangling with 200 pounds of cats at one scour hole, he catches only one here and one there.

SPAWN PERIOD

By the time the water temperature exceeds 50°F, blues start their gradual and inexorable progression to spawning sites. The spawn on the Missouri River encompasses nearly 7 weeks and, during this period, continuous waves of new participants invade the spawning grounds, he says. Some observers suspect that a few of the males that remain near spawning sites mate with more than one female.

Both males and females prepare the spawning bed, but after the female deposits her eggs and the male fertilizes them, it's the male's bailiwick to keep the nest clean, oxygenate the eggs, and protect the nest from creatures that seek to consume the eggs and fry. Traditionally, the last male leaves his spawning nest around July 15.

During the spawn, many of the fish become emaciated and are blemished with sores and scars. From Jamison's perspective, this 7-week spell is the most difficult period of the year to consistently catch big blues. Nevertheless, he occasionally drives the barb of a Gamakatsu Octopus hook into the jowls of a blue cat of substantial proportions.

He attaches an 8-ounce egg sinker above an 18-inch leader of 80-pound Dacron, affixing the leader to a 10/0 Gamakatsu Octopus hook with a snell knot.

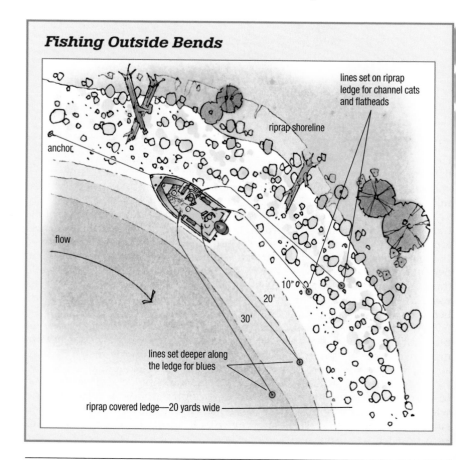

Fishing Outside Bends

lines set on riprap ledge for channel cats and flatheads

riprap shoreline

anchor

flow

10"

20'

30'

lines set deeper along the ledge for blues

riprap covered ledge—20 yards wide

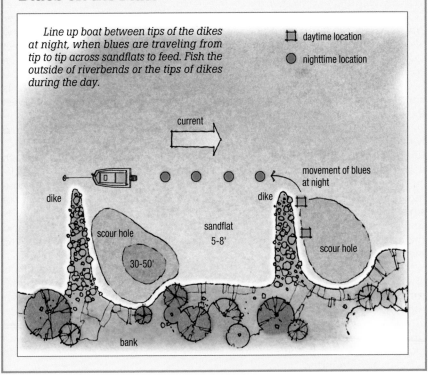

Blues on the Flats

Line up boat between tips of the dikes at night, when blues are traveling from tip to tip across sandflats to feed. Fish the outside of riverbends or the tips of dikes during the day.

⊟ daytime location

⬤ nighttime location

current

movement of blues at night

dike

dike

scour hole

sandflat
5-8'

scour hole

30-50'

bank

His choice of baits ranges from freshly cut shad, carp, or goldeye to live green sunfish and chubs.

When the river flows from normal to no more than 2 feet higher, he fishes outside riprap riverbends during daylight hours. Rather than probe the steep or nearly vertical sections of these bends, he focuses on gradually sloping areas, concentrating primarily on notches and depressions along these banks. Blues in these areas are searching for, preparing, or guarding a nesting site.

Jamison and a partner employ a total of four rod-and-reel combos, placing one over the drop-off and allowing the bait to settle into about 25 feet of water, while three other outfits work the gradually sloping topography of the riprap, plying water as shallow as 4 feet. At these riprap bends, he doesn't fish a fruitless section for more than 30 minutes, he says.

These areas can be fished at night, but they usually are replete with snags, and getting snagged, breaking lines, and tying rigs compounds the inherent chores of night-fishing. Moreover, the necessity to move every 30 minutes is difficult to accomplish at night.

Therefore, at night, during the early stages of the spawning season and toward the end of it, Jamison prefers to fish the flats in 4 to 8 feet of water between wing dams, the same environs he works for blues during summer. During the early days of the spawn, he says, "some fish are still actively feeding and covering a lot of ground looking for spawning sites.

Also, near the end of the spawn, some fish have spawned and are once again actively feeding."

At night, the flats are easier to fish than the riprap bends because of fewer snags. And if an angler is anchored at a bountiful flat, he can stay there all night and allow the blues to come to him.

When working a flat, Jamison changes the length of his leader to 24 inches. The speed of the current, he notes, is what dictates the length of the leader. According to his formula, an 18-inch leader is for fast water, a 24-incher for slower currents. He also substitutes a 3- or 4-ounce No-Roll sinker for the egg sinker on the flats.

But he regularly utters an important disclaimer about working flats during the heat of the spawn: "The flats are typically dead—no-fish zones—from June 15 to July 1, when most of the fish are spawning. Believe me, I've spent years and many, many fruitless nights figuring this out."

During those spawning seasons when the river flows high and hard, Jamison moves to L dikes, also called trail dikes. Many of the blues have moved there, he says, taking refuge from current and debris that accompany the high water by moving inside the L-shaped wing dams. If the water stays high throughout June, the blues also spawn in the crevices and depressions of the riprap that line the inside of these dikes.

He fishes an L dike by anchoring his boat on top of it and then placing his baits at various spots along the inside edge, using a 24-inch leader and a 4-ounce flat sinker. In his experience, L dikes are productive both night and day at high-water times during the spawn.

Even though Jamison pigeonholed the spawning season as his most trying and least fruitful period of the year, he still manages during every spawn to enjoy a Donnybrook with some 30-pounders—during the spawn of 2002, he caught and released a 65-pounder.

WINTER INTO SUMMER ON THE MISSISSIPPI

The angling duo of Mark Farrow and Luke Steen caught 151.6 pounds of blue and channel catfish from the Mississippi River near Ft. Madison, Iowa, to win the 2004 Cabela's King Kat Tournament Trail National Championship. They bested the second-place finishers by 24 pounds, and their 40.75-pound blue won the honors for biggest catfish.

Mississippi River blue cats relish deep-water abodes surrounded by fast current. During the dead of winter, when ice appears around Alton and St. Louis, Farrow and Steen fish downstream near Cape Girardeau, Missouri. From December to the middle of March, Steen notes, the number of blue cats that inhabit some deep holes can reach astronomical proportions, and some of the best wintering holes are at wing dikes. Along a series of wing dikes, the one that has a deep hole above and below its tip is often best, he says.

As the water temperature slowly escalates in late March and into early April, the blue catfish become ready to leave their wintertime holes. Some of the blues in the Mississippi from St. Louis, Missouri, to Keokuk, Iowa, migrate upstream, heading toward the holes at the tailraces below locks and dams.

Other blue cats roam the deep-water ledges along the outside bends of the river channel in 20 to 25 feet of water. To fish such a ledge, Farrow and Steen anchor their boat on the ledge with the bow pointed upstream and their rods across the

Winter on the Ohio

During the dead of winter, the water temperature of the Ohio River below Markland Dam, located just upstream from Madison, Indiana, hovers around 38°F. Jeremy Leach, an experienced Ohio River angler from Lexington, Indiana, says that even though winter isn't his favorite fishing season, it possesses one great asset the other three seasons lack. The whereabouts of channel and blue catfish are relatively easy to pinpoint: They inhabit the deepest holes in the river. On the portions of the river that Leach fishes, channel catfish are more numerous than blues and flatheads.

An ideal wintering hole on the Ohio River, in his eyes, is along an outside bend of a river channel a quarter-mile long and 60 yards wide. At one spot, it's 15 yards from the shoreline and its farthest point from the riverbank is about 60 yards. The topography of this locale consists of a flat, much of it covered with 5 feet of water. The flat stretches from the shoreline to the hole and then abruptly plummets from 20 feet of water into 40 feet. In addition, a power plant regularly discharges a stream of warm water into the river just upstream from the hole, and Leach notes that industrial and power-plant discharges often attract scores of catfish. The channel and blue catfish reside along the back of the hole next to the precipitous drop-off. Flathead catfish reside in this hole, too.

Other than at a riverbend, Leach says that during the winter deep holes below locks and dams can shelter a throng of blue and channel cats, as well.

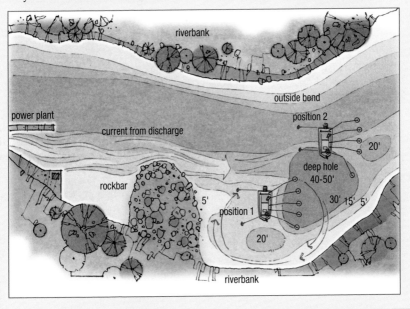

stern. The boat is positioned so baits can be placed at various depths and areas along the ledge to intercept cats as they meander and forage.

Proper anchoring tactics, they note, are one factor that separates topnotch blue-cat anglers from run-of-the-mill fisherman. Another essential element is the right bait, but if the boat isn't properly anchored so that these baits can be precisely presented, the finest bait is worthless.

The most significant post-winter change occurs after the first massive spring rain causes the river to rise. Most high-water situations commence in mid-April and continue into June. After a springtime deluge causes the river's water level to rise 10 feet or so, outside bends become unfishable. Not only is the current too swift to properly anchor the boat along a ledge on an outside bend, but it's cluttered with debris.

When these outside bends can't be fished, Farrow and Steen explore the ledges along the inside bends of the river. Many of the best ledges are in about 22 feet of water. They anchor the boat and present their bait on inside ledges during high-water spells the same way they do on outside ledges during low water. Besides probing deep-water ledges during the spring, they also fish deep water adjacent to wing dikes , noting that some hold blue catfish year-round.

SPAWN PERIOD INTO SUMMER

About the time that high water recedes in mid-June, some blue cats spawn. Farrow estimates that the spawning season lasts until mid-July. He and his partner prefer not to catch blue catfish that are more concerned with procreation than with foraging, so they never probe spawning locales. Instead, they keep fishing deep-water haunts. Although their catches are never substantial, they manage to tangle with a few blues even during the doldrums of the spawn.

Besides the bountiful numbers of blue cats that abide along the deep-water ledges and holes adjacent to wing dikes, Farrow discovered in 2002 some deep-water

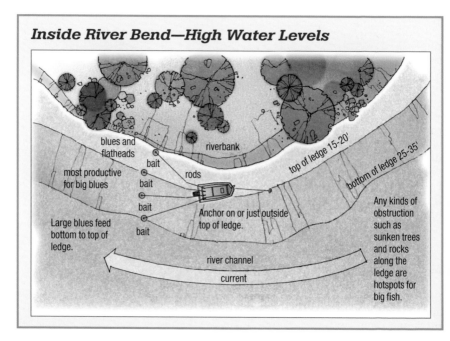

Inside River Bend—High Water Levels

blues and flatheads
riverbank
top of ledge 15-20'
bottom of ledge 25-35'
bait
rods
most productive for big blues
bait
bait
Anchor on or just outside top of ledge.
Any kinds of obstruction such as sunken trees and rocks along the ledge are hotspots for big fish.
Large blues feed bottom to top of ledge.
bait
river channel
current

riverbank

bait — 20' channel cats
bait — 25' big blues
rods bait — 30' and flatheads
bait — 35-40' most productive for big blues

Anchor boat on or just outside top of ledge.

Current cuts into bank carving steep ledge.

top of ledge 10-20'

bottom of ledge 35-40'

top of ledge 10-20'

bottom of ledge 35-40'

river current

river channel

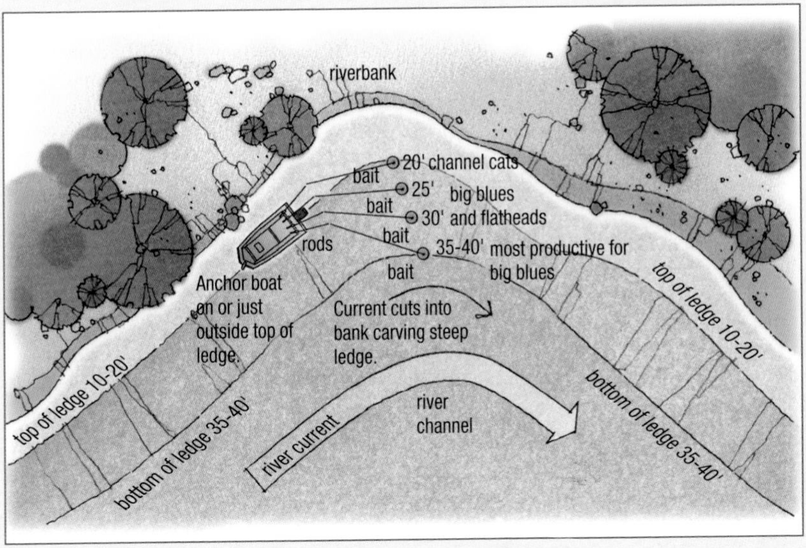

lairs that often hold impressive numbers of big blue catfish, a unique series of dikes, which anglers need a sonar to pinpoint. Because they're situated in the middle of the river, Farrow calls them midriver dikes. Not fished by many other anglers, the top of these dikes is about 20 feet deep, dropping quickly into about 40 feet of water.

The best midriver dikes are two that are about a long cast apart, they note. Farrow and Steen anchor their boat on the upstream dike, placing the anchor on the steep upstream side. The rope is tied to the boat's bow so that the boat floats just above the top of the upstream dike. So placing it, they can fish along both the upstream and downstream sides of that dike, and make casts to probe the upstream side of the downstream dike.

Blue catfish can hold at a variety of spots along these midriver dikes. The blue cats along the upstream side can be found suspended in 20 to 30 feet of water, with the best locales at the ends or tips of the dikes; because they are in the middle of the river, each dike has two tips to check.

These midriver dikes hold blue catfish from mid-June through September, and Farrow and Steen have caught and released as much as 300 pounds of blue catfish during a 4-hour outing, with many specimens weighing 35 pounds and the biggest reaching 60.

LATE SUMMER AND FALL PATTERNS

MISSISSIPPI RIVER, MEMPHIS

James "Big Cat" Patterson of Bartlett, Tennessee, has been fishing for blue catfish for almost 30 years, guiding professionally for the past decade on the Mississippi River in the vicinity of Memphis, Tennessee. Most of his days are spent pursuing trophy blues, although he's also wise to the ways of the river's channel

Farrow and Steen's Riggings

Farrow's favorite rod is a vintage #3 Berkley E-Cat, which sports an Abu Garcia 7000 baitcast reel spooled with 60-pound-test Stren Super Braid. Steen works with the same rod and reel, but prefers to use 40-pound-test Berkley Big Game monofilament.

When plying blue-cat abodes in 25 to 35 feet of water buffeted by a heavy current, Farrow opts for an 8-ounce flat slipsinker. After he strings the line through the sinker, he threads on a bead and then attaches the top eye of a 1/0 barrel swivel to the braided line with a palomar knot. To the bottom eye of the swivel, Farrow executes another palomar and affixes a 36-inch leader made from 40-pound-test Stren High Impact monofilament. The rig is finished by attaching a hook to the leader with a palomar knot.

Farrow uses two styles and two sizes of hooks: a 7/0 and 8/0 Kahle and 8/0 Gamakatsu Octopus. When he uses three or four chunks of one-inch-thick skipjack herring steaks, the Kahle hook allows the chunks of bait to lie on the bottom. But when he baits with a gizzard shad head or a fillet from a 7-inch shad, he uses the Octopus hook. He chooses the same hook when he baits with a 5-inch skipjack herring, which he hooks through the eyes.

Steen likes red Daiichi circle hooks, ranging in size from 6/0 to 10/0. Rather than setting the hook, he allows the catfish to impale itself on the circle hook.

Both anglers favor fresh skipjack herring as bait. Along the areas they fish on the Mississippi, skipjack can be found only from mid-April to mid-October. When skipjack can't be had, Farrow and Steen use gizzard shad. When neither shad nor herring can found, they use pieces of Asian carp.

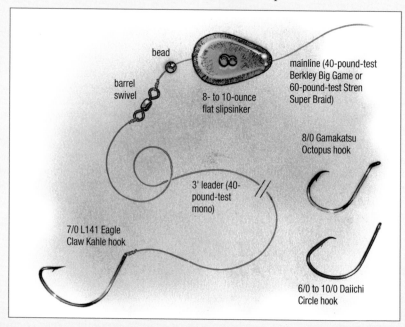

bead

barrel swivel

8- to 10-ounce flat slipsinker

mainline (40-pound-test Berkley Big Game or 60-pound-test Stren Super Braid)

8/0 Gamakatsu Octopus hook

3' leader (40-pound-test mono)

7/0 L141 Eagle Claw Kahle hook

6/0 to 10/0 Daiichi Circle hook

Walking a Revetment Bank

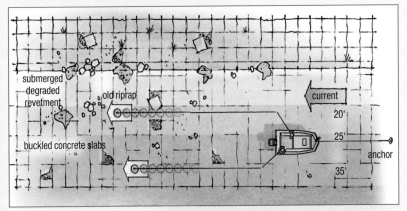

submerged
degraded
revetment

old riprap

current

20'

25'

buckled concrete slabs

anchor

35'

Walk baits back by lifting rod tip slightly and letting the current carry baits downstream over bottom. Walk in short increments while thumbing the spool.

PHOTO I BILL DANCE

and flathead catfish. He's an accomplished tournament angler, too, with big finishes at a variety of events.

Revetment banks—Patterson is familiar with the numerous wing dams jettying from shore into the Mississippi, and has caught many notable blues from the scour holes around these structures. "Wing dams can be good any time of the year, but they're also feast or famine," he says. "The best ones have well-defined holes, but those are becoming scarce because many of the older dams have filled in with sediment, and the remaining good ones get fished so heavily that it's sometimes hard to get on a good spot." So Patterson often focuses on alternative locations that might hold blue cats.

"Some of my favorite spots to fish in summer and early fall are faster current areas adjacent to revetment banks," he says. Expansive revetment blankets, consisting of concrete slabs tied together with cable, are laid along the shoreline and often covered with riprip for added stability. Revetment is installed by the U.S. Army Corps of Engineers to stabilize and protect highly erodable riverbanks where the force of the current is greatest.

"These banks provide structure and cover attractive to big blue cats and their prey, especially where older sections of revetment are falling apart," he notes. "Over time, riprap is redistributed, cables break, and the water washes out holes between and under the slabs where they've broken apart. In other places slabs have buckled, creating areas of current protection near bottom that hold big blues.

"I avoid fishing revetment banks when the current's so fast that I can't use any sinker weighing less than a pound," he says. "In summer and early fall, I prefer fishing a lower water stage, bringing the bank closer to the channel edge in about 35 to 40 feet of water. At lower river stages, the current is still swift along revetment banks and the blues like the current, but I can fish them with sinkers of 12 ounces or less."

Patterson uses primarily skipjack herring for bait, either freshly caught or previously vacuum-sealed and frozen for later use. He baits with the head, chunks or steaks from the larger back portion, or with fillets. Before steaking, the entire belly-meat section, including entrails, is cut out and wrapped together with rubber bands, creating another dandy bait. At times, he also uses whole gizzard shad.

Baits are delivered on three-way rigs with a 7/0 to 10/0 Kahle or wide-gap hook, tied to an 18- to 24-inch section of 60-pound-mono leader, and a 3-ounce or heavier casting or cannonball sinker tied to a 20- to 30-pound-test dropper, with current speed dictating sinker weight. While fishing from an anchored position and for weights up to about 4 ounces, he uses 7-foot heavy-power Quantum Cabo PT rods. In faster currents requiring heavier sinkers, he switches to 7½-foot medium-heavy to heavy-power Quantum Big Cat rods. He prefers using stiffer rods for feel and hook-setting power. Quantum Cabo PT level-wind trolling reels spooled with 65-pound Stren Super Braid complete the setup.

"Along a typical revetment bank, I anchor in about 25 to 30 feet of water, positioning baits along the slope from about 25 to 40 feet deep. One of the most effective presentations in summer and early fall is to 'walk' baits behind the anchored boat. If I'm fishing alone, I set one bait to fish stationary while I walk the other," he says.

After a short cast behind the boat or after releasing the rig boatside, he thumbs the open spool while the bait drifts slightly downstream and to bottom. Once bottom is felt, the spool is again thumbed and the rod tip lifted slightly, to allow the current to carry the sinker and bait downstream in short increments of 6 inches to a foot.

"It's important to feel the sinker thump bottom as you walk a bait," he says. "Some of my clients not familiar with feeling bottom, continue to let out line on a snagged rig; so the current carries line downstream while the rig is stuck in one spot. Because the right sinker weight helps maintain bottom contact and feel, I bring sinkers in the range of 3 to 12 ounces to suit different current speeds. Sinkers that are too light move too quickly; ones that are too heavy don't allow the bait to move downstream on the subtle lifts. The feel of sinker on bottom is also what makes a stiff and sensitive rod important," he notes.

"Walking is a great way to stay in contact with your bait and for identifying bottom objects like rock, concrete slabs, and other cover that accumulates in revetment areas," Patterson says. "Baits can be walked effectively as far back as 200 feet, and I think this mimics natural food items that slowly tumble downstream over bottom. The sinker thumping bottom might also attract catfish to the bait. The farther downstream the bait is and the flatter the line, the more slowly you can walk the rig. As a general rule, the faster the current is flowing, the harder a blue cat strikes a walking bait."

Drifting sandbars—From summer into early fall, Patterson's preferred method for locating and catching big blue catfish is to drift the Mississippi's expansive sandbars. "The best sandbars are those with rollercoaster bottoms," he says, "with depths typically ranging from 25 feet on the tops of the sand humps to 45 feet in the troughs. I've caught blue cats drifting in water as shallow as 15 feet and as deep as 94 feet."

Big Cat's rigs for drifting are three-ways, with a Kahle hook tied to an 18- to 24-inch leader of 40-pound mono, and a 20- to 30-pound mono dropper of the same length to hold the sinker—4 ounces in most cases, which is usually plenty

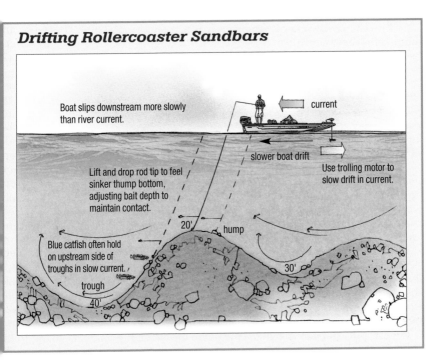

Drifting Rollercoaster Sandbars

Boat slips downstream more slowly than river current.

current

slower boat drift

Use trolling motor to slow drift in current.

Lift and drop rod tip to feel sinker thump bottom, adjusting bait depth to maintain contact.

20'

hump

Blue catfish often hold on upstream side of troughs in slow current.

30'

trough

40'

to feel bottom. He prefers the cannonball-style sinker for drifting because it makes a good thump on the sand, using a 7-foot medium-heavy to heavy Quantum Cabo PT trigger-handle casting rod, and a Cabo PT trolling reel spooled with 40-pound-test Super Braid. Clients can hold the lightweight rod for long periods without fatigue, and the graphite is sensitive for feeling sinkers on bottom. He baits drift rigs with golfball-sized chunks of skipjack.

"I use a controlled drift, slowing the drift with a trolling motor while keeping the bow pointed upstream," he says. This method, often referred to as "slipping," allows baits to be fished more vertically and on a shorter line, helping to control them while maintaining feel and contact with bottom. "Drifting is best using a short line, with the bait bouncing bottom about 20 feet downstream of the boat. The line's usually at about a 10-degree angle. It's important not to jig the rig too aggressively. Subtle lifts and drops of the rod tip are just enough to help the bait scoot along on bottom in the current. The steep line angle also keeps the bait swimming downstream slightly above bottom, while the sinker thumps it along the way," he explains.

Most of Patterson's catches while drifting occur on the upstream portions of the drop-off from a hump into a hole. "When approaching a hole, it's important to slow the drift and let out line to maintain contact with bottom, keeping the steep line angle. The extra time also allows blues to find the bait. They often hit it on the fall as line is let out to reach bottom," he says, "and they commonly swim straight up with the bait in their mouth, which is why I like a fairly long rod to take up slack in a hurry."

He relies on good electronics to adjust the depths of his rigs to work bottom, as the depths change over the series of humps and troughs, and also uses a GPS unit to adjust course to stay on trails of productive drifts.

"If I'm fishing with clients who have a difficult time maintaining contact with bottom while on a controlled drift, I switch to dragging baits over the same sandbar areas," he says. "It's an easier way for beginners to fish, and it's also effective. I shorten the sinker dropper on three-way rigs or use Carolina rigs to drag baits. The sinker dragging bottom creates a plume that might be an additional trigger. When blue cats take a bait, they're notorious for swimming downstream towards the boat, so it's important to watch for slack line that often indicates a bite. Reel up slack quickly and set the hook."

MISSOURI & MISSISSIPPI RIVERS, ST. LOUIS

Carl Roberts, St. Louis, Missouri, is a quick study in locating and catching big blue catfish. He wasn't exposed to fishing growing up—rather, he played a variety of sports until three knee surgeries sidelined him. Then he took up catfishing, beginning as a bank angler. After a couple of years he bought his first boat and caught a chronic case of the catfishing bug. He now guides professionally and is a serious competitor in catfish tournaments.

He primarily targets big blues, although he fishes for channel catfish, as well. Most of his pursuits are in the lowermost reach of the Missouri River—from its mouth at the Mississippi upstream to Weldon Springs, Missouri; and from the Mississippi north of St. Louis upstream to Grafton, Illinois. Although he finds daytime fishing productive, his day job forces him to be on the water most often during the evening and after dark.

Roberts puts skipjack herring at the top of the list for big blue cats. In the areas he fishes, this baitfish typically begins to appear in late March to early April. "I catch them on small curlytail jigs with a red head and white body, but other colors like chartreuse and black work well, too," he says. "I also use Sabiki rigs with four jigs, sometimes catching multiple skipjacks at a time. The best spots are where they concentrate in turbulent water below dams and around wing dams. As the river cools in October and November, they can be caught at warmwater discharges." He vacuum-seals and freezes whole baitfish to keep year-round.

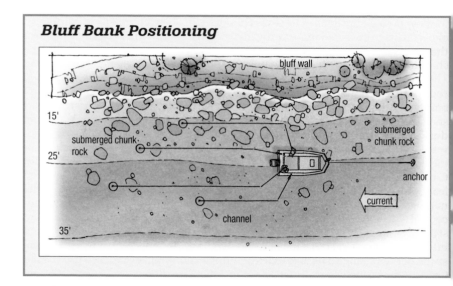

Bluff Bank Positioning

Bridge Piling Setup

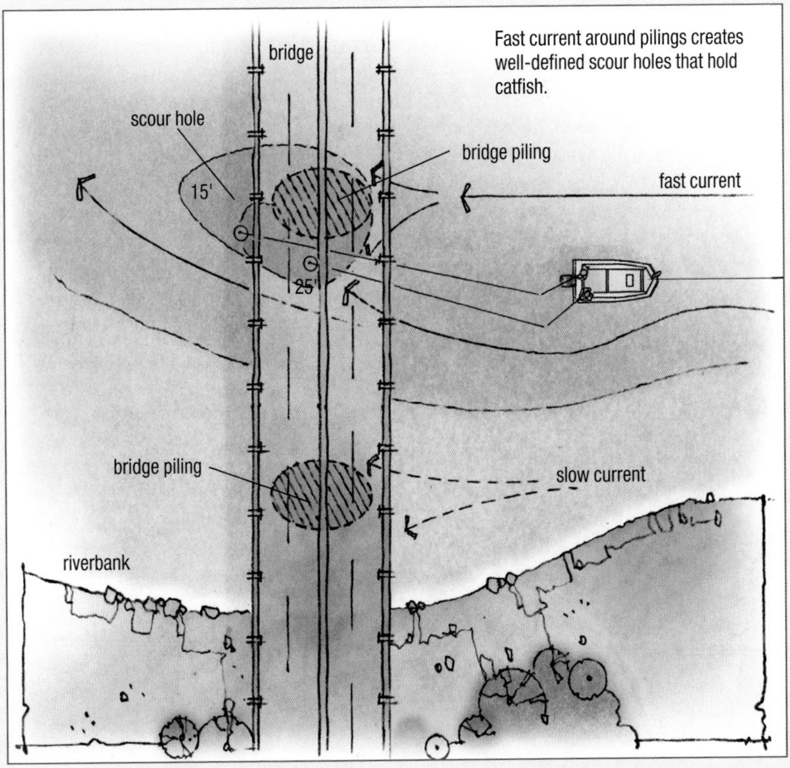

Fast current around pilings creates well-defined scour holes that hold catfish.

bridge

scour hole

15'

bridge piling

fast current

25'

bridge piling

slow current

riverbank

Bluff banks—While he also fishes wing dams when conditions are right, some of his favorite spots for targeting big blue cats are the bluff banks scattered along the lower Missouri. "The bluffs are always my first stop," he says, "because the characteristics of bottom along these banks attract big catfish."

Over long periods of time, weathering and erosion have loosened chunks of rock that fall from the bluff and accumulate in the river. "The larger chunks on bottom serve as current deflectors, with catfish holding downstream of them. You snag and lose a lot of rigs, but the catches outweigh the costs of losing lead. I also duck behind bluff banks to fish when high winds prevent effective fishing in open-water areas," he says.

To fish the bluffs, Roberts uses slipsinker rigs consisting of an 8/0 Gamakatsu Circle hook tied on a 12- to 18-inch leader of 50-pound-test Berkley Big Game. The leader is tied to a strong barrel swivel connected to 80-pound Spiderwire Stealth mainline, after sliding on a No-Roll slipsinker from 3 to 8 ounces, depending on current. He pours his own No-Rolls using Do-It Molds. "I prefer the No-Roll sinker style when fishing rocky areas, because flat sinker design keeps it from settling into and snagging in cracks less often than egg sinkers," he says. He uses Shakespeare Ugly Stik Tiger rods matched with Shakespeare Tidewater T20L or Abu Garcia 7000 C3 reels.

The river next to a typical bluff is about 18 to 20 feet deep. Roberts pinpoints likely catfish holding areas along the bluff and anchors about 30 to 40 yards upstream. "I set baits to cover depths where the chunk rock has settled, which is in about 20 to 25 feet as the bottom slopes from the bluff into the channel. I let baits drift along bottom in current, allowing them to settle behind larger chunk boulders. If my rig snags, I let it fish, because blue cats often pull it free when they strike," he says. He relies on a 15-pound Digger Anchor to hold steadfast in current over bottoms from sand to rock. Jerking the rope on the Digger trips a mechanism to straighten the flukes for easier retrieval.

Bridges—"The big concrete pilings that support the bridges spanning the rivers are good spots for big blue cats," Roberts says. "The best pilings have a lot of fast current rushing by. The fast water scours holes, and the pilings break current on the downstream side. I anchor about 40 yards upstream from the piling and cast, letting baits drift and settle in the scour hole on the side of the piling and also behind it on the downstream side.

"Blue cats hole up in these areas eating food that drifts along and gets washed behind the pillars," he says. One of his favorite bridge pilings has a scour hole about 24 feet deep on one side that wraps slightly around the downstream end to a depth of about 16 feet. An 80-pound behemoth blue, Roberts' largest, was caught on a chunk of skipjack placed behind that bridge piling in April of 2006.

No fisherman hits the bull's-eye for big blue cats each time out. Blues can be nomadic, moody at times—and conditions can make their whereabouts and eagerness to feed unpredictable, often sending the most experienced catters off course. Focusing on good locations and fishing them with the most effective presentations should put you on better target to more and bigger catfish.

Flatheads

TACTICS THROUGH THE SEASONS

Preseason for flatheads extends from late winter through early spring—the end of the Coldwater Period on the In-Fisherman Calendar of Fish Activity. It's not the best time of the year to target big flatheads or big numbers of smaller fish in most parts of the country. Many small- to medium-size rivers in the North still are covered with ice, and flatheads are tucked in tight behind rocks, timber, and each other, enjoying the end of a long winter's nap. Even their reservoir cousins in the Midsouth are more dormant than active, particularly during periods of frigid weather.

Eventually, when water temperatures begin to rise and river flows stabilize, the general mood of flatheads everywhere improves as they emerge from wintering holes and begin looking for food. This is the beginning of the Prespawn Period, which will offer flathead anglers some of the finest fishing of the season, both for size and numbers of fish. Depending on where you live, however, this beginning may be several weeks or even months away. Want to satisfy your flathead craving right now? Then head for a big river.

Large rivers can intimidate catmen accustomed to the intimacy of smaller streams. The transition from a small river with visible riffles and holes to wide, deep waters like the Mississippi, Ohio, Missouri, or Tennessee rivers may seem overwhelming. But take a closer look at a manageable stretch of water, and you'll likely see many similarities to your favorite catfish river. A hole may be 50 feet deep instead of 10, or 500 yards long instead of 20, but that's just a matter of scale. Narrowing your search to the most productive areas is key to locating flatheads during early season in any river.

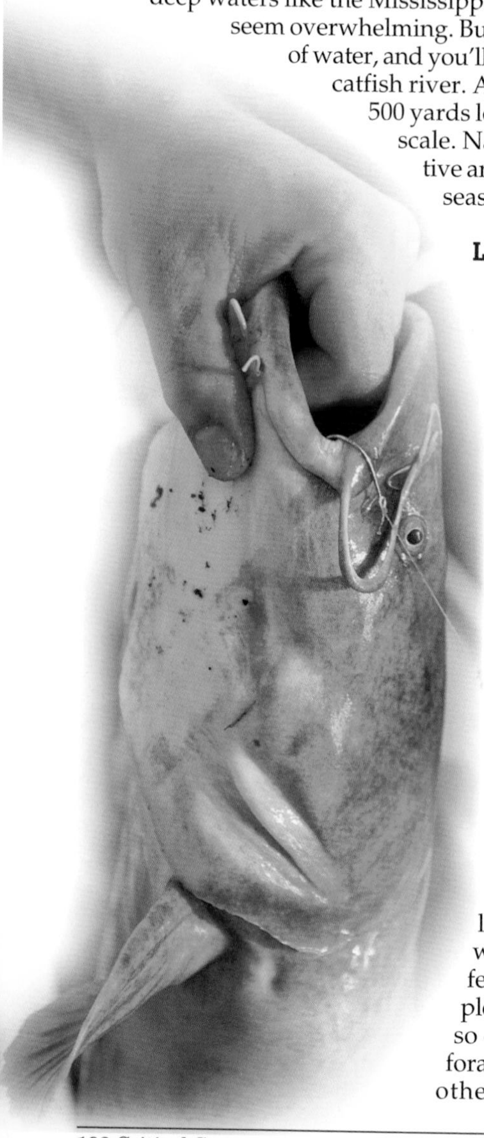

LOCATION IN PRINCIPLE & PRACTICE

During winter and through early spring, most flatheads in big rivers inhabit deep holes, which provide slightly warmer temperatures than other areas and better protection from current. In northern rivers like the upper Mississippi and Missouri, flatheads may hibernate for weeks or even months. In more southerly waters like the lower Missouri or Ohio rivers, the fish behave similarly during frigid weather.

Flatheads may resume feeding during periods of mild weather, even if water temperatures rise only a few degrees, and late-winter warming trends that last for days or even weeks often urge catfish to feed. Even in the North Country, a warm southwest breeze in February or March can melt thin ice and warm the water enough to activate flatheads. Medium-size livebaits, fresh portions of cutbait, and sourbaits are effective.

Once water temperatures climb into the low- to mid-50°F range, often coinciding with heavy spring rains, flatheads begin feeding more heavily. Wintering holes offer plenty of security and comfort but little food, so cats begin seeking areas that concentrate forage species. Large minnows, shad, and any other fish species of appropriate size and

Typical Big River Pool

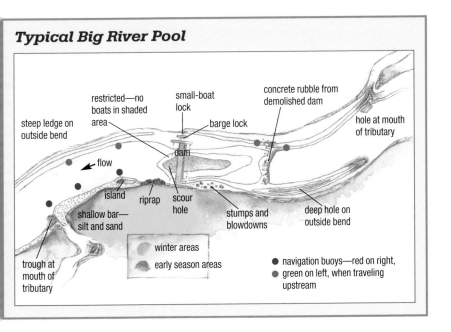

steep ledge on outside bend

restricted—no boats in shaded area

small-boat lock

barge lock

concrete rubble from demolished dam

hole at mouth of tributary

flow

dam

island

riprap

scour hole

shallow bar— silt and sand

stumps and blowdowns

deep hole on outside bend

trough at mouth of tributary

winter areas

early season areas

● navigation buoys—red on right,
● green on left, when traveling upstream

---

abundance—from white suckers to white bass—are important prey. Increasing river current forces baitfish to hold behind shoreline snags, wing dams, and in deep outside bends.

Deep Structure—Flatheads won't move far from wintering holes, even if sufficient forage is available nearby, because wintering areas provide depth and protection from current. The lower third of a typical big-river pool usually harbors the deepest and slackest holes. Begin your early-season search in this section, near the main river channel, surveying the bottom with sonar for structural elements that provide cover and deflect current.

Ohio River guide Frank Van Winkle of Batavia, Ohio, targets flatheads at the base of flooded dam foundations. Though the tops of these structures lie 20 feet or more below the surface, they still function as barriers to catfish and other species moving upstream from wintering holes. Van Winkle speculates that flatheads follow the main channel upstream until they reach these dams, then hold along the face of the dam or behind large chunks of concrete.

Shoreline Barriers—By mid-spring, heavy runoff often

Live or fresh-cut baitfish are effective during the early season.

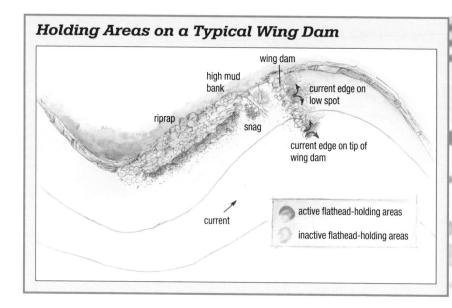

Holding Areas on a Typical Wing Dam

wing dam

high mud bank

current edge on low spot

riprap

snag

current edge on tip of wing dam

current

active flathead-holding areas

inactive flathead-holding areas

makes anchoring in the main channel, or presenting baits in deep water, difficult. In fast water, look for shoreline bars on inside bends or at creek mouths. While the current in the middle of the river is fast, water traveling outside the main channel is slowed by shallow water and numerous obstructions that restrict flow and push the current back toward the channel. These areas also provide cover for baitfish that in turn attract and hold flatheads until water levels begin to fall.

Shoreline barriers are particularly important in channelized rivers like the lower Mississippi and Missouri. Snags and brush have been removed from large sections of these rivers, and oxbows, side channels, and sloughs have been sealed off from the main river, creating a deep, swift chute with little cover. Wing dams and riprap banks may provide the primary catfish habitat in these river stretches.

Wing Dams—A study on the use of wing dams on the Missouri River, conducted by the Missouri Department of Conservation, revealed that active flatheads prefer to hold along the edge where fast and slow currents meet. Distinct current edges occur behind low spots atop and at the tip of the wing dam, where fast water from the main channel pours over the slackwater behind the dike. Inactive flatheads usually hold behind such obstructions.

Of particular interest are the wing dams on the Missouri and Mississippi rivers, where sections have been removed to allow water to flow through. These notched wing dams offer an additional current edge that holds big flatheads, particularly during high water. Another kind of wing dam common on the Missouri River is a trail dike, built along outside bends to prevent bank erosion. A riprap wall extends from the tip parallel to the shore, providing additional cover for flatheads and their prey.

Tributary Mouths—The mouths of large tributary streams also act as barriers. Lake Pepin, a 25,000-acre impoundment in Mississippi River Pool 4, is formed by the delta of the Chippewa River, which partially blocks the flow of the Mississippi, creating a lake-like environment with little current upstream. Similar deltas on other big rivers offer relief from current and concentrate baitfish that eventually spawn in the smaller rivers. Catfish hold in the slackwater of the tributary mouth, gorging on shad and other forage.

PRACTICAL PRESENTATIONS

Baits—Cutbait usually is the best choice for blue and channel cats, but it also can outproduce livebait for flatheads during early season. The best cutbait bite often occurs when lethargic flatheads are emerging from their wintering holes, and again when their activity level peaks in late spring or early summer, though many catmen continue to use cutbait throughout the season. Several nightcrawlers threaded on a hook also works well at this time. When water levels begin to stabilize and flatheads begin to feed more exclusively after dark, livebait usually is once again the top choice.

Wild baitfish, especially those caught by hook and line or by cast-net from the river you're fishing, are most effective, as they live longer in a baitwell and on the hook. They also react more strongly when a predator approaches than do baitfish from a bait shop. Gizzard shad, bullheads, carp, and panfish are effective baits. Match the size of your offering to the size of the fish you're after, keeping in mind that a record-class flathead can eat a bigger bait than most freshwater anglers can cast with their stoutest rod and reel.

Rigs—Most situations can be met with a simple sliprig, consisting of a bell sinker held in place above a hook with a barrel swivel. Use just enough

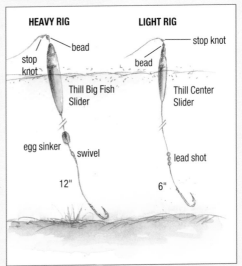

Slipfloat Rigs

Three-Way Rig

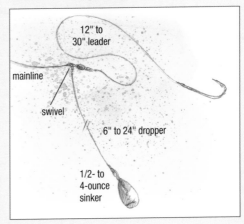

Sliprig

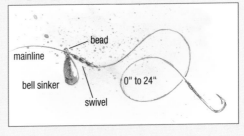

leader to attract fish without hanging up, keeping in mind that long leaders allow more bait movement, but they also tend to snag more often than short leaders. Six to 12 inches usually is sufficient length for anchoring livebaits near heavy cover, but a 30-inch leader can be used in areas where snags aren't a problem.

Three-way rigs are another versatile option. Use a 6- to 24-inch dropline anchored by a bell or bank sinker heavy enough to keep the bait on bottom. A 1/2-ounce sinker may be sufficient in shallow water, but 4 to 8 ounces may be needed in fast water. The leader should be slightly longer than the dropline—usually 2 to 3 feet. Use a dropline with a lighter breakstrength than your mainline and leader to retrieve most of your rig, if the sinker hangs up.

Finally, float rigs are effective for searching areas with slow to moderate current, or for working baits over broken bottoms like riprap that would quickly consume most bottom rigs. A small, thin float like the Thill Center Slider works for small portions of cutbait. The more bulbous Thill Big Fish Slider excels for big livebaits. Weight larger floats with a 1/2- to 2-ounce egg sinker threaded on the mainline above a barrel swivel and 12-inch leader. Don't drift baits too quickly, though, since flatheads in cool water seldom chase baits.

Water Temperature and Early Season Flatheads

The thermographs in this figure show daily water temperatures from January to July for a typical flathead river in the Upper Midwest. Trends cover the same time periods in back-to-back years.

The temperature patterns can be used to describe potential flathead behavior and how it might compare in different years in this river. A good starting point is winter, when flatheads are assumed to be inactive at wintering sites.

Water temperature climbing into the upper 40°F to 50°F range is a good sign that flatheads are becoming more active and moving from wintering sites. In the first year, this happens around March 7, but it's delayed a month in the second year, when those temperatures aren't reached until about April 8. This shows how temperature might affect the start of the early-season transition.

In the first year, the water temperature hovers around the low 50°F range for about four weeks, during which time the water dives back into the mid- to upper 40s on two occasions. The month-long period of colder water likely slows movements to prespawn areas. During the two periods when temperature plummets back into the 40s, flatheads might retreat downriver, temporarily settling into holes, until warming water sends them upstream again.

During the second year, flathead movement to prespawn sites likely starts later (early April) and occurs over a shorter period, because the water temperature increases steadily and more quickly, unlike the ups and downs experienced in the first year. By late April, water temperatures for both rivers are in the 60°F range, and most flatheads are probably in river reaches where they'll eventually spawn.

For most of May, when temperatures are steadily climbing through the 60s, flatheads should be moving among cover spots to feed and search out spawning locations. This is the period of fine fishing that's often experienced during the latter part of the Prespawn Period.

PRIMETIME IN SMALL RIVERS

Up North by mid-May and into June, and from April into May farther south, when water temperatures breach 60°F, flatheads are generally settled into river reaches where they eventually spawn, although "settled" is a relative term compared to the movement activity during the Spring Coldwater Period. They're still moving, hopscotching among spots like big snags and rockpiles, to feed and scout out spawning areas. But their metabolism is ramped up during this latter part of the Prespawn period, flatheads are feeding heavily, and the fishing is often as good as it gets.

SCOUTING SMALL RIVERS

For *In-Fisherman* editors, a typical trip for flatheads to an unfamiliar stretch of river usually begins with a day of fishing for channel cats. The same weather and water conditions that increase flathead metabolism also improve the channel cat's feeding mood, but being more abundant in most rivers, channel cats are more likely to feed during the day. They also bite willingly during the

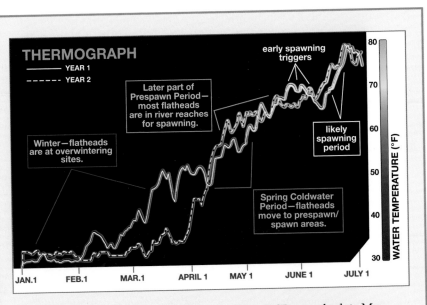

Temperatures cycle around the mid-60°F to 70°F range by late May, with catfish now more in a spawning mode. Spawning probably occurs in early to mid-June during both years, when water's consistently warming to around 70°F and above. Although not on this graph, in the following year, spawning temperatures weren't reached until about the second week of July.

Measuring water temperature throughout the early season can help you sort out at least one detail affecting flathead activity and location. If you don't have a source for temperature data where you fish, a thermometer can be one of your best investments for decoding the season.

RIPRAP FLATHEADS

The Missouri River contains more miles of riprap than any other freshwater river in the world. Critics say the riprap—placed there by the U.S. Army Corps of Engineers—has altered the ecological balance of the river, but catfish use it for feeding, refuge, and spawning. Anglers have learned that riprap areas harbor catfish and have devised unique ways to catch them from these rocky river margins.

Years ago LeRoy Kadel, an ardent walleye angler, wrote to *In-Fisherman* Editor In Chief Doug Stange, explaining his new passion for catching flatheads in riprap along 30 miles of the Missouri River between Council Bluffs and Missouri Valley, Iowa. Kadel says that he never fishes around wing dams any more, nor probes other traditional catfish hideaways. He now fishes riprap on the outside bends of the river, in currents of 10 mph and in depths from 50 to 75 feet.

To fish these deep, fast stretches, he ties his boat to a piling near the head of the bend and wields a 9-foot rod with a heavy-duty reel and 20-pound-test line. To this he attaches a three-way swivel with a 2-foot leader of 17-pound-test line fixed to one eye of the swivel. On the other

Riprap Rigging for Flatheads on Rivers

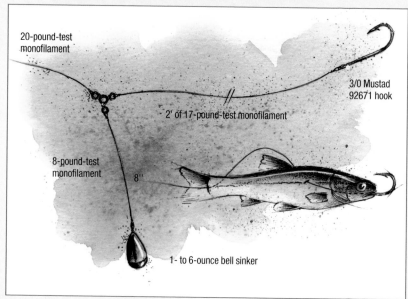

20-pound-test monofilament

3/0 Mustad 92671 hook

2' of 17-pound-test monofilament

8-pound-test monofilament

8"

1- to 6-ounce bell sinker

To rig a chub or bluegill, run the hook through the body 1 inch ahead of the tail and pull line through. Run hook through ahead of the dorsal fin and pull line through. Pass hook through gill and mouth about 1 inch. Pull line tight, pull loop over tail, and pull loop tight.

Riprap Positioning

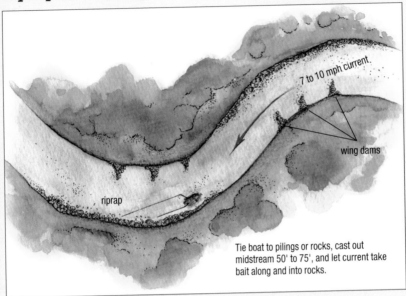

Tie boat to pilings or rocks, cast out midstream 50' to 75', and let current take bait along and into rocks.

eye, he ties an 8-inch piece of 8-pound-test mono sporting a hefty bell sinker. For bait, a 4- to 6-inch chub placed on a 3/0 Mustad 92671 hook is key.

Kadel makes long casts aimed at the mainstream of the river. After the bait hits the water, the swift current is allowed to carry it to the riprap, where it bobs among the rocks. He catches flatheads weighing 4 to 8 pounds with regularity, but once in a while he catches a 20-pounder.

Half a state away and many miles downstream from Kadel's honey holes are John Jamison's favorite riprap lairs. This angler from Spring Hill, Kansas, has spent more than a decade exploring the ways of Missouri River catfish, from St. Joseph to Jefferson City, Missouri. Along the way and at specific times during the year, he's found blues and flatheads milling around riprap.

In late March or early April, when the water temperature reaches 55°F, Jamison finds blue catfish haunting the riprap along the outside bends of the Missouri. Near the end of May, when the water temperature climbs into the upper 60°F range, he locates blues searching for spawning sites in the same riprap. But once they start spawning in June, it's so difficult to catch these blues that he switches his attention to small flatheads, instead, most weighing 1 to 3 pounds. He plumbs riprap along riverbends, using lightweight tackle baited with fillets of fresh shad, which in June flatheads can prefer over livebait.

Prespawn Period, allowing us to cover many spots quickly as we evaluate a long stretch of river.

In most of the small rivers we've fished, it's possible to explore a 10- to 15-mile stretch and catch lots of channel cats during a typical early summer day. The purpose of the excursion, however, isn't just to catch channel cats, but rather to see and evaluate lots of water. Again, the biggest flatheads in most rivers tend to fall into the largest and deepest holes with the most cover. It's impossible to

Barging In on Flatheads

Winter doesn't release its grip on the Ohio River's flatheads until the water temperature hits 50°F, and often the fish don't stir until that temperature reaches 55°F. During a normal April, it takes about two weeks for the temperature to escalate 5 degrees. When the water temperature hovers around 55°F, most flatheads are found either immediately above or below a deep hole. If the river is up and the current is swift, however, flatheads seek refuge around current breaks, which Jeremy Leach, expert catfish angler from Lexington, Indiana, regularly finds around barges and barge pillars. Such areas are also easy spots in which to anchor a boat.

Leach describes one of his favorite flathead coverts as a tie-off station for barges that lies about 100 feet off the shoreline. The river's topography at this spot consists of a long ledge that runs perpendicular from the riverbank toward the river channel and then turns to run parallel to the river. Along the ledge, there's a 27- to 30-foot hole that's 50 yards wide and 150 yards long. Most of the catfish mill about the segment of the ledge that runs parallel to the river channel.

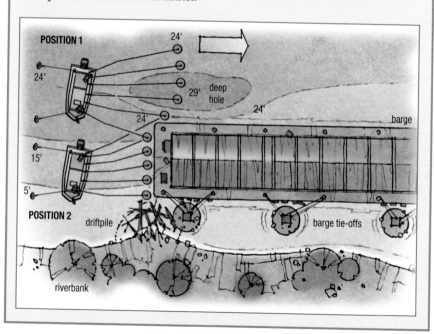

In-Fisherman Editor In Chief Doug Stange: "Presentation is important, but only after you've solved the location puzzle. Understanding the flathead's habitat preferences throughout the day leads naturally to the right location, which, in turn, points to an appropriate presentation."

make judgments about how good a particular hole might be if you don't know what lies around the next bend.

Most holes occur along sweeping outside bends, where the river makes a sharp turn. The best bend-holes usually follow a long, relatively straight stretch of river with fairly uniform depth and current. These holes are scoured by the current pushing against the bank and the river bottom. Trees and other debris that fall into the water in the straight stretch also tend to collect along the outside bend, providing overhead cover and protection from current for flatheads and their prey.

Holes also occur behind riffle areas in relatively straight river stretches. Water moves through long, featureless runs at the same speed, creating a channel of fairly uniform depth; but when the current encounters a harder rocky bottom that doesn't erode, the river becomes shallower and current increases. When the bottom again changes from rock to sand or silt, this faster water shoots over the riffle and scours out a hole. Sediments gradually settle to the bottom as current speed slows and another run begins.

Flatheads and channel cats often prefer different holes. Since most rivers support more channel cats than flatheads, competition for food usually is higher among channels. This forces channel cats into feeding stations that afford the best opportunity to grab edible items drifting in current. In some small rivers, channel cats may feed more often in riffles than in holes. Flatheads, meanwhile, usually are attracted to larger holes with more cover that provide more security and harbor more baitfish. Overhead cover from rock outcrops, downed timber, or manmade structures also seems more important to flatheads than to channel cats.

Selecting the best hole within a long river stretch still requires comparative judgments. If you're going to spend an entire night at a spot, you can rule out smaller and shallower holes, even though they may contain good cover. But what to do when you identify two or more prime flathead holes that are several miles apart? On a bigger river, you might fish both holes during a single night, but navigating smaller streams after dark can be difficult and dangerous. Wiser to choose the best hole and set up there for the night.

Flatheads are most active during the morning and evening twilight periods, but can be caught almost any time of the day or night—if you know where to look. Here's Doug Stange at the start of a good day on the Minnesota River.

If one of these holes is located in an otherwise desolate stretch of river, it might just contain many flatheads and certainly some of the biggest fish. But a prime hole located in a prime stretch of river usually attracts more flatheads. These stretches are more diverse, support a larger forage base and, in turn, hold more catfish. However, if fishing pressure in this hole is high, it's probably best to fish the more remote hole.

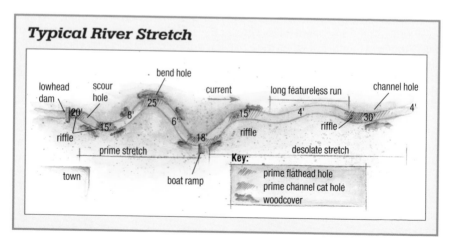

Typical River Stretch

PRIMARY PRESENTATIONS

Once you decide on a hole, you should set up an hour or two before dark. Flatheads prefer to feed under the cover of darkness during most of the warmwater season, but there are exceptions. When fish first begin to emerge from their wintering holes, for example, they often take smaller meals during daylight hours. And when their activity level peaks during the height of the Prespawn, they can be caught during the middle of the afternoon on pieces of cutbait intended for channel cats. The hour or two before dusk is prime again during early fall.

Most holes can be fished effectively from a boat anchored near the head of the hole, but you can fish from shore if water levels permit. We typically set up camp on the inside bend, usually the low-bank side of the river on a bend hole. The most obvious feeding stations are the head, and the leading edge of a snag at a cutbank on the opposite shore. The core or center of the hole, the shallow flat on its inside perimeter, and shoreline eddies behind the snag or other current breaks also can be productive, depending on water level.

Slackwater tends to be the home of flatheads that are in a neutral or negative feeding mood, while active cats work closer to the main current, though during high water flatheads don't hold in the faster flows. Heavy current pushes them into eddies formed behind shoreline obstructions, where they can feed more efficiently. During low water, on the other hand, active fish more often position in the deeper water near the core of the depression.

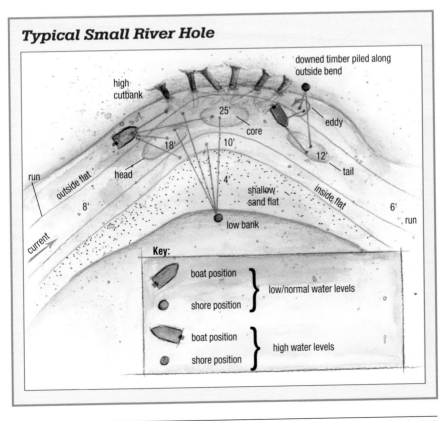

Typical Small River Hole

downed timber piled along outside bend

high cutbank

25'

core

eddy

18'   10'

12'

run   tail

outside flat   head   4'   inside flat

8'   shallow sand flat   6'

run

current   low bank

Key:

boat position } low/normal water levels
shore position

boat position } high water levels
shore position

The biggest problem associated with fast water is that it makes presentations more difficult. A rig cast across fast water at the head of a hole to an eddy on the opposite shore may anchor there for a short time, but eventually, current pushing on the line moves the rig out of the eddy into heavier flows. Fishing at closer range from a boat or from the high bank on the outside bend is necessary for a precise presentation.

Release rigs allow you to fish key spots more precisely and to fish more spots at one time. A downrigger or planer-board release clip tied to a limb extending out over the eddy is the simplest option. You can use a boat to deploy the rigs, dropping them vertically into the spot we intend to fish. The line above the rig is attached to the release clip, which holds the rig in place until a fish begins to move off with the bait. Then put the reel in freespool, moving the boat to the anchor location or to a position on the opposite shore.

The terminal rig usually is a standard slipsinker setup. Slide a 2- or 3-ounce bass-casting sinker on your mainline, followed by a bead and a barrel swivel. Tie a short length of leader material to the other rung of the swivel, then add your hook. A 12-inch leader is about right for most conditions. Longer leaders allow the bait too much movement, especially when positioned near heavy cover. A shorter leader or even none at all—letting the sinker slide right up to the bead—is a good choice near snags or in faster current. This keeps the bait on a short leash and forces it to struggle away from the weight of the sinker.

BAIT & TACKLE

Big, lively, wild baits are vital. Suckers raised in bait ponds don't live as long on the hook or react as strongly when a flathead swims close, as do wild, 10- to 15-inch suckers caught by hook and line from the river you're fishing. Big, green sunfish, creek chubs, and small carp also are effective baits. Perhaps the best baits of all are bullheads. They don't have to be big—5- to 8-inchers are perfect. Run a 7/0 to 10/0 hook through the thinnest part of the tail muscle, leaving the hook point exposed, to ensure good penetration on the hook-set.

Simple, sturdy hook designs like the Mustad 92671 and Eagle Claw 84 are good options. Sharpen hook points with a file and reduce the barb slightly for easier penetration. Premium hooks with smaller barbs and needle-sharp points are more expensive, but usually worth it. The Owner SSW, Daiichi Heavy Duty Bait Hook, and Gamakatsu Octopus are fine flathead hooks. The VMC 7299 is another good hook— less expensive than other premiums but sharper than standard hooks.

Large wild baitfish, often those caught by hook and line from the river you're fishing, attract attention and draw strikes.

Once baits have been set, place rods in holders on the boat or in

Rods go in rod holders or bank sticks with the freespool button engaged and the clicker set.

ground spikes on the shore, with the freespool on and clicker engaged. Most heavy-power rods with medium to medium-fast action work for flatheads. We've caught lots of big fish on muskie rods, saltwater boat rods, and heavier, general-purpose rods like those in the Shakespeare Ugly Stik line. Shakespeare's Ugly Stik Custom USCC 2270 M is a favorite for flatheads around heavy cover. Their Tiger series rods are another good option. Also check out rods available in St. Croix's Premier Musky line, Quantum's Big Cat, and Cabela's King Kat Pro selections.

Couple these rods with a tough, dependable baitcasting reel with a smooth drag and large line capacity. We've used Shakespeare Tidewater reels for years, and now they offer their Arsenal Series. The Arsenal has all the features needed for small-river flathead duty—a powerful gear ratio, a clicker loud enough to wake you up from a light snooze, and a multi-disc drag system. The AR20AL reel is rated for 330 yards of 20-pound mono, but handles all the 50-pound line you need. Penn's International 975, Abu Garcia's 6500C3 and 7000C3, and Quantum's Iron IR430 are other top choices.

Use a good abrasion-resistant mono in 40- to 50-pound test. Berkley Big Game, Stren High Impact, and other premium lines have proven to be tough. Twenty-pound test works for smaller fish and might land you a big one, but chances are when a big one hits you'll wish you had heavier line.

HOOKING, LANDING & RELEASING

If the hole you're fishing hasn't been fished by other anglers recently, the action may start an hour or so before dark, when the sun drops just below the tops of the trees and the light is perfect for a photo. Fish may continue to bite for a few hours after dark, with a lull sometime during the night. Two options here—trailer the boat and check into a motel for a decent night's sleep, or stick it out and wait for the action to resume a few hours before dawn. We usually wait. Sleep is a fair price to pay for a big flathead.

When a fish takes, wait just long enough to know it has the bait, has turned, and is moving away from you. Don't wait for it to swallow the bait—it may move into a snag after taking the bait or may be hooked too deeply to release. As it moves away, set hard, rod tip high, and hold on. Don't give any line unless you have to. Keep the fish's head pointed toward you and away from the snag. Fights with flatheads on heavy tackle usually don't last long but are memorable for their intensity.

You can certainly catch a 20-pounder from a small river this summer. And once you break 20, catching a 30 won't be too difficult. Get a bait in the right place at night and you'll catch them, maybe even most of the fish in the hole. A few 20s, a 30, and maybe even a 40 from one hole during one night is a dream come true for many anglers. But we can't in good conscience keep all those fish.

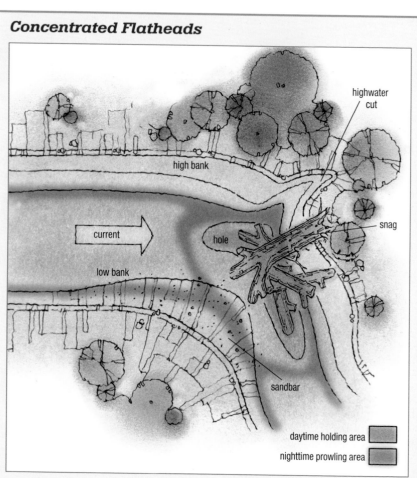

Concentrated Flatheads

highwater cut

high bank

current

hole

snag

low bank

sandbar

daytime holding area

nighttime prowling area

Flatheads often cover a large area while searching for prey after dark. Successful fishing depends on being in the right spot at the right time—choose spots wisely or be prepared to wait. During the day, though, most flatheads hold in the densest available cover. Put a bait where they can find it, and you'll get bit.

A 20-pound flathead in some small rivers may be 20 years old, and it might take even longer for the river to replace that fish. Flatheads are especially vulnerable during the Prespawn Period when big fish are so focused on eating that they can't help taking a well-presented bait. Capture the moment with a photograph and slide the fish back into the water. Return next season, when the same fish is a little wiser and definitely bigger.

NOTES ON FLATHEAD FEEDING

Flatheads, especially big ones, often feed after dark once summer sets in. A radiotelemetry study conducted by John Skains and Dr. Don Jackson of Mississippi State University reinforces the theory that flatheads in rivers carefully select their lair and tend to hold in it during the day. At the beginning of the study, 10 flatheads were captured from the Big Black and Tallahatchie rivers in Mississippi and implanted with radio transmitters.

Researchers learned that during daylight, flatheads generally were sedentary in one of their home areas, which typically contained wood-cover. Only one fish was found moving during daylight, and this occurred at 3:30 p.m. on an overcast day. All the fish had at least one home site and usually two or three. No radio-tagged fish shared home sites, though the boundaries of their ranges sometimes overlapped.

When the fish moved at night, they tended to travel along the shoreline, heading in one direction throughout the night, then returning home before daylight. The maximum distance for a nighttime foray was just under a mile, but sometimes they remained in their home site all night.

The tagged flatheads usually held in areas with reduced current both day and night, often in deep eddies, ranging from 2 to

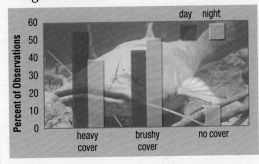

A Day & Night Difference

Big Black River

Tallahatchie River

Flatheads in the Big Black and Tallahatchie rivers tended to hold in heavy or brushy cover during day-light hours, but often made short forays at night. Some fish even moved through long featureless runs after dark, likely enroute to areas with substantial cover and abundant forage.

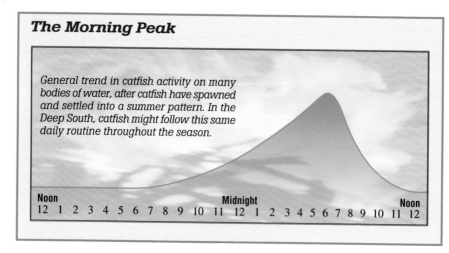

The Morning Peak

General trend in catfish activity on many bodies of water, after catfish have spawned and settled into a summer pattern. In the Deep South, catfish might follow this same daily routine throughout the season.

Noon
12 1 2 3 4 5 6 7 8 9 10 11 **Midnight** 12 1 2 3 4 5 6 7 8 9 10 11 **Noon** 12

20 feet and most often from 6 to 10 feet. Surprisingly, no day or night depth-preferences were noted.

During the day, flatheads primarily held in brushy areas or dense snags. At night, their nocturnal forays often kept them around cover, but active fish often moved through clear areas. In the unaltered Big Black River, fish held in denser cover—which was more available—than in the channelized Tallahatchie River.

SUNRISE CATS

Many anglers overlook what often is the hottest of all potential daily feeding periods, from about 4 a.m. to 8 a.m. The actual length of the period isn't so important as knowing that it exists and that it may focus catfish activity so that you can take advantage of it. This period isn't magical, just good on many catfish waters.

Some anglers believe that early morning is a catch-up period for catfish feeding activity. The fish have all night to feed, but apparently they don't always get the job done, or perhaps they just prefer feeding during the morning.

Fishermen often dwell on the flathead's tremendous senses of smell and taste, but understanding that catfish also have good vision helps explain the potential intensity of this catch-up feeding period during the early morning. Flatheads also operate well in dingy water, using their senses of smell, taste, hearing, and feeling; and when the water clears even slightly, they rely on vision, too.

Like other predatory fish, flatheads at night likely have a significant vision advantage over most prey species. They probably see even better with a bit of light, and continue to have a vision advantage over their prey during the morning twilight period. The big fish, the ones that have lived 10 or 15 years, know the morning period can be prime-time feeding, a catch-up bite, or a hurry-up-and-feed bite, given the approaching, intense daylight.

The midnight shift can be good, but it gets old when you have to work the next day. Time it right, and on some waters you might catch more flatheads during the hours just before and after dawn than you would by fishing all night.

FLATHEADS DURING THE DAY

Many catmen catch a flathead or two each season during the day, often on a piece of cutbait intended for a blue or channel cat. This usually occurs toward the end of the Prespawn Period, when the fish's metabolism is in high gear; but few flathead specialists target flatheads during the middle of the day, particularly during summer.

Dean Opatz, of Jordan, Minnesota, is Chief Deputy Sheriff and part-time flathead guide. He fished exclusively at night for many years, until a lack of sleep and an increasingly demanding work schedule forced him off the water after dark. And then he learned that he could catch more flatheads during the day than he could at night.

Opatz admits that flatheads are more active at night but adds that they're easier to find during the day. Tracking studies seem to support this idea: Flatheads often cover a large area when prowling after dark, but usually remain holed up in a dense patch of cover during the day.

The problem night fishermen face is deciding where to set up to intercept actively feeding fish. Every home site probably has one or two high-percentage spots, but it's impossible to know when a flathead will move through those areas. It might swim upstream instead of downstream during a nocturnal foray, or engulf a big baitfish before it finds your bait. The only way to know for sure is to sit and wait.

Most flathead anglers know the sit-and-wait routine well, but patience usually is detrimental when fishing during the day. Opatz says the best bite usually occurs between 10 a.m. and 2 p.m. When the sun's high, the biggest fish usually are buried in the biggest, nastiest-looking snags in the river. These fish seldom move for a bait but usually will eat a livebait or fresh piece of cutbait dropped in front of their barbels.

Opatz waits only five minutes or so at each spot but says that most fish bite within a minute or two. The key is getting the bait as tight as possible to the snag. That's the reason he prefers cutbait to livebait: A lively baitfish often wraps the leader around limbs and branches, while a baitfish fillet snags less often, even when cast into the densest cover.

In-Fisherman Publisher Steve Hoffman hoists a daytime cat.

Big River Options

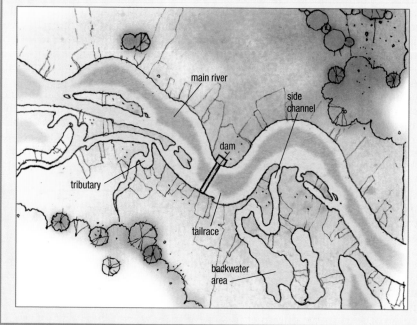

Many flathead anglers know that the density of the cover is more important than the depth of the hole. Opatz caught three big flatheads one fall from a spot less than 4 feet deep, and the flat surrounding the small depression was less than 2. All the fish were holding under the rootwad of a massive cottonwood, the dense roots providing overhead cover, allowing the fish to hold in shallower water than they usually prefer.

From this and similar experiences, Opatz has developed a location strategy based on time of day. When he hits the water at first light, he usually begins fishing 100 yards or more above a big snag. As the sun continues to climb and the fish swim toward their home sites, Opatz moves closer to the wood. By about 10 a.m., he's bouncing his sinker off the snag on his casts.

SUMMER FLATHEADS—GUARANTEED PATTERNS IN BIG RIVERS

Flatheads are more difficult to find in big rivers than they are in smaller farm-country rivers. In terms of habitat, however, rivers of any size generally consist of an endless series of riffles, holes, and runs. The idea is that the current accelerates over shallow riffles, scours a hole when it encounters softer bottom, and then flattens out in a uniform run.

Not all holes follow riffles. Some of the deepest holes occur on sharp riverbends, where the current scours the outside of the bend. These bend holes often are the most productive areas on small rivers because they collect logs and other debris that flatheads use as cover. But these features are easier to see on smaller rivers.

Spend a day on the Mississippi, Missouri, or Ohio, and you quickly realize that this pattern is much less obvious. That's not to say it doesn't exist—there still are shallow hard-bottom areas, deep holes, and uniform runs—but you can't always see them. Studying hydrographic maps and sonar displays is the best way to visualize the bottom. Better yet, get off the main river, into backwater areas where flatheads are easier to find and catch.

BACKWATER AREAS

Finding and catching flatheads in big rivers doesn't have to be difficult. The upper Mississippi River—and probably several other larger rivers across the country—contain a maze of backwater lakes, dead-end cuts, side channels, and tributary streams. These backwater areas often are the best option for flathead anglers from late spring through early fall.

"The best locations within these backwaters are similar to the spots you'd fish in a small river, including holes, snags, and cutbanks," says Dirk Wassink, an avid catfish angler from Hull, Iowa, who often fishes the middle portion of the upper Mississippi River. "Any area with moderate depth, overhead cover, and protection from current probably holds flatheads at some point during the season. They don't always need deep water or heavy cover but almost never hold in fast water.

"The best holes in the backwater areas that I fish range from about 10 to 25 feet deep, but depth seems secondary to the quantity and quality of the cover," he says. "I wouldn't hesitate to fish a shallower hole with a big snag piled along the outside bend, or ignore a perfect-looking hole that lacked sufficient cover. The right combination of these elements is what makes a good flathead spot."

Many flathead anglers anchor in these holes or at the heads of holes, which often occur on outside bends. This tactic works during normal or low-water levels, but when the water's high, the current usually is too fast along the outside bend. Fast current makes boat control and bait presentation difficult and the area less attractive to flatheads. "The shallower the hole, the more likely I am to place baits in the deepest part of it," Wassink explains. "On smaller tributaries and side channels, it's often possible to spread baits out from an anchored position, placing one bait at the head of the hole, one in the core, and a couple more on the adjacent shallow flat.

"The more time I spend on the water, the more I believe it pays to think shallow. Flatheads often hold in the thickest available cover during the day and then patrol shallow flats after dark. These flats are located along the inside bend on larger tributaries, or above or below the hole in most side channels.

"Flats rank among the most productive spots on the river section that I fish. A prime flat is 3 to 15 feet deep, has slow to moderate current, a cutbank along the outside bend, and a nice current seam created by scattered wood or other debris. All of these attributes aren't necessary for a flat to hold fish, of course, but more is better. The presence of baitfish helps, too.

"Whether I'm fishing flats or holes, I survey the area with my sonar unit before I anchor," says Wassink. "Fancasting with a sinker sometimes reveals cover elements that I didn't see on sonar. Cast a 2-ounce sinker across a hole or flat, let it sink, and then slowly retrieve it along the bottom. The sinker transmits bottom composition and cover better than most electronic tools.

"This gives me an idea where to place my baits. If I find a sunken log lying parallel to the current, for instance, it can guide fish to a bait presented next to it. Or I might discover a terrible tangle between the spot where I intend to anchor and the spot where I plan to cast. In this situation, I usually rethink my presentation. I always

Tricks of the Trade

Here are a few tips that we've learned over the years:

■ Scout during the day, fish at night. When you first begin fishing a big river like the Mississippi, consider leaving your rods at home and spending a weekend evaluating a long stretch of river.

■ Scout during low-water periods. Scouting during winter is especially productive. River levels usually are at their lowest levels of the year, revealing the shallow cover that attracts flatheads during summer.

■ Use lively baitfish. Bullheads, chubs, and suckers: All are effective flathead baits as long as they're active. If a baitfish isn't struggling, give the line a tug. If the bait still doesn't swim, replace it.

■ Look for beavers. I'm not sure why, but I often see lots of beavers cruising around at night in my best flathead spots. The reverse also is true: I rarely see beavers in areas that don't hold flatheads.

■ Look for old snags. Ancient logjams are what you're looking for, not freshly fallen trees. Old trees collect drifting timber and other debris and host lots of invertebrates that attract baitfish.

■ Keep moving. Catching flatheads requires patience, but if you haven't been bit in a couple of hours, move to another area. Develop a milk run of spots that you can safely navigate after dark.

■ Watch your rod tip. Learn the difference between a struggling bullhead and a bite—it's the only way to keep your blood pressure regulated. Also realize, though, that baitfish tend to struggle when a predator approaches.

assume that the fish of a lifetime is going to bite every time I make a cast. If I don't believe I can land such a fish in a particular spot, I won't try to hook him.

"I prefer to anchor my boat perpendicular to the current, with one rope tied to a bow cleat and a tied near the stern," Wassink says. "This technique provides a more stable fishing platform, and also allows lines to be spread across a hole or flat. Rod holders are convenient but not necessary, as long as your reels are equipped with a freespool baitclicker.

"Sometimes I'll concentrate on cover—particularly large snags—rather than holes or flats. I usually anchor directly behind big logjams after dark, centering the boat on the current seam formed by the tip of the snag. Logjams washed by moderate current are better than those in slackwater," he adds.

Wassink points to the confluence of a small feeder creek with a larger tributary stream as a good spot to try. "I haven't had great success fishing tributary mouths—the area where tributaries dump into the main river, but the same type of spots often produce well in tributaries and side channels.

"All these complex backwater spots—those associated with deep holes, shallow flats, lots of cover options, and current breaks—always seem to attract the most and the biggest flatheads. Areas lacking one or more of these elements might hold fish, but not as many and probably not any of trophy size."

MAIN RIVER AREAS

Flatheads have more habitat options in the main river, which makes finding them more difficult. Tailrace areas, wing dams, riprap banks, mid-depth holes, and other areas all hold fish at various times throughout the season. The key is deciding when to target flatheads in the main river versus fishing for them in backwater areas.

Wassink says that main-river areas often produce flatheads as soon as water levels begin to subside in late spring. But they don't produce as many fish or as many big fish as backwater areas until July, he says; and on big-river stretches without expansive backwaters, flatheads are limited to the main river.

"When I refer to main-river areas, I'm not talking about the main channel," he explains. "I never fish the water between the navigational buoys. It's too dangerous, especially at night. Recreational boats are hazardous, but barges are deadly. On the stretch of river that I fish, seeing three or four barges a night is common, but anglers on some river sections might see a couple of barges every hour.

"I limit my search to four areas on the main river, all of them in fairly shallow water. My best spots are flats associated with side channels. Usually there's a large flat on the main river and a moderately deep hole where the side channel begins. The best spots have plenty of submerged timber and enough current to keep your anchor rope tight in an upstream wind," he says.

Inside main-river bends also produce good numbers of flatheads, Wassink points out. On

Big River Safety

Nothing's better than fishing a big river on a clear, moonlit night. Add a bit of rain or fog, though, and things can get dicey. Add an encounter with a wing dam, deadhead, or barge and they get deadly. A few safety tips:

- Don't run in heavy fog. If heavy fog sets in when you're fishing, you might be able to idle back if you're fishing near the ramp. But if you need to make a long run, wait until morning. And don't forget to call home.
- Study navigational rules. Most states produce some type of boating guide. Pick one up and read it, especially the sections on buoys, wing dams, and barge traffic.
- Check water levels first. Use the Internet or a call a baitshop before you leave home. High water always is dangerous, and rapidly rising levels often flood the river with deadheads and other debris.
- Organize your boat. Stow your tackle and equipment properly so you can quickly find what you need without stepping on your favorite rod. Keep a sharp knife near your anchor rope, too, in case you need to move in a hurry.
- Rig your boat right. Minimum equipment includes a sonar unit, spotlight, flashlight, and cell phone or marine radio. A GPS with mapping capability and interior boat lights also are nice to have.

some inside bends, drifting timber gets lodged on shallow sand flats; in others, trees simply topple over from the bank onto the flat. He fishes these areas the same way he fishes flats in side channels and tributary streams, anchoring just below the snag and spreading baits downstream.

"Outside river bends also are effective during low-water periods, but there usually is too much current during high to normal water levels," he says. "Use sonar or cast a sinker to verify the presence and location of submerged timber before you begin fishing, and then anchor your boat immediately below the cover. Inactive fish hold in snags during the day and then cruise the downstream flat at night.

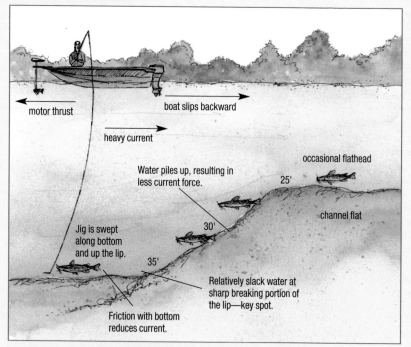

Tailrace Tactics

motor thrust

boat slips backward

heavy current

Water piles up, resulting in less current force.

occasional flathead

25'

channel flat

Jig is swept along bottom and up the lip.

30'

35'

Relatively slack water at sharp breaking portion of the lip—key spot.

Friction with bottom reduces current.

The boat is moving at same speed as surface current, drift corrected with forward thrusts of the electric motor to keep jig vertical.

"Straight river stretches are my least favorite areas, but they sometimes produce a good fish or two, especially shallow flats with scattered timber. Rock also is a good flathead attractor, so be on the lookout for wing dams and rockpiles associated with uniform flats."

TAILRACE AREAS

Wassink recalls one particular year when fishing on the main-river portion of the upper Mississippi was great from the end of July through mid-August, when water levels dropped and the flatheads abandoned shallow cover. "August typically is a good month on the stretch that I fish, but the low water had me stumped. I heard reports that some anglers were catching flatheads from the tips of wing dams, but my efforts weren't successful.

"I moved upstream, searching for spots. When I reached the tailrace, I remembered reading an article in *In-Fisherman* years ago on jigging for flatheads. Doug Stange also had done a television segment on this presentation, which involved working a jig-and-minnow over the tailout area of the scour hole below the dam.

"Instead of using a spinning rod and light monofilament line, I opted for flathead-grade gear: a 7½-foot flippin' stick and sturdy baitcasting reel spooled with 65-pound superline. The thin-diameter superline provides excellent bait control and sensitivity along with high break-strength. The line also provides incredible power, which allowed me to quickly muscle a flathead to the boat and get back to fishing.

"I probably fished the scour hole eight or nine times over several weeks, usually during the last three or four hours of daylight," he says. "When I fished alone I typically caught one or two; if I brought a partner along, we usually caught two or three. Not fantastic numbers but not bad for daytime fishing, especially when my traditional spots weren't producing anything at night.

"The average size of the fish was good, too. Three of the biggest each weighed about 40 pounds, and one tipped the scale at 52 pounds. Interestingly, I didn't catch any channel cats while jigging.

"My best bait was a 1/2-ounce jighead and 5-inch Kalin grub. I tipped the jig with a 4- to 5-inch creek chub or sucker. I'm not sure why, but chubs seemed to produce better than suckers. I also caught a few fish on plain jigheads tipped with a minnow.

"With the water so low, I assumed the flatheads would be scattered throughout the scour hole. I was wrong. Every time I caught a fish, I punched in a waypoint on my GPS unit. Most of the fish came from an area no larger than 50 square yards. I caught most of the fish in the tailout area in 18 to 28 feet of water, and no fish in the deep water in the core of the hole.

"Hits were bone-jarring. Two or three fish were snagged, but the rest engulfed the bait. Set the hook on a big flathead directly below the boat with no-stretch superline, and you're in for a memorable battle," Wassink says.

"Obviously, there's more room for experimentation with this tailrace pattern, but I do know this: It's not difficult and it's a lot of fun. Other anglers couldn't believe that I was targeting flatheads with jigs, and they were even more surprised when they saw me landing big fish.

"That 52-pounder, by the way, was the last fish I caught that season. It was mid-October and the water temperature was 59°F. The memory of that fish was just enough to carry me through the winter."

FAVORITE FALL TACTICS

We've learned a lot about flatheads in recent years, but much of their behavior during fall remains a mystery. We know, for example, that flatheads in rivers and reservoirs crowd into cover-laden holes in mid- to late fall. The specific water temperature that coincides with this movement varies by region; in the mid-50°F range seems about right in Minnesota, but 65°F may be cool enough to get fish moving in North Carolina.

Many anglers still wonder, though, why certain holes attract huge congregations of fish while similar holes in the same area seem to hold no flatheads. The fish surely are able to detect subtle differences that we can't. A difference in bottom composition, current velocity, or even a slight change in temperature or oxygen levels may make one hole more attractive than others. But we don't have definite answers.

Even when fish are found, catching them can be hit or miss. Several fish might be caught from a small river hole one afternoon, yet it will be devoid of fish the next day under what seem to be similar weather and water conditions. The same is true on lakes and reservoirs, where anglers often experience a flurry of late-season activity, followed by several days or even weeks of poor fishing.

Where in Small Rivers

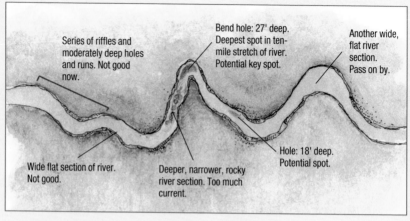

Series of riffles and moderately deep holes and runs. Not good now.

Bend hole: 27' deep. Deepest spot in ten-mile stretch of river. Potential key spot.

Another wide, flat river section. Pass on by.

Wide flat section of river. Not good.

Deeper, narrower, rocky river section. Too much current.

Hole: 18' deep. Potential spot.

During fall, catfish drift downriver to wintering holes. Holes in middle and lower river sections more likely hold cats, but the quality of the hole matters. If it's one of the deepest holes in a section of river, it likely harbors some cats—and probably many—during fall. But, flatheads apparently don't always use the deepest holes, sometimes moving into only moderately deep holes with rock or woodcover.

Sliprig

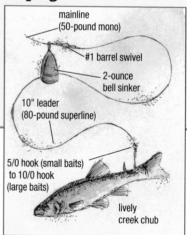

mainline (50-pound mono)

#1 barrel swivel

2-ounce bell sinker

10" leader (80-pound superline)

5/0 hook (small baits) to 10/0 hook (large baits)

lively creek chub

Flatheads may feed less frequently as the cooling water slows their metabolism, but this doesn't explain why so many fish seem to feed at the same time. They may be tuned into some subtle change in barometric pressure, water clarity, or other factor we're not aware of. Or perhaps the answer is simpler, such as baitfish being more available at certain arbitrary times.

What we do know is that fall can bring some good flathead fishing, particularly for big fish that may, after several weeks of heavy feeding in preparation for winter, be near their peak weight for the year. Anglers armed with these strategies and the confidence to keep fishing when the fishing's slow might be rewarded with the trophy of a lifetime.

FISHING SMALLER RIVERS WITH DOUG STANGE

Stange: The key to fishing in the fall is the same as during summer, only more so—find the right hole, and often there won't be many good holes. Identify the location of potential holes by surveying a large section of river during summer. Once that's accomplished, you have a good shot at finding and catching flatheads in the fall, so long as the water isn't too high, dirty, or cold.

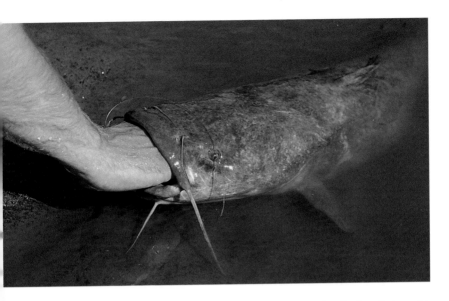

Livebait or fresh cutbait continues to be the best option for flatheads in cold water. I've never had success with prepared catfish baits for flatheads. Crawlers sometimes work well during spring, but I haven't done well with them in fall. Frogs also can be good at times, but they're not magic. Cutbait—strips of freshly filleted sucker or other oily baitfish—works just as well, particularly if you're after channel cats, too. But if you're targeting flatheads, livebait's the way to go.

Creek chubs are good during fall. In spring, on the other hand, chubs haven't worked well for me. They seem fragile and die easily, particularly just before spawning, when the males have horny protuberances on their heads. They also aren't active then. By fall, chubs become hardy—and wild. Big ones measure 10 to 12 inches. The bigger the bait, the better, when the water's still in the 60°F range. Six- to 8-inch baits are fine, as the water cools into the 50s and upper 40s.

Bullheads also are a top bait, perhaps the best bait on many small rivers, but they're often hard to get during fall. Seven- to 8-inchers are fine, early on. Later, 5-inch baits are better. Wild suckers are good, too. So are narrow-bodied panfish like green sunfish. And in waters where shad are a staple forage, they remain an option during fall—particularly big gizzard shad.

I hook my livebaits just under the skin about halfway between the dorsal fin and the tail. I match hook size to bait size, so at least a 7/0 hook (better, a 10/0) is necessary for the largest baits. A 5/0 works fine for smaller baits. I still use the same hooks I've been using for over 20 years, the Mustad 92671 and Eagle Claw 84. I touch up the hook points with a file and bend down the barbs slightly to make running the hook through the baitfish easier.

Typical terminal rigging consists of a bell sinker sliding freely on the mainline, stopped by a swivel about 10 inches above the bait. I use at least 50-pound monofilament for flatheads, even during fall. The 10 inches of leader is 80-pound superline—like Stren Super Braid or Spiderwire Stealth. Superline is more supple than mono and therefore makes a better leader. It also makes a fine mainline, but it is more expensive than mono.

Active cats often move to the head of a deep hole to feed, but during late fall, they usually don't swim up into heavy current or move shallow enough to enter

Where in Big Rivers

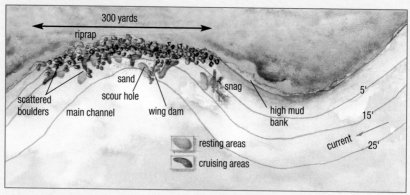

Inactive flatheads tend to hold tight behind snags, boulders, and other cover. Semiactive fish, though, may cruise through the hole looking for an easy meal. The base of the riprap, on the edge of the drop-off and the slack water cushion in front of wing dams and other structures, are key spots for cruising fish.

Three-Way Rig

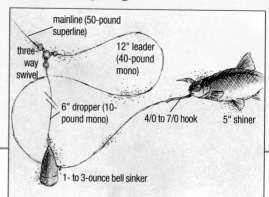

a riffle. Set at least one bait at the head of the hole in deeper water just away from current. Set another in the middle of the deepest part of the hole. And set other baits in slack, deep water alongside the hole.

The biggest fish I've caught in small rivers during fall have come from the portion of a hole where sand meets rock. One of the best spots I fish has a sandbank on the inside bend of the hole, while the outside bend is broken granite. Most of the inactive fish hold in the granite crags. When they feed, they swim right along the sand bank. If you're in a good hole, just wait them out.

Can't say for sure what the best part of the day or night is for flatheads where you might be fishing. I take most of my fish from about 3 p.m. to 8 p.m. Wherever you fish, I'd be surprised if the hour before and the hour after sunset aren't key times, particularly as the water continues to cool toward late-fall lows.

FISHING LARGER RIVERS WITH STEVE HOFFMAN

Hoffman: After fishing for flatheads in wintering holes throughout the Cold-water Period, I'd rate late fall and early winter as the most productive portion of the season for fish numbers and size. Cooling water temperatures at the beginning of this period serve as a catalyst for fish that have been largely static since they finished spawning in midsummer. In the upper Mississippi River pools I most often fish, they begin to move from side channels and backwater lakes into the main river. On the lower Mississippi and Arkansas rivers, fish may be moving from oxbows or other connecting waters, and in channelized rivers like the lower Missouri and Ohio, they may move toward slackwater holes at the lower end of pools or tributary mouths.

On navigable rivers segmented by dams, tailrace areas are one of the first places to look during the fall transition. While filming an In-Fisherman Television segment during a mid-October warm spell, we found that flatheads holding in the scour hole below the dam still were feeding aggressively after dark. Stillfishing with big livebaits on the tailout lip of the hole was productive, but we caught more fish by drifting 8- to 10-inch suckers on three-way rigs onto the flat behind the lip.

The fall season, however, is a time of transition, and patterns often don't last long. The cold rain that fell intermittently during our filming session cooled the water by several degrees. The next night we returned to the same location and found that the fish either had moved again or just refused to bite. My guess is, the fish feeding on the mid-depth flat had either moved to the core of the scour hole or to some other wintering area. A few warm, late-fall days might encourage them to resume feeding, but those warming spells are rare across the northern edge of flathead country.

The fish continue to feed in these wintering areas, particularly when water temperatures still are in the high 40°F to low 50°F range. But finding them can be difficult. They tend to spread throughout the river and connecting waters during summer, so the 10 best spots in a 5-mile river stretch might all hold some flatheads. But during winter, that same stretch might harbor none. The advantage is that once you find a flathead, you've probably found lots of them.

WINTER FLATHEADS

John Lehto of Somerset, Wisconsin, is one of the pioneering anglers of how and where to catch flatheads in cold water. When he retired a few years ago, Lehto set a goal of catching a Wisconsin-record flathead. He'd already caught several big fish while targeting walleyes and sauger in the spring and fall, so he figured those same spots would produce a trophy fish during the traditional summer season, too.

He soon found that fishing with livebait after dark required more patience than he was willing to give, so he abandoned his quest. While trolling crankbaits along a riprap bank for walleyes the next fall, though, he caught another nice flathead. He made a second trolling run across the same river section and caught another. His quest was reborn.

What's most significant about Lehto's initial catch is that it occurred in late October, after the water temperature had dropped below 50°F. This is the time when flatheads are moving toward deep, slackwater holes where they spend the winter in a semi-dormant state—yet, flatheads continue to feed periodically throughout winter, especially during periods of moderate weather. And if only a small percentage of the fish are actively feeding at any time, good catches still are possible because of the large number of fish confined to a small area.

Once Lehto began targeting flatheads in earnest, he kept a record of his catch throughout the season, along with date and water temperature. November, when water temperatures on the rivers he fished ranged from 41°F to 44°F, was best for numbers of flatheads. He and his partner boated 160 fish, including one over 60 pounds and the rest over 50. Daytime air temperatures during this period remained above freezing, and the water level was mostly steady.

The water continued to cool in early December as colder weather set in, and the river level began to fall. Lehto boated almost 2 dozen flatheads in 7 days of fishing the first half of the month, but from mid-December through the end of January, air temperatures rarely climbed above freezing, and he chose to let the cats rest instead of contending with ice on his rod guides and dangerous ice floes.

Back on the river in February, he recorded water temperatures from 37°F to 39°F. Most anglers assume such frigid water is cold enough to shut down flatheads completely, but Lehto and company picked up where they had left off, boating 32 flatheads in 6 days, including three trophies weighing 48, 50, and 69 pounds. That last fish was large enough to meet his goal of establishing a new state record but he released it, since no certified scales were available on the river.

March brought gradually warming water, as temperatures crept up from 38°F to 46°F. Surprisingly, the first 5 days produced 54 flatheads, while the remaining 5 days, with warmer water, produced only 11. Lehto believes rising river levels toward the end of the month were more to blame than rising water temperatures for the poor fishing, but says the fish may also have roamed more in warmer water. Two trips in April, one at the beginning of the month and one at the end, yielded only two flatheads, as the water temperature approached 50°F.

KEY WINTERING AREAS

Lehto's favorite winter spots are holes from 15 to 25 feet deep, with hard bottoms and light to moderate current. Flows during winter usually are light, but flatheads still seek areas with current-deflecting cover like wood or, better, rock.

Outside bends with riprap on sharp-breaking shorelines seem particularly productive, especially if a few submerged trees or a wing dam are associated with the hole.

In most of these spots, the riprap extends from above the highwater mark on shore down the breakline into about 15 feet. Rocks scattered over a predominantly sand bottom provide ideal resting areas for flatheads and other species. On some banks, the rock extends less than 100 yards, making it easy to probe the entire ledge for active fish. In other areas, the riprap runs for more than a mile. Identifying key holding spots within these general areas is necessary for consistent fishing.

Lehto usually scans the edge of the drop-off with sonar to locate snags, boulders, and other cover that serve as a current break for flatheads. He spends most of his time probing the water immediately behind these breaks, but also drifts through the head and tail of the hole in search of roaming cats. Flatheads holding away from current breaks usually are more active, but if walleye or sauger are holding in these areas, the cats are tight to cover.

In large rivers segmented by dams, the population often is divided between both halves of the pool. Many commercial fishermen have caught loads of wintering flatheads in the deep slackwater immediately above the dam, while others have caught good numbers of fish in the scour hole below it. The most important attributes for flathead wintering areas are adequate depth, proper bottom composition, and numerous current breaks.

It's interesting that the best areas also are in or near the main river channel. In those that Lehto fishes, many backwater lakes, sloughs, and side channels are available to the fish. Most of these areas have at least some deep water, supporting a substantial population of panfish and other forage species throughout winter; but they lack current during low water and most are covered in ice by midwinter. Flatheads seem to prefer areas with some current in winter.

PRESENTATION IN PRACTICE & THEORY

Jigs—Watching Lehto fish for flatheads, it would be easy to mistake him for a walleye fisherman. Sitting in the back of the boat, he operates a transom-mount electric motor with one hand while he jigs with the other hand. All the while his eyes are fixed on the sonar screen to keep the boat slipping with the current right on the edge of the channel drop. As soon as his jig touches bottom and the line goes slack, he pops it up again with a quick flick of the wrist.

One major difference is that most walleye anglers tip their jigs with a live minnow when the water temperature dips below about 50°F. Lehto, on the other hand, keeps right on jigging with plastic, adding a bit of one commercial scent or another to trigger fish attracted to the motion and vibration of the jig. The key, he says, is to not let flatheads get a good look at an artificial offering. Keep it moving and they'll strike out of reflex before they realize the bait's a fake.

He uses a variety of soft plastic bodies but isn't sure that it makes much difference to the fish. Shad-shaped baits 4 or 5 inches long are a definite favorite, but he's also had success with big tubes and curlytail grubs. He doesn't think color is too critical, either, but usually goes with yellow, green, and chartreuse baits since they're most visible in turbid water. He's also experimented with rattles inserted into the plastic bodies but isn't convinced they produce more fish.

Lehto rigs plastics on 5/8- to 1-ounce jigheads that have a keel-weighted shape to fight current and a hook heavy enough to hold a substantial flathead. In-Fisherman also has had success with 1- to 2-ounce saltwater-style shad heads

Least Aggressive

three-way rig

jig & minnow

tube body

shad body

large grub or
curlytailed shad

bladebait or
spoon

Most Aggressive

from Owner, Lunker City, and other manufacturers. Color doesn't seem to matter, though most anglers feel more confident with bright colors in dirty water.

We've long advocated fiberglass rods for catfishing, but jigging for flatheads is better done with a heavy-power graphite rod. Lehto prefers a fast-action muskie bucktail rod from 6½ to 7 feet long, but a heavy flippin' stick also works. The sensitive blank is needed to detect bites and to feel the bottom, so the jig can be hopped above rocks and other obstructions. A stiff tip also allows you to drill the hook into a flathead's jaw before it can reject the bait.

Lehto usually opts for 40-pound monofilament mainline and a 30-pound leader connected to it with a barrel swivel. Snags are common in rocks and wood, so he wants to leave as little line as possible connected to a snagged jig. Braided and fused-filament superlines also work. Monofilament is sensitive enough for vertical-jigging and also is more abrasion-resistant than superlines of the same breakstrength.

Blades & Spoons—Bladebaits and heavy jigging spoons may be a better option for vertical-jigging in some situations, especially during extended periods of moderate weather, when flatheads seem most active. Drift downstream with the current, hover in place, or move slowly upstream with the electric motor along the edge of the break, as you work these baits along the bottom. One- to 2-ounce lures are often needed to stay down in current.

Blades and spoons work differently than jigs. Both usually are fished more aggressively and are designed to trigger active fish. Blades vibrate best as the rod tip is sharply raised a foot or two, then they drift back to bottom on a semitight line. Most hits occur as the bait is raised. Spoons, on the other hand, wobble on the downward flutter, the point of the presentation that produces most strikes.

The major drawback to using blades and spoons is that they're more prone to snagging in rocks and wood. Jigs often can be finessed out of rocky crevices or pulled over branches and stumps, whereas the treble hooks on a bladebait or spoon are more prone to catch and hold. However, they still deserve a place in your box, if only for relatively clean-bottomed areas.

Three-Ways—Three-way rigs are a popular option for stillfishing during summer, but they're also an effective way to present livebait near bottom while drifting. Attach one eye of a three-way swivel to your mainline and the other two to a leader and sinker dropper. Make the leader and dropper lines short to keep baits near the bottom and to minimize snags while drifting. Using lighter line for the dropper also allows you to salvage the rest of the rig if the sinker hangs.

A 4- or 5-inch shiner on a 5/0 hook is a good setup, but small suckers and other livebaits also work. Avoid larger baitfish used during the warmwater season, since a flathead's slower metabolism probably favors smaller meals. Walleye anglers often use three-way rigs to hold floating minnow imitators near bottom, which might also be effective for flatheads.

Holding the bait in place from an anchored boat is an option if you're confident fish are holding below, but drifting probably will account for more fish. Slip downstream through the hole using a subtle lift-drop motion to maintain bottom contact with the sinker, and keep the bait near bottom. Moving upstream also is an option, provided you use a heavy enough sinker to bump the bottom as you go.

Three-way rigs are the most subtle presentation option, so move slowly to keep the bait in the strike zone long enough for fish to react. Letting the rig sit for long periods in slackwater pockets behind rocks and other current breaks may trigger strikes from lethargic fish when nothing else will. It's seldom necessary to give line when a fish takes the bait, so set the hook as soon as you detect a strike.

SNAGGING & HARVEST

Many of the big flatheads reportedly caught during the Coldwater Period are snagged. River walleye anglers in the North and reservoir bass anglers in the South probably snag thousands of flatheads every winter while targeting their favorite species. In some areas, though, anglers specifically target flatheads with weighted treble hooks, jigging spoons, and other lures designed to snag rather than entice fish to bite.

Lehto says that about 25 percent of his fish are snagged, but adds that the exact percentage varies throughout the season. When the fish are more scattered at the beginning and end of the Coldwater Period, most are hooked in the mouth. On one November trip, for example, only one of eight fish caught was snagged (under the bottom jaw).

When flatheads group tightly together behind cover during spells of nasty weather, it's almost impossible to work a lure through a hole without snagging a fish or two. This is another reason Lehto doesn't fish when the weather's cold, preferring instead to wait until the next stretch of warmer weather that will get the fish moving enough to chase a jig.

Whether big flatheads are caught or snagged doesn't matter, of course, if all those fish are harvested. Fish caught from these winter concentrations are the fish that—once spring arrives—spread throughout the river and its tributaries to reproduce and provide sport for countless anglers. Exercise discipline, then, by practicing selective harvest, releasing big fish and keeping a small fish or two for the table.

In-Fisherman's Internet Fishing Content Director Jeff Simpson with a coldwater flat.

Tailrace Tactics

**FIRST-RATE
FISHING
BELOW DAMS**

t's no mystery why some of the best catfishing of the year often takes place in a tailwater area, beginning around April in the South and lasting well through June in the North. It's gluttony. And it's love. In that order. For a fat cat's penchant for chow is hardly affected by the lusty advances of even the loveliest catfish of the opposite persuasion—at least not until the very end, when nature cannot be ignored. Even then, though, even when a bully big male cat is guarding his brood in a hole in a cutbank, food's welcomed with a bite and a burp when it rolls close by.

Tailwaters may be large or small, turbulent or gently flowing, shallow or deep, dangerous or safe, depending on the size of the river and the subsequent size, construction, and purpose of the dam. All tailwaters are dangerous in high water. The water immediately below the turbines of large hydro stations, though, where water boils for all the world like cauldrons from hell, holds a special terror. Lowhead dams, too, are always dangerous, particularly so because many of them don't look as if they are. But get sucked into the turbulence below and you can kiss your life goodbye, even if you're wearing five life jackets.

Cats move upriver during high-water periods in spring. If, for example, a river's free of ice by March, the water temperature is poking into the 50°F range by mid April and cats are on the move. Hole by hole, run by run, shallow section by shallow section, cats move until they hit barriers. A barrier may be a particularly shallow portion of river. It may be a tremendous buildup of fallen timber stretching across a river. Eventually though, it usually is a dam.

A cat consolidation of sorts is going on, the opposite of what happens by late summer. Say a river's 50 miles long. By late summer, catfish relate to the deepest holes in the river; but those holes often are evenly spread throughout all 50 miles of river. Once late spring arrives, though, once cats have had a chance to move, most of them are somewhere in the upper third of the river.

Cats don't all group in tailwaters. But a lot of them at least make it there and stay for a while to feed before gradually moving back downriver to spawning areas, perhaps the same areas where they've spawned before. At any one time, then, once plenty of water is moving during spring, the catfish population in a tailwater area is constantly being replenished by catfish arriving from downriver. And again, because of the supreme feeding conditions in most tailwaters, most cats stay at least for a while.

The amount of fishing pressure makes a difference in the number of available fish in smaller tailwaters. Once cats reach a tailwater, the consolidation continues as they are moved by current into prime feeding areas. There may be few such locations in smaller tailwaters, a dozen in larger ones. Rarely, though, are there many prime spots, and you need to recognize them. We'll get to that.

Once the fish stationed in those areas are caught, it takes awhile for the spots to be replenished. During peak prespawn movements in spring, this may take several days. When the water's low in summer, it takes a major rain to replenish spots with catfish. Periods between good fishing may last more than a month.

Once you learn to read current, you know exactly where fish might be. Then you need to probe those spots to see what kind of structure lies below. That usually determines how many cats can be there. Once you're anchored right, you'll catch most of the cats feeding there, which during June is most of the cats most of the time.

BAITS AND TACKLE

Tailrace catfish feed on both live and dead baitfish. Smaller fish species are disoriented by the turbulent waters below dams, making them easy prey. When baitfish pass through dam turbines they're often chopped into palatable slabs that catfish feed on.

During spring, therefore, it's rarely necessary to use anything but chunks of cutbait of a size appropriate for the cats being pursued. In small rivers, the best choice may be as simple as a freshly killed 4-inch baitfish. Cutting off the tail helps to keep the bait from spinning in current. Slash the sides of the a time or two to get those succulent juices flowing. Slip the hook through once near the tail end, leaving the hook point exposed to ensure a good hookset. Use a #4 or #2 hook like the Eagle

Tailrace Casting Rod and Three-Way Rig

John Blain of Deepwater, Missouri, is a caster who likes to tangle with big blue cats. To catch them at Truman tailrace, which is 250 yards wide, an angler must be able to toss a bait more than 100 yards. Blain uses a 13-foot Lamiglass casting rod with either a Daiwa SL20SH reel or a Garcia 7000 reel. His reels are spooled with 20-pound-test monofilament. To the line, he affixes a 4/0 Kahle hook and a 4-ounce bank sinker.

The configuration of the hook and sinker is similar to a Wolf River rig, but Blain doesn't use a three-way swivel. Instead, he ties a catfish breakaway knot that has a 6-inch loop knot, to which the hook is attached by a Palomar knot and an 18-inch section of line to which a snap and bank sinker are affixed. According to Blain, the best casting bait for blue cats is a shad head no bigger than a large thumbnail.

With current, most blues are caught as the bait drifts downstream about a foot or two off bottom in 20 feet of water. This is accomplished by casting at a quarter upstream and allowing the bait to drift. On the drift, the sinker occasionally becomes anchored on the bottom. If it anchors at the right lair, the best cat of the day often is taken.

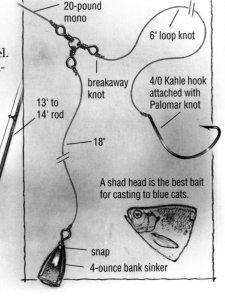

20-pound mono

6" loop knot

breakaway knot

4/0 Kahle hook attached with Palomar knot

13' to 14' rod

18"

A shad head is the best bait for casting to blue cats.

Garcia 7000 or Daiwa L205H

snap

4-ounce bank sinker

Claw 84 or the Mustad 92671—simple, affordable, sturdy hooks. There are lots of snags, so buying boxes of a hundred saves money. Cats up to about 10 pounds take a piece of cutbait (suckers and shad work great), something about 1 inch x 1 inch x 1/2 inch thick. Increase those dimensions by half an inch at most for bigger catfish. Going any larger makes it difficult to fish it properly in current.

Leave the hook point exposed by slipping it once through the corner of the skin of the cutbait. A 2/0 hook is just right for fish from 6 to 10 pounds or so. For bigger fish, go with a 3/0 hook. Sharpen hooks with a file and reduce the barb to make sure the hook sets easily. Eventually, when the largest flatheads switch to livebaits, you'll need heavier rigging.

Common Tailrace Options

G ood spots usually are in deep water at the head of a deep hole, at a river bend, or at a rock slide next to a bluff. A ledge often is an important ingredient in a good hole. Once the whereabouts of the cats are determined, the boat is anchored about 40 feet upstream.

Anglers use 20- or 30-pound line. Some anglers use live shad, but old-time flathead anglers in the Midwest still prefer a live goldfish, a spunky green sunfish, or a bullhead. Occasionally, an old-timer hooks into an impressive bunch of flatheads by using a gob of nightcrawlers. Most anglers use cut shad or carp for blue cats and channel cats. From an anchored boat, either cast or drop vertically, allowing current to wash the bait downstream to cat lairs.

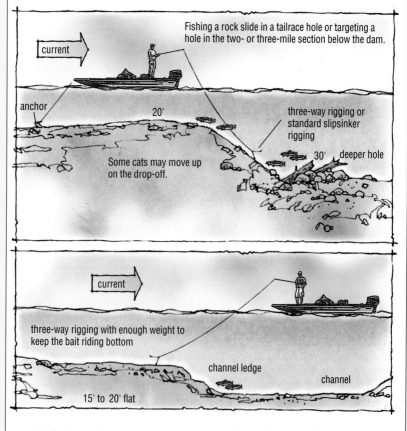

Fishing a rock slide in a tailrace hole or targeting a hole in the two- or three-mile section below the dam.

current

anchor

20'

three-way rigging or standard slipsinker rigging

Some cats may move up on the drop-off.

30'   deeper hole

current

three-way rigging with enough weight to keep the bait riding bottom

channel ledge

channel

15' to 20' flat

Drift along the channel edge or work down the gut of the old river channel, using three-way rigging to present a shad head, a portion of cutbait, a plastic dipworm and dipbait, or livebait. Bait choice depends on the season and the catfish species being pursued.

Weight your bait with a bell sinker, preferably the kind called a bass-casting sinker, which usually has a swivel on top. Egg sinkers don't work well because they don't stay in place on bottom and you can end up with twice as many snags. There's no way to completely eliminate snags, though, so make your own sinkers, or at least buy in bulk. Keeping on hand a supply of weights from 1 to 8 ounces covers most tailwater situations.

One of the biggest mistakes catmen make is worrying about the length of leader between the hook and sinker. This is needless worry because no leader is necessary. Let the sinker slide right up against the hook. The resulting rig looks, casts, and fishes almost like a leadhead jig—exactly what you want. Too much leader causes a loss of feel, lack of control, and subsequently snags. If the swivel eye on top of the sinker is so big that the eye of your hook sticks, use a bead to cushion this connection.

Once you learn to read current, you know exactly where fish might be.

Use current to move this rig along the bottom. If your rig's just heavy enough and you hold your line just tight enough to stay in constant contact with current, your rig moves through prime current spots so you can feel everything down there. Lift the rig over rocks and slide it through sand and gravel pockets. Snags are minimized, while presentation is maximized.

The most important part of this process, though, is the acquired ability to judge more than bottom content, which is secondary to current in determining where fish are. You can use this rig to read current conditions. Specifically, first look for and then feel for current tunnels.

CURRENT TUNNELS

Current edges are formed: Where flows moving in opposing directions meet, and where flows moving at different speeds and consisting of different volumes of water meet. Current tunnels are formed near bottom along these edges or at the rear or tailout of holes gouged by the turbulence of the tailwater, creating areas of relative calm in turbulent water. Catfish use these tunnels as a current refuge. They can move easily through them, and feed more efficiently. Food that washes into these areas moves slowly through, making it easily accessible to the catfish holding there.

Current tunnels may be either flat, relatively indistinct in shape, or oval and much like a tunnel. The flat tunnels usually form where flows moving in opposite directions meet. The circular tunnels form where flows are moving the same direction at different speeds and with different volumes of water. Most tunnels are no more than 15 to 20 feet long.

The obvious spot for circular tunnels is immediately below the dam. If a pillar separates one lock from another, and if only one of them is running water, the pillar creates a current edge where a large volume of water crushes and runs over a lesser volume of water moving in the same direction.

In most major dam areas, so much water is running or it's so deep that it's impossible to safely fish close to the dam. Lowhead dams don't, for the most part, have many pillars, and getting too close is dangerous. And stay away from areas of massive turbulence. Anchoring is unsafe in some situations, too. Ask folks who know about local conditions. And when in doubt, don't anchor. Always have a knife on hand to cut the anchor line in an emergency.

To fish through a current tunnel, anchor in the slower water on one side of the most turbulent flow, as close as possible to the head of the current edge. Cast

Current Edges & Tunnels

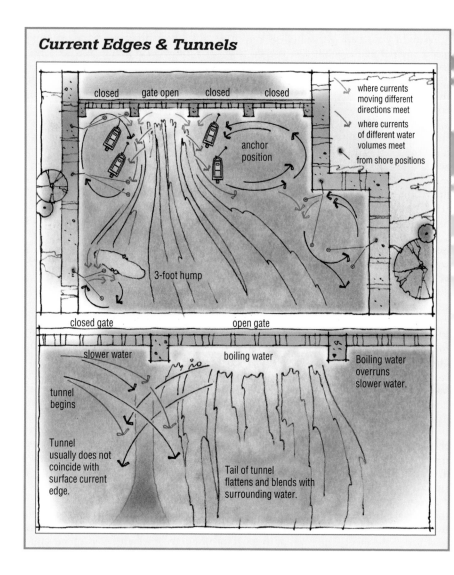

closed gate open closed closed

where currents moving different directions meet

where currents of different water volumes meet

anchor position

from shore positions

3-foot hump

closed gate open gate

slower water boiling water

Boiling water overruns slower water.

tunnel begins

Tunnel usually does not coincide with surface current edge.

Tail of tunnel flattens and blends with surrounding water.

your bait to the head of the current edge, usually just behind a pillar, and tighten your line to the bait. The objective is to locate the head of the current tunnel and to keep your bait anchored there, or at least move your bait through it as slowly as possible.

A good sense of feel with your rig allows you to identify the location and length of current tunnels. Cast to the crease at the head of the current break. The rig sinks through stronger current, eventually hitting bottom where it's surrounded by slower-moving water with faster water coursing above it. Holding your rod tip at about 2 o'clock, tighten your line to your rig lying on bottom. Your sinker should be just heavy enough so turbulent water sweeping against most of your line drags your bait slowly along the bottom. Hit a current tunnel and your bait stops, at least momentarily. Sometimes the rig anchors where it first hits the tunnel. Other times, when the boat isn't in perfect position, the bait is dragged along the edge of the tunnel or swept out of it. With experience, you'll be able to judge what's happening.

Hit the head of the tunnel, keep your bait there for two minutes, and you'll feel the solid *cawonk!* of a cat. Drop your rod tip a foot or two toward the fish as it begins to move away, and then set. Big cats don't miss when a bait's in a tunnel. And little cats don't dare fin where monsters tread.

Chances are, several good fish are working each tunnel. They move forward through it until they reach the head, then sweep back to the area near the tail end and work forward again. Picture the tail of a tunnel waggling around like the bottom of the cone of a tornado. The farther back in a tunnel your bait is, the more turbulent the water and the more difficult for cats to find your bait.

Pancake tunnels are most common. They lie along current breaks where currents moving in opposite directions meet. These can be fished from a boat or from shore, using the same presentation described above. A float may also be helpful in moving a bait along or through these flatter and longer tunnels. Catfish aren't so likely to always lie at the head of these tunnels, so it takes longer for fish to find your bait. It shouldn't take longer than 10 minutes in a spot, though. Fish along areas and move on—or at least try a different portion of a current area.

Hold the rod tip high to minimize the amount of line in the water. Again, don't ever keep your bait in the same spot for long. Let it settle, let it drag, get it to hold. Wait no more than five minutes. Move the bait again to be sure you're searching for cats, and to be sure it hasn't tumbled into a crevice where fish can't find it. In large and turbulent tailwaters like those found behind TVA dams and behind the locks on the Ohio and Mississippi rivers, few rigs hold bottom better than the breakaway design, which usually consists of a light dropline and sinker that snags bottom as it drifts along. A cat takes the bait and the drop rigging breaks, freeing the catfish to fight without weight on the line.

Another approach is to use a boat to run up into the fast water. Stop along a current crease and when the boat starts drifting at the same speed as the current, drop your bait vertically to the bottom. Use your motor to keep the boat moving just fast enough to keep your bait vertical. Again, you're moving the bait along in the slower water on bottom.

Some of the hottest territory is the tailout of the hole gouged immediately below the dam. When your bait hits this area, it slows even more as it enters the tunnel that runs along the drop-off lip coming up from the deep water in the hole. This tunnel runs the length of the rear of the hole, but there's no way to fish it perpendicular to current. You can only drag baits through it by drifting downriver. Once your bait's swept up onto the flat at the end of the tailout hole, reel up, motor back to the end of the turbulence, and begin again.

These basic principles apply to situations found in every tailwater, but other tactics are bound to develop, given the peculiarities of each location. Always be willing to try what's working locally, but don't be afraid to buck the status quo.

CATCH MORE FROM SHORE

Every year, thousands of catfish anglers gather below dams. But many of the agencies that manage these structures prohibit boat traffic within the first hundred yards or more of the tailrace—particularly on dams below large reservoirs, which often concentrate the highest numbers of cats—making it difficult to reach the best fishing areas.

Working the Washout Hole and Tailout Area

Catfish hold in the relatively slack water along the lip of the washout hole. Most congregate along the lip in the tailout area of the washout hole. They tend to hold close to the bottom, but usually can be seen on a sonar, graph, or liquid crystal display unit.

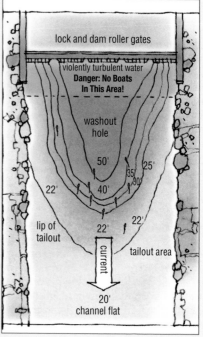

lock and dam roller gates

violently turbulent water
Danger: No Boats In This Area!

washout hole

50'

35'
25'
30'

22'   40'

22'

lip of tailout   22'   22'

current

tailout area

20'
channel flat

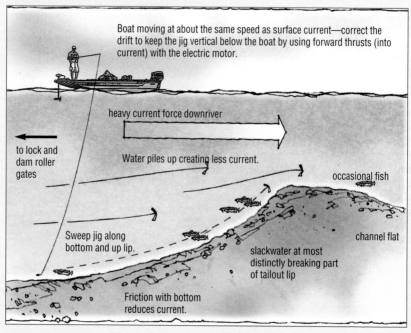

Boat moving at about the same speed as surface current—correct the drift to keep the jig vertical below the boat by using forward thrusts (into current) with the electric motor.

heavy current force downriver

to lock and dam roller gates

Water piles up creating less current.

occasional fish

Sweep jig along bottom and up lip.

channel flat

slackwater at most distinctly breaking part of tailout lip

Friction with bottom reduces current.

Even shore anglers face a greater challenge than most observers realize. Many bank fishermen these days are equipped with 10- to 12-foot surf rods and large-capacity spinning reels spooled with 30-pound line. Without an understanding of the fundamentals of distance casting, though, few are able to cast much farther than anglers using shorter rods and lighter rigs. Casts of 100 yards or more are often necessary to reach catfish.

Most tailrace fishing also is confined to a few small public-access areas, usually maintained by a state fishery agency or the Army Corps of Engineers. When the discharge from the dam reaches optimum levels and the fish population below these structures peaks, most of these access areas are as crowded as a trout stream on opening day. Even under the best conditions, though, just a few anglers usually catch the bulk of the fish.

CASE STUDY: KEYSTONE DAM

Tim "Tiny" Smith of Drumwright, Oklahoma, a veteran competition distance caster and catfish guide, has a reputation for catching fish from shore in the tailrace below Keystone Dam near Tulsa. While many shore anglers use off-the-shelf surf rods rated for 2 to 4 ounces of lead, Smith's custom sticks are designed to cast a pound or more. The rods he uses are 12 to 14 feet long, constructed of a boron-graphite material that's as strong as fiberglass composites but much lighter. The faster action and stiffer tip section also allow him to cast lighter rigs with much more force than he could with inexpensive rods with a softer action.

Tee 'em high and let 'em fly.

Smith began his tournament casting career with spinning gear, but prefers casting outfits for big cats. Each of his rods is equipped with an Abu Garcia Ambassadeur 7000, which he favors

Keystone Dam

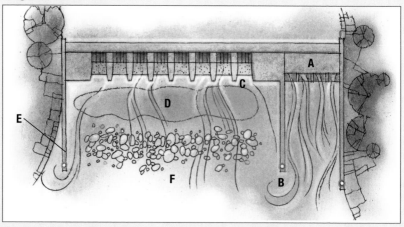

A—Generator Turbines. *This area usually holds a few active fish, particularly during warmer months when shad and other baitfish are washed through from the lake.*

B—Current Tunnel. *This is where the fast water from the turbines and slackwater from the closed floodgates meet. Active fish usually hold along the wall and along the edge of the washout hole, looking for dead and injured baitfish swept through the turbines.*

C—Floodgates. *Throughout most of the year, these gates are open only enough to allow a small trickle of water to flow through. The gates with the most flow usually hold the best numbers of actively feeding cats.*

D—Washout Hole. *The scour hole below the floodgates holds fish throughout most of the year. Active fish tend to hold at the head or edge of the hole, particularly when the flow is heavy, while neutral or negative fish tend to favor the core of the hole.*

E—Floodgate Wall. *This area experiences at least a small bit of current almost all of the time, which in turn attracts cats. At night, the lights on the corner of the dam also attract insects, baitfish, and flatheads.*

F—Rockbar. *The large rocks strewn across the riverbed below the washout hole attract active fish that feed on baitfish holding near the boulders.*

for its large line capacity and durability. These reels also sport a smooth, dependable drag system and a bait clicker for detecting bites while the reel's in free spool.

Smith spools with 30-pound Breakaway monofilament, which has a thin diameter for its test rating. This gives him the strength needed to wrestle big cats out of the rock and rubble littering the river bottom, but still allows for enough line capacity to make incredibly long casts.

Bait—The best bait for big cats often is whatever forage is abundant in a particular body of water, that is, whatever the cats are accustomed to eating. Shad, carp, and sunfish top the list in most areas. Smith usually prefers shad, which he catches in a cast net and keeps alive in a baitwell set up in the back of his truck.

Smith prefers to use shad heads because they're usually more effective and stay on the hook better during a long cast, but he doesn't hesitate to bait with shad sides when the bite's slow—just in case the fish have developed a temporary preference for fillets. During most trips, though, he baits with the heads, which he hooks up through the bottom lip and out a nostril to keep the offering looking natural in current. He also changes baits every 10 to 15 minutes to ensure they're fresh.

Rigging—Smith's typical rigging is designed to keep his bait off the bottom where it would quickly be lost to snags rather than cats. He begins with a 5-ounce bell or bank sinker tied to a short length of 17-pound mono. The other end of the sinker dropper terminates in a loop, which is threaded through a similar loop at the end of his mainline. Should the weight become snagged, the dropper line can be broken with a steady pull, and the rest of the rig can be retrieved. Above the mainline loop, he attaches a 2/0 O'Shaughnessy hook on a dropper knot.

Smith also uses a slipfloat rig when blue cats are suspended off the bottom. The rig is constructed as before, except that a lighter 1- to 2-ounce sinker is used, along with a weighted slipfloat on the mainline above the terminal rigging. The sinker riding below the hook allows him to detect more light bites than he could with a standard slipfloat rig. Any movement of the bait is immediately indicated by the float.

He also uses a hook clip to aid casting distance and accuracy. The clip is fashioned from

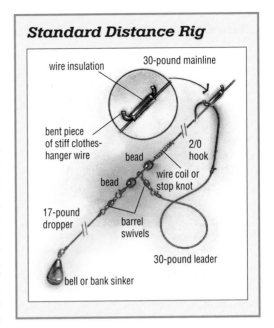

Standard Distance Rig

wire insulation
30-pound mainline
bent piece of stiff clothes-hanger wire
bead
2/0 hook
bead
wire coil or stop knot
17-pound dropper
barrel swivels
30-pound leader
bell or bank sinker

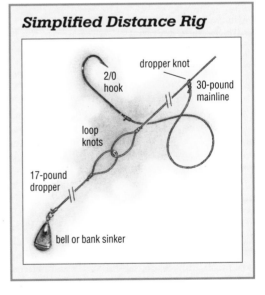

Simplified Distance Rig

dropper knot
2/0 hook
30-pound mainline
loop knots
17-pound dropper
bell or bank sinker

a short length of a wire coat hanger attached to the mainline with a piece of insulation from a 110-volt electrical wire. The baited hook rides in the bend of the wire during the cast, but instantly releases when the bait hits the water. The hook clip eliminates the helicopter-type spinning of the bait during the cast, which may dramatically decrease casting distance and cause terminal tangles.

Hooking and Landing—For setting hooks at long distances, timing is critical, and power is a must. With the long rods typically used for 100-yard casts, though,

Tim Smith's Flathead Rigging

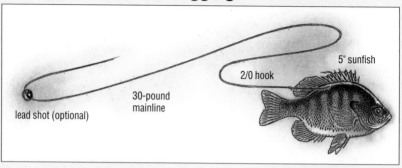

lead shot (optional)

30-pound mainline

2/0 hook

5" sunfish

S mith usually targets big blue cats, but occasionally sets up for flatheads when conditions are favorable. In this situation, he favors live sunfish about 5 inches long, instead of cut shad. He also removes about half the scales to allow the bait to release more scent.

He runs a 2/0 hook through the back of the bait, under the dorsal fin. This allows the freelined bait to move around in a natural manner to attract prowling flatheads. A short lob cast delivers the bait to a likely area, and the free spool bait-clicker controls its movement.

When the clicker indicates a fish has picked up the bait, Smith engages the reel and waits to feel the weight of the fish. He then sets the hook sharply and keeps steady pressure on the line until the fish is brought to net. This rig occasionally produces big blue and channel catfish looking for a lively meal.

a swift lift generates ample force to drive the hook into catfish flesh. When they feel a bite, many anglers immediately rear back on the rod with all their might, often tearing the lips off the fish that engulf their bait. Unfortunately, most of their swings result in missed fish. Smith, meanwhile, merely lifts the rod sharply from 9 to 12 o'clock and rarely misses a fish.

From almost 200 yards away, an 8-pound blue cat feels like a trophy. Reeling in that much line along with a 5-ounce sinker and a decent catfish soon becomes a challenge for arms and shoulders. Fighting fish with a long rod becomes a game of strength. Fast-action rods flex and bob every time the fish surges, rolls, or shakes its head, leaving your arms to absorb the shock. As the fish continues to struggle, though, the stiff rod and tight drag eventually take their toll, and the fish usually is played out in less time than with a shorter, softer rod.

Once the fish is turned, you can begin regaining line. For many anglers this is the most physically demanding part of the process. The fish no longer is struggling so hard, but reeling in even a spent fish for more than 100 yards in heavy current soon becomes tiring. Begin with the rod tip at the 12 o'clock position and reel down to 9 o'clock, keeping the line tight at all times. Now slowly lift the rod back to 12 o'clock and repeat the process again and again until the fish is within reach.

As a cat approaches the net, it often garners enough strength for one more drag-slipping run. The rod tip surges down and line peels quickly from the spool.

This final leg of the fight usually is short-lived. The trademark blue cat battle ends with the fish rolling into the net. After a quick photograph, slide the hard-won trophy back into the water so both angler and fish can recuperate.

CASE STUDY: STOCKTON DAM

Stockton Lake, near Stockton, Missouri, has long been considered one of the state's top walleye waters. And while the walleye fishing is exceptional, the Little Sac River below Stockton Dam remains a relatively untapped catfish fishery.

This dam, though, is a bit more difficult to fish than Keystone Dam or those below other large impoundments. At Stockton, shore anglers fish from the top of wall almost 40 feet above the water, which requires a few specialized tools to assist catmen in hooking and landing fish. These tools can't be purchased from tackle shops or catalogs, but they're fairly easy to construct.

This scenario makes landing fish more difficult. Even with 40-pound line and a stiff, heavy-power rod, a 10-pound fish can be almost impossible to hoist up the steep wall without the proper net. An 8- or 10-foot extension handle may work for shorter drops, but beyond that range, the net becomes too heavy and cumbersome.

Stockton Dam regulars use a net constructed of a bicycle wheel that functions as a frame and a bag from a large landing net. The wheel is attached to the net with a length of nylon rope threaded through the edge of the bag and around the wheel, then knotted firmly in place. The net is then lowered on a heavy rope over the side of the wall when a fish is hooked, and the wide diameter of the wheel allows even large fish to be netted with ease.

Tackle—Rod and reel selection among Stockton tailrace anglers varies, but the relatively few anglers who catch most of the fish generally agree that 8-foot medium-heavy-power rods are the best choice. Large-capacity spinning reels spooled with heavy line—up to 50- or in some cases even 60-pound test—complete the combo. The rest of their tackle consists of 3- to 5-ounce sinkers, which are enough to anchor rigs in all but the heaviest current, and 2/0 wide-gap hooks. A few anglers have also begun to use similar-sized circle hooks with excellent results.

The same riggings used by Tim Smith below Keystone Dam would be effective at Stockton, too, but local anglers usually rely on sliprigs or three-way rigs. The sliprig is the most popular option because it's easier to tie and modify as current conditions change throughout the day. During heavy flows, anglers shorten leader length so the bait's easier for cats to grab and hangs up less often on the snaggy bottom. In slacker conditions, though, a longer leader allows more bait movement, which may attract more cats.

A three-way rig often is a better option in the heaviest flows. A short, 6-inch leader keeps the bait from flailing about wildly in the current and keeps the bait from tangling around the mainline while casting. The length of the sinker dropper usually is about twice the length of the leader to keep the bait riding just above the bottom, though a longer dropper often is used when cats are holding higher in the water column.

Location—When fishing any tailrace, location usually is the most important factor. You can't catch fish if your bait isn't where the cats can find it. At certain times below many dams, though, so many fish are concentrated into tailraces that almost any section produces at least a few small fish. But below most small dams like Stockton, most of the fish—particularly the bigger fish—hold in key areas.

The obvious spot is the deep washout hole directly below the floodgates. This usually is the deepest hole in the tailrace and probably for many miles below. At Stockton, this hole also is sweetened with manmade brushpiles that attract and hold baitfish throughout much of the year. The baitfish, in-turn, attract and hold catfish.

Fresh cut portions of oily baitfish, such as shad or suckers, on a sliprig are the best option for this area most of the time. At night, however, many anglers prefer a slipfloat rig to catch cats feeding on baitfish, which are gathered near the surface to feed on insects attracted by the lights on top of the dam.

The generator turbines on the other side of the dam are another prime location for cats in warm weather. Shad and other baitfish pulled through the turbines from the lake attract hordes of

Drifting and trolling are gangbuster techniques below dams. Keep a few fish for supper and release the rest.

hungry cats in many tailraces. When fishing this area, most anglers opt for a lighter weight rig, so it drifts along the bottom in the faster current. This allows anglers to cover more water and contact more active catfish.

The pillar between the floodgates and the turbines functions as a current break, which serves as a resting area for cats in a neutral or negative feeding mood. Fish holding in this area seldom are as aggressive as those holding in faster flows, but the area usually holds more fish, and few pass up the opportunity for an easy meal.

Most anglers modify their rigging to accommodate the speed of the current and the activity level of the cats. In this case, that means a heavier weight to anchor baits in key areas, rather than letting the bait drift along the bottom. This is particularly effective in cold water, during cold fronts, or during other conditions that cause tailrace catfish to turn a bit sullen.

DRIFTIN' & TROLLIN' BELOW THE DAM

Keep rods in holders while trolling, and don't touch 'em till a big cat loads 'em.

Catfish tournament pro and guide Phil King of Corinth, Mississippi, is a genuine river rat. He has the kind of catfishin' savvy that only comes with hard time on the water. Like the rivermen who floated the mighty Tennessee before the dams were built, [cliché and restated better immediately] King works with the current, lets it carry him to the fish, then tames it just enough for a precise presentation. His anchorless techniques have paid off well in tailwaters.

One reason for King's success is that he knows catfish

aren't always sitting on the bottom. Many fish suspend, and his approach is one of the surest ways to catch them. He employs two basic methods that should produce during much of the season in tailraces.

REVERSE DRIFTING

King uses this method to probe the main river when current is being generated at the dam. It allows him to cover key structural elements such as holes, humps, rockpiles, ledges, and bars at a pace he chooses, regardless of how slow or fast the water is moving. Reverse-drifting is an excellent way to locate big concentrations of catfish, and it's King's primary "numbers" technique. He and two clients boated 400 pounds of cats in a single day using this method, and don't sell it short for trophy cats, either. Because reverse-drifting allows considerable control over boat speed and bait presentation, saturating a deep log or rockpile with a mess of shad guts or a fresh, juicy skipjack fillet is far easier than with other anchorless techniques.

Reverse-drifting is accomplished by pointing the nose

Tennessee River catfish guide Phil King with a 20-pound blue cat that was suspended over a rock hump.

of the boat into the current and using a bowmounted trolling motor either to hold the boat stationary or allow it to slip slowly downstream. The method works best with lightweight shallow-draft boats, like King's aluminum jon. His trolling motor provides enough power for most fishing conditions, but if the current is really racing immediately below the dam, he launches in slower current a few miles farther downriver. Once the drift of the boat has been slowed, an accurate bottom-bumping presentation is possible, even in deep water (King routinely targets 20- to 50-foot depths).

To catch cats suspending within a few feet of the bottom, a common scenario in tailrace current, King chooses his tackle carefully. He uses medium- to heavy power 7½-foot King Kat Pro rods and Ambassadeur 6000 or 6500C reels spooled with 60-pound Spiderwire Stealth or similar braid. "Braided line's low diameter offers greater strength with less drag in current, and its almost total lack of stretch allows for feeling the lightest bites," he says. "My strike-to-hookup ratio increased 100 percent when I switched from mono to braid."

Reverse Drifting

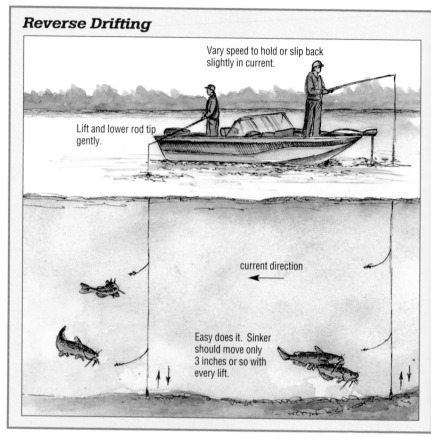

Vary speed to hold or slip back slightly in current.

Lift and lower rod tip gently.

current direction

Easy does it. Sinker should move only 3 inches or so with every lift.

Reverse Drifting Rig

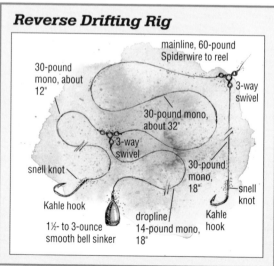

mainline, 60-pound Spiderwire to reel

30-pound mono, about 12"

3-way swivel

30-pound mono, about 32"

3-way swivel

30-pound mono, 18"

snell knot

Kahle hook

snell knot

1½- to 3-ounce smooth bell sinker

dropline 14-pound mono, 18"

Kahle hook

King's reverse-drifting rig is designed to snare unsuspecting cats suspending from 1 to 5 feet off bottom. His Kahle hooks are tied with a snell knot; this moves the hook point into position perfectly when rod pressure is applied and results in only a few missed strikes. While the leader is 30-pound mono, the sinker dropper is 14, which allows quick breakoffs should the weight become lodged between rocks. To allow for better bottom feel and fewer hangups, use a smooth, cylindrical bell

Trolling

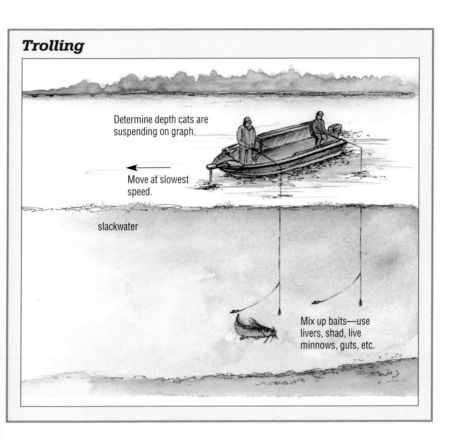

Determine depth cats are suspending on graph.

Move at slowest speed.

slackwater

Mix up baits—use livers, shad, live minnows, guts, etc.

sinker, not a triangular sinker or one with ridges on the sides, he advises.

King floats downstream until he spots likely fish-holding structure on his graph or sees fish suspending near the bottom. He then motors back upriver and baits up with shad guts, skipjack fillets, chicken livers, live shad, or a live yellowtail (a local baitfish). Usually he puts two different baits on each hook leader and rigs each rod with a different combination of offerings until he determines

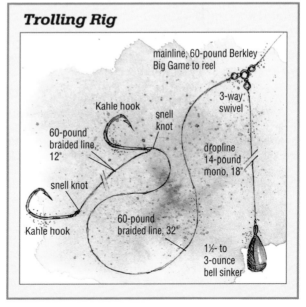

Trolling Rig

mainline, 60-pound Berkley Big Game to reel

3-way swivel

Kahle hook

snell knot

60-pound braided line, 12"

dropline 14-pound mono, 18"

snell knot

Kahle hook

60-pound braided line, 32"

1½- to 3-ounce bell sinker

what the fish prefer. Once he drifts back over the potential hot spot, he lowers the sinker to the bottom, engages the reel, lifts the rod tip slightly, and lowers the sinker back down to the bottom. "The key is to move the sinker gently, only 3 inches or so off the bottom, then let it back down easy," King says. "If you're not getting bites, you're probably either jerking the sinker too high or letting it clank back down too hard. Easy does it—just lift and lower, lift and lower. When you feel a bite, set the hook hard."

Make constant depth adjustments when probing irregular bottoms. "If you can't feel the sinker tapping bottom, immediately let out more line until you do; and you'll need to retrieve line when you come across a hump or rockpile. Try to adjust your drift so your line is directly under the boat at all times," he says.

If current speed permits, King uses his trolling motor to move laterally across the structure as well as straight down. "This works especially well along a ledge or channel drop-off, or when you're having trouble pinpointing fish on a big piece of structure like a bar."

TROLLING

King relies on trolling in slow to slack current, finding it especially productive in the "deadwater" pool that forms adjacent to current boils below dams, during periods of heavy generation. Here, big catfish often stack up to gorge on disoriented baitfish washing in from turbulent current boils nearby. Trolling, he says, is his primary big-fish technique.

He finds that catfish suspend considerably higher off bottom in slack water than when current is present. "It isn't unusual to find big cats suspending 15 feet deep in a 30-foot hole. These fish tend to be slower to bite than cats in current, and trolling is the best way to catch 'em. It allows you to soak the bait right in their faces for an extended time."

Besides shad guts, livers, and cutbait, King uses live baitfish extensively for trolling. Prior to fishing, he dons his life jacket and motors carefully to the turbulent water directly below the dam, where he uses a homemade net with a basket formed from stiff chicken wire to capture fresh baitfish. Usually one or two dips will snare enough bait for several hours of trolling.

Like reverse-drifting, trolling is an electric motor technique, but because of little or no current, it's less demanding on the boat operator. He simply adjusts his trolling motor to the slowest speed that permits forward movement; meanders around the slackwater pool until he spots suspending fish on his graph, and then lowers baited lines down to the fish's level.

King uses sturdier tackle for trolling—7- and 8-foot solid fiberglass rods and Ambassadeur reels spooled with 60-pound Berkley Big Game line. He places up to 7 rods in Driftmaster holders strategically positioned around his boat, and instructs his clients not to touch them until a fish has loaded on. "No premature jerking, please," he insists while demonstrating the method. "Let the rod bend so far that the last guide is underwater before you pick up the rod."

The terminal rig is different from that used in reverse-drifting. For trolling, King uses 63-pound braided line on the leader and larger Kahle hooks to hold the bigger baits monster cats often prefer.

Whether fishing from shore or casting, drifting, or trolling from a boat, tailwaters can produce big-time, with a cat consolidation peaking during the early part of the season into early summer. For fishermen, the call is clear and so is the direction to head for good catfishing—below a dam near you.

Chapter 12

Unique Environments

COASTAL CONNECTIONS

TIDAL AND BRACKISH-WATER CATS

Over the past couple of decades, some of the hottest blue-cat fishing has surfaced in tidal rivers, particularly along the mid-Atlantic seaboard. Non-native blue cats forage on plentiful gizzard shad and herring, leading to some of the most productive fisheries today. In rivers such as the James and Potomac in Virginia, and the Cape Fear in North

Carolina, among others, anglers are tangling with big numbers of trophy-class cats. Yes, the blue tide has come in, and there's good fishing all the way to where rivers meet salt.

As an example of the burgeoning fisheries, blue catfish were stocked in the James River in the 1970s and really took off in the 1990s. "Blues were putting on 10-pound increments each year, says Bob Greenlee, district fishery biologist with the Virginia Department of Game and Inland Fisheries. "Fifty-pounders were unheard of in the 1990s; now 70s are common and a handful of 80s are caught each year. The state record 95-pound 11-ounce blue was caught in the James in June 2006," he says. "There's an unbelievable biomass of blues out there. We see electrofishing catch rates up to 2,000 fish per hour."

WEIR ON THE JAMES RIVER

Jimmy Weir, a blue cat specialist from Virginia Beach, Virginia, has a knack for producing big blue cats in almost any weather or water condition and is a consistent performer in local tournaments. He and his partners have logged 10-fish creels pushing close to 300 pounds. Time now to follow his approach to finding and catching big blue cats in tidal rivers. His tactics are deceptively simple, having been refined through years of experience, and should help you catch more and bigger blues from the lakes, rivers, and reservoirs you fish.

CREATING & SUSTAINING A TROPHY FISHERY

In-Fisherman Publisher Steve Hoffman: Many catmen are surprised to learn of the abundance of trophy blue cats in the James, Rappahannock, and other tidal rivers. Why are the cats in these rivers getting so big, so fast?

Weir: Tidal rivers like the James contain diverse habitat—huge flats, small tributary creeks, and lots of main-channel habitat like holes and steep ledges. The two major rivers that feed the James, the Appomattox and Chickahominy, also contain similar habitat and support their own populations of resident blue cats. This diversity, coupled with an abundance of baitfish and a strong catch-and-release ethic, has made the James River one of the best rivers for blue cats anywhere.

Hoffman: As the average size of blue cats in the James River has increased, anglers seem more willing to release big fish—those weighing 40 pounds or more. How have local catfish tournaments promoted the release of large blues?

Anglers seem more willing to release big fish.

Weir: Many of the best anglers in this area fish tournaments, and most realize that this is a finite fishery. The resource will continue to improve only if we conserve what we already have. Rules requiring the release of big fish should be mandatory for all tournaments. All of our Virginia Catfish Association tournaments require fish to be weighed alive, but we realize that rules alone aren't good enough. Keeping a 30- to 40-pounder or bigger fish alive requires a large livewell with a good circulation system.

Livewell systems with this kind of capacity aren't a factory option on most freshwater boats, but transforming a 120-quart cooler or other container into a suitable livewell is easy. All you need is a 750-gallon-per-minute, through-transom pump; about three feet of 3/4-inch hose; a short piece of 3/4-inch PVC pipe; and a 3/4-inch PVC end cap. Drill a series of holes in the PVC pipe and mount the spray bar inside the cooler. If the water is changed every hour or so, large cats can be kept alive for several days.

Hoffman: Many tournament organizers I've talked with claim that live-release tournaments lack support, particularly in the Southeast. They say participants and spectators want to see numbers of big fish—dead or alive.

Weir: That lacks vision. No fishery can support numbers of trophy fish and unlimited harvest indefinitely. These tournament promoters should reduce the creel limit to increase fish survival, particularly on big fish venues. At our tournaments, participants are allowed to weigh only three fish. Five fish were permitted a few years ago, but the average size of the fish has increased dramatically.

BIG FISH LOCATION

Hoffman: You tend to fish each spot differently, depending on water conditions and the activity level of the fish. What are your basic location and presentation guidelines?

Weir: I consider how fish behave in their environment. When I'm fishing secondary channels or feeder creeks, for example, I know the fish are there to eat. I employ a run-and-gun approach by setting up on deep holes or hard structures like trees or docks for no longer than about 30 minutes. If I don't get bit by then, I move. Since these areas tend not to be as deep as main-river spots, though, I also know the fish will be more suspicious. I motor around the core of the hole, then drift back into casting range by releasing more anchor rope.

Creeks and side channels are especially productive during the Coldwater Period from early winter through midspring. By the time water levels start to stabilize, I begin looking for fish in the main-river channel. Blue cats have gained something of a cold-water reputation in recent years, but some of my best fishing for big fish on the James River occurs during midsummer when water temperatures reach peak levels. This is when blues move onto shallow flats adjacent to the main channel to feed after dark. Be there with the right bait and you'll get bit.

THE RIGHT EQUIPMENT

Hoffman: You consider a boat to be one of your most important pieces of fishing equipment. What features should catmen who fish big rivers for big cats be looking for in the ideal catboat?

Weir: I prefer a wide-beamed catfish boat, about 20 feet long. This type of boat is plenty stable when two fishermen are landing a big fish on one side of the boat. It also has enough room for a large livewell and other gear. But my ideal boat also must have a shallow draft so I can navigate across shallow bars at the mouth of tributary streams, particularly during low tide. There's no such thing as one boat ideally suited for all conditions, but my Carolina Skiff is the best compromise I've found.

Hoffman: You use a simple sliprig for most situations, but you're quite particular about your terminal components. What type of hooks and sinkers do you use?

Weir: I use a 6/0 Mustad 37160 hook almost exclusively, because the wide-gap design allows for large baits and it holds up well to big fish. Then I attach a 2-foot

> *Blue cats have gained something of a cold-water reputation in recent years, but some of the best fishing for big fish occurs during midsummer when water temperatures reach peak levels.*

piece of 50-pound monofilament leader to the hook with a snell knot. The rest of my rigging consists of a 3- to 5-ounce flat river sinker held in place above the leader with a barrel swivel. Flat sinkers don't roll around on the bottom like egg sinkers, but I prefer the line to run through the center of the sinker instead of using a separate line attachment eye.

TAKE TIME FOR BAIT

Hoffman: You're even more passionate about bait than you are about sinkers. How important is good bait for blue cats?

Weir: Good bait is absolutely essential for big fish, particularly during weekend tournaments when fishing pressure is high. I typically spend two to three hours gathering enough large shad for a day's fishing, and I never regret a minute of it. When bait's not abundant in shallow water, I move back and forth across ledges along the main river channel while watching sonar for large schools of baitfish. I keep an eye out for big-fish arches too, since this can help pinpoint the depth where blue cats are feeding.

The James River is blessed with a huge population of gizzard shad, a reason this river produces so many big blue cats. Some throws of an 8-foot cast net yield so many shad that I have to struggle to pull them over the gunnels. Shad from about 8 to 14 inches long are the best bait year-round. I get two baits out of a shad this size by cutting once behind the gill plate and again in front of the tail fin. Some days, blue cats seem to prefer shad heads, while other days, the body section produces more fish.

I also use live 8- to 12-inch eels, or larger eels cut into 3- to 5-inch pieces. This bait is particularly effective during the Spawn Period or during summer when water temperatures reach peak levels. Eels can be kept alive on a bed of ice for more than 24 hours, and cut eel can be stored in a freezer for weeks or even months. Another advantage to using eels is that frozen chunks work almost as well as fresh ones.

BASS ON THE CAPE FEAR

Anglers like the legendary Ed Davis are rare. He used to prowl portions of the Cape Fear River near Fayetteville, North Carolina, catching oodles of humongous blue and flathead catfish, including several state and line-class records. In the late 1990s, however, Davis was waylaid by Amyotrophic Lateral Sclerosis, tragically keeping him at bay and ultimately taking his life, in 2004.

Alfred Bass, a 32-year-old from rural Elizabethtown, North Carolina, knows he can't fill the void that Davis' death left in the angling community along the Cape Fear River and across much of the Southeast. Nevertheless, Bass plies some of the same waters that Davis once fished, and he does it with a fervor and expertise that Davis would have saluted.

The Cape Fear begins at the convergence of the Deep and Haw rivers in central North Carolina and flows for 202 miles, coursing southeasterly through the communities of Lillington, Fayetteville, Elizabethtown, and Wilmington. Ten miles northwest of Wilmington it merges with the Black River; then the confluence of the Northeast Cape Fear River occurs in Wilmington, where the river turns south and flows another three miles before it enters the Atlantic Ocean.

In the 1930s three locks and dams at Tarheel, Elizabethtown, and Riegelwood were constructed, making the river navigable upstream to Fayetteville. Thus from Riegelwood to the coastal estuary below Wilmington, it's a tidal river. Davis's favorite water was between Fayetteville and Elizabethtown, a stretch that could

Alfred Bass hoists a tidal Cape Fear blue.

yield trophy-sized catfish any month of the year. Alfred Bass fishes the entire river, but primarily from Elizabethtown and Wilmington.

BLUE CAT PURSUITS

In January and February, when the Cape Fear's water temperature ranges between the upper 40°F to lower 50°F range, Bass focuses on blue catfish below Riegelwood, on the river's straight stretches near its juncture with the Black River. He occasionally ventures as far downstream as the coastal estuary and as far upstream as Riegelwood.

Bass pursues flatheads and channels during the remainder of the year—flatheads from March to October and channels in November and December. Two elements determine his blue-cat winter fishing. First, it corresponds with the spawning run of American shad up this river; second, he finds blues a more dependable catch during the coldwater period when fishing for flatheads and channels is more difficult.

During the winter, blue catfish in tidal waters find shelter from heavy-current flows in deep holes in the lower portions of some of the tributaries that feed a tidal river. According to Weir, one of the nation's savviest blue-cat anglers, this fact holds true on the James River as long as its tributaries don't become too cold and freeze. When the tributaries become too frigid, Weir says blue catfish migrate out of the tributaries to find refuge in some of the deepest holes in the James.

Weir, who fished with Davis on the Cape Fear, notes that the Cape Fear is different from the James. It's not as big and lies much farther south, allowing it to be warmer. So instead of plying the Cape Fear's tributaries for blue catfish during winter, Weir says Davis probed ledges adjacent to big, deep, main-river holes. Unlike many river scenarios, the Cape Fear's best wintertime spots, Davis found, weren't associated with riverbends but with straight stretches.

Bass agrees with Weir, saying that he spends January and February catching blue cats that inhabit deep holes associated with major ledges. A ledge is the key;

Timing Late-Season Blue Cats

Alfred Bass finds January and February, when water temperatures are in the upper 40°F to low 50°F range, the best months to fish for blue cats on the Cape Fear River. But in rivers of the nation's heartland where winter strikes earlier and harder, good fishing starts sooner.

James Patterson, catfish guide and tournament angler from Bartlett, Tennessee, says that on the Mississippi River near Memphis, Tennessee, a good late-season bite starts when water temperatures fall below 50°F. "Good fishing lasts into about December until the water cools to the upper 30s," he says. "Around mid-November, blues start bunching up in numbers in eddy currents around wing dikes. Fishing can be great once you find groups of blues."

Catfish guide Jim Moyer says that on his home waters—the Cumberland and Tennessee river systems—he starts catching numbers of blue cats again when water temperatures drop below 60°F until they reach the upper 40°F range

later in December. "The first frost usually indicates the start of the season," he says. "On the Cumberland and Tennessee, November is a great month. Tributary drawdowns pull baitfish out to the deeper main river. The best spots for blues are drop-offs, ledges, and humps, and I also catch some around wood." On the Mississippi farther north in Iowa, a stretch that Moyer knows well, good fishing can start as early as October. He finds ledges, humps, and wing dams good bets.

he suspects it breaks the current, giving blues and baitfish a place to rest. He pursues blue cats only during the day.

To find them along a ledge, Bass watches his sonar as he slowly zigzags his 24-foot Smoker Craft pontoon boat along the ledges and across the river holes. He describes the process as "looking for a little channel, followed by a ledge surrounded by baitfish."

The baitfish are American shad, which are seasonal on the Cape Fear, running from January into April. During this period, Bass baits up with shad. If they're scarce he uses sunfish, white perch, jumbo shiners, or American eel.

The Cape Fear once brimmed with American eels, a favored bait with Ed Davis. Nowadays, the eel population has declined. Bass buys his from a local bait store, preferring 10-inchers that he cuts into and fishes on a circle hook.

Drifting for Suspended Blues

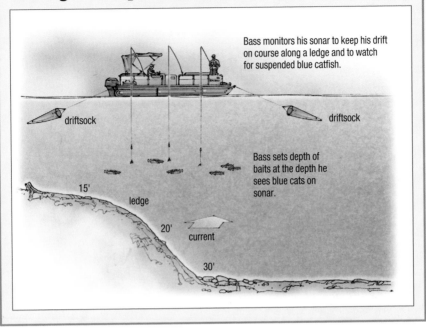

Bass monitors his sonar to keep his drift on course along a ledge and to watch for suspended blue catfish.

driftsock

driftsock

15'

ledge

Bass sets depth of baits at the depth he sees blue cats on sonar.

20'

current

30'

Bass finds that an outgoing tide is best: At its peak, the current's pace is torrid. The speed of flow dictates the size of bait used. When the current's strongest, he uses a piece of shad weighing about 12 ounces on a 12/0 or 14/0 Mustad circle hook, with the hook centered along the bottom edge of the bait. When baiting with a shiner fillet, the hook can be placed at either end of the fillet. If he uses whole and live shad, the hook goes through both eye sockets or through the flesh above the tail. When the current slows, he uses smaller pieces of shad about an inch in diameter.

DRIFT-FISHING TACTICS

Bass drift-fishes if his sonar reveals that baitfish and blue catfish are suspended or widely scattered along a ledge. Wind isn't a factor in his drifting, but current speed is. If the current is strong, he uses two driftsocks, one at the bow and another at the transom. In slower current, he uses one driftsock and attaches it in the middle of his boat's starboard side. His tackle consists of a heavy-action 7-foot Shakespeare Ugly Stik Tiger Lite 2200 rod and an Abu Garcia 6500 reel spooled with 30-pound-test Yo-Zuri Hybrid line.

When blue catfish are scattered on bottom along a ledge, Bass uses a three-way rig that allows the sinker to bounce across bottom. The rig consists of a small barrel swivel and either a 2- or 4-ounce No-Roll slipsinker that's threaded onto a 6- to 10-inch dropline. On the dropline below the sinker, he threads on a glass bead that is held in place by another small barrel swivel. The mainline is then threaded through the top barrel swivel on the dropline. A 90-pound-class barrel swivel is then tied onto the mainline, and a 1- to 2-foot leader of 30-pound-test Yo-Zuri Hybrid, sporting either a 12/0 or 14/0 Mustad circle

Bass' Three-Way Rig

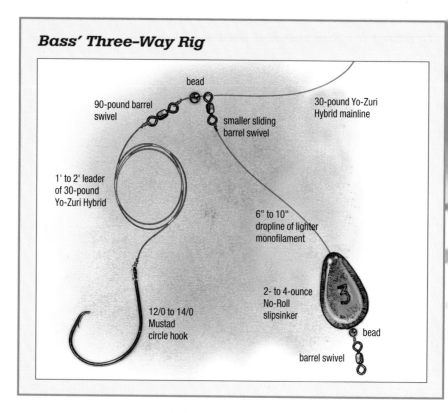

bead

90-pound barrel swivel

smaller sliding barrel swivel

30-pound Yo-Zuri Hybrid mainline

1' to 2' leader of 30-pound Yo-Zuri Hybrid

6" to 10" dropline of lighter monofilament

2- to 4-ounce No-Roll slipsinker

12/0 to 14/0 Mustad circle hook

bead

barrel swivel

hook, is tied to the other end of the swivel. Sinker size and dropline length are determined by the speed of the current.

If blue catfish are feeding aggressively, Bass drifts with two rods. If they're difficult to entice, he uses as many as eight rods. He drifts with rods in Driftmaster rod holders and sets the drags on his reels at the maximum tension.

SUSPENDED BLUES

Occasionally the Cape Fear's blue catfish rise off bottom and suspend. In a hole that's 30 feet deep along a ledge, Bass has seen blues suspended as shallow as 10 feet and as deep as 25.

To catch them, Bass replaces his three-way rig with a slipsinker rig, which consists of a 2- to 4-ounce No-Roll slipsinker, a #3 glass bead, a #5 Rite Angler Barrel Swivel, a leader made of 30-pound-test Yo-Zuri Hybrid Line, and either a 12/0 or 14/0 Mustad circle hook. He fishes these rigs vertically, with baits placed at the depths where the blue catfish suspend.

As Bass drifts, he positions his boat over the ledge and monitors his sonar to correct his course with the outboard motor. When a blue catfish engulfs one of his baited circle hooks, he waits until the rod tip is about to touch the surface of the water before he removes it from the holder. He doesn't set the hook; by waiting for the blue catfish to pull the rod tip toward the surface of the water, the hook embeds in the corner of the catfish's mouth. As he removes the rod from the rod holder, he loosens the drag to fight the fish. He redrifts a ledge until the blue-cat bite ceases.

Bass' Slipsinker Rig

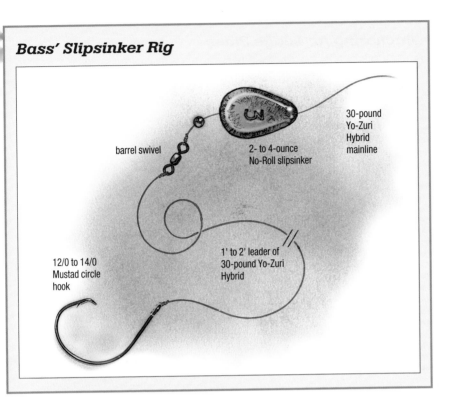

30-pound
Yo-Zuri
Hybrid
mainline

barrel swivel

2- to 4-ounce
No-Roll slipsinker

1' to 2' leader of
30-pound Yo-Zuri
Hybrid

12/0 to 14/0
Mustad circle
hook

ANCHORING TACTICS

Bass fishes from an anchored boat when his sonar shows baitfish and blue cat-fish tightly congregated near the bottom along a ledge. He positions his boat broad-side to the current, using two Super Hooker Anchors designed for 24- to 30-foot boats. One anchor is situated at the front of the boat and the other at the rear. The boat is anchored on top of a ledge and within 75 to 120 feet of where he spotted a concentration of baitfish.

If the tide is slack, he places five baits on the downstream side of the boat and five on the upstream side. His ten casts range in length from 75 to 120 feet. At a ledge that's 15 feet deep with a 30-foot hole, he places two baits on top of the ledge in 15 feet of water, two at 19 feet, two at 24, two at 28, and two at 30 feet in the basin of the hole.

Except for the length of the leader, Bass' rods, reels, lines, and terminal tackle are the same as on the slipsinker rigs he uses while drifting for suspended fish. At slow current periods, he attaches a 3-foot leader to the barrel swivel. When the current's fast, he uses a 6-inch leader. He fishes with fewer rods in heavy current and his casts are made in the direction of flow.

After casting, he places the rods in rod holders and allows the striking catfish to load the rod to embed the circle hook, just as he does while drifting. If he doesn't get a bite within 30 minutes, he moves to another spot.

On a normal day's fishing, Bass tangles with a dozen 20-pound blues. He reports that the Cape Fear's population of trophy blue catfish has increased substantially in recent years. His biggest weighed 76 pounds.

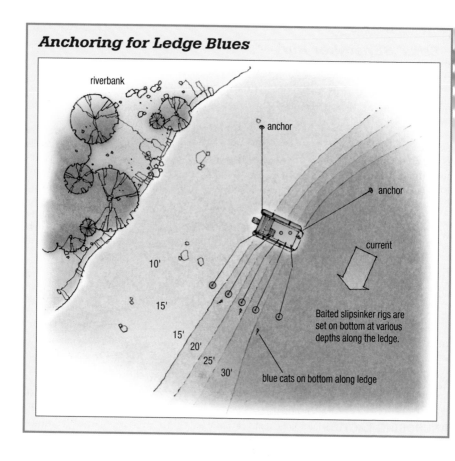

Anchoring for Ledge Blues

riverbank

anchor

anchor

current

10'

15'

15'

20'

25'

30'

Baited slipsinker rigs are
set on bottom at various
depths along the ledge.

blue cats on bottom along ledge

BRACKISH-WATER BLUE CATS

Most anglers never consider coastal waters for catfish. Saltwater may seem alien to those familiar with fishing freshwater reservoirs, rivers, and streams, but many brackish (part salt, part fresh water) marshes and bay systems harbor sizable populations of blue cats during winter, creating a virtually untapped opportunity for prime fishing.

Tagging studies and sampling projects conducted by officials with the Sabine National Wildlife Refuge in Hackberry, Louisiana, have found the salt content in coastal waters during winter months compatible for blue cats. Blues have a higher tolerance for saltwater than do flatheads and channels, and they fare well in coastal areas during winter when forage is abundant.

The Gulf Coast offers dozens of options for catfishermen in pursuit of these brackish-water blues. Some of the best spots are in the vast, lonely marshes and tributaries of Southwest Louisiana and Southeast Texas. Here, a small but dedicated core of anglers moves from inland waters toward the coast when water temperatures plummet.

Some of the techniques employed to bag these blues go hand in hand with well-known catfish strategies, while others may seem a little odd. In the right situation, though, they can be deadly.

PRIMARY LOCATIONS

One of the best spots to locate brackish-water blues is a large, marshy drainage where a river and bay meet. This kind of spot offers two key ingredients to success—strong tidal movements and abundant forage species.

During incoming tides, look for catfish around points at the mouth of the bay and river. Many of these spots have washouts created by current, which are several feet deeper than surrounding waters.

Cats bunch up in these holes, which often are filled with potential prey items such as menhaden and blue crabs. Another spot to consider during incoming tides is the river channel itself, which often extends into the bay. When viewing a surface map, it may seem that the river ends where the bay begins, but things can look different when viewed through a depthfinder or when studied on a detailed topographical chart.

On Lake Calcasieu near Lake Charles, Louisiana, the Calcasieu River channel gradually declines about 200 yards into what most people consider the bay. Such spots can, at times, be tremendously productive.

During outgoing tides, look to marshy drainages for the most consistent catfish action. As baitfish are displaced from the marsh, catfish gather at key junctures like the mouth of the drain and sloughs that wind into the marsh.

Within marsh systems, one of the most likely locations to find cats is where several small drainages meet. These current-laden spots often form eddies that are natural magnets for catfish. Since crabs, shrimp, and menhaden that dwell in marshes during winter can't navigate well in current, they become displaced into eddies. Blue cats often hold around these eddies, waiting for prey to come to them.

WINTERKILLS, DRIFTING, AND WADING

Air temperatures along the Gulf Coast can range from around 70°F down to the 20s during winter, so large baitfish kills often occur, especially of menhaden and shrimp. Often, a warm spell occurs, and baitfish move into the shallows of the bay where the water warms quickest. These warm spells may be followed by a brutal cold front that sends water temperatures plummeting and kills many baitfish.

These fishkills, similar to those in northern waters, attract cats. The spots with the greatest potential for fishkills are where shallow and deepwater meet at the mouth of the bay, and along shallow, flat shorelines on the main body of a bay. Commercial shrimpers who dredge these areas often talk of bringing up tons of dead, rotting baitfish.

The flats can be especially productive during a high tide on a warm winter afternoon. Since flats usually are barren of fish-holding structure, covering lots of ground is important. One way to do this is to freeline a bait while slowly moving through the area with a trolling motor. Another good way is to position the boat along the outer edge of the flat and drift with the tide.

Some anglers prefer to wear Neoprene waders and wade the flats. This is an especially good method when a falling tide reveals catfish actively feeding in the shallows, their dorsal fins sticking out of the water. At times the fish may be caught by sight-casting with popping cork rigs. It's a rare occurrence, but the sheer excitement of it makes it worth looking for.

When wading for cats, wear the proper attire. Wade-fishing belts can give back support and plenty of places to carry gear needed for such a demanding method of fishing. Walking through chilly waters can tire muscles quickly and give anglers even in the best of shape sharp back pains.

Primary Locations

One warning about wading in coastal bays: Don't just find a goodlooking spot, hop overboard, and start wading. Some spots may have mud deeper than the water. Poke and prod the area with a pole or paddle to test the strength of the bottom. Also, look for areas that have large stands of roseau cane, which typically grow near a hard bottom.

BAIT CHOICES

Shrimp—One of the all-around best baits for brackish blues is shrimp. Fresh shrimp is difficult to get during winter, but it's definitely superior to dried or frozen shrimp. You can buy fresh shrimp from fishmarkets or grocery stores. It's more expensive, but the shrimp usually are larger and in far better condition.

Mullet—Mullet are fairly easy to catch with casting nets during winter and are an excellent bait choice. Avoid frozen mullet, though, because it easily tears off the hook.

Menhaden—Menhaden is another top choice for brackish-water blues. It's usually available in adequate supply at coastal bait shops.

Crab—Crab may seem like an unusual choice for catfish bait, but it works. Many catfish caught in coastal ecosystems have a bellyful of crab remains.

Squid—Frozen squid is readily available at coastal bait shops, and it suffices for catfish bait. Squid isn't one of the best baits, but it freezes well and is difficult to remove from a hook. Use it as a last resort.

TERMINAL RIGS AND TACKLE

Hang-ups usually aren't as big a problem in coastal areas as in inland waters. Debris may collect in the mouth of a river, but the marshes and shallow flats usually don't hold many snags. In these areas, the best riggings are simple—a Kahle-style hook and a slipsinker rigged above a swivel.

Floats are useful in some applications, especially for drifting over open flats. The best floats are weighted popping corks used chiefly for speckled trout in bays.

Multiple Drainage Areas

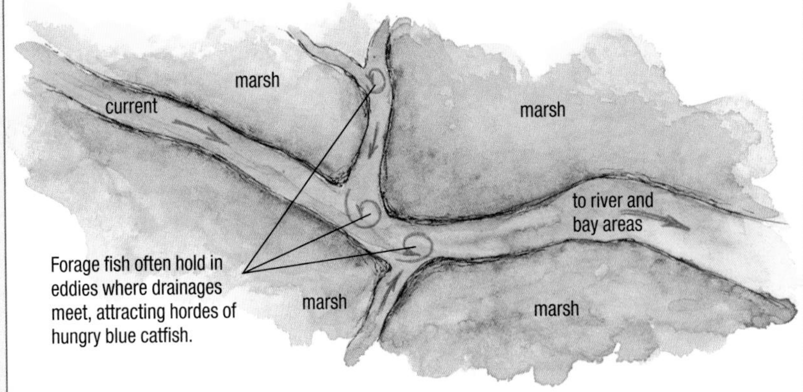

marsh

current

marsh

to river and
bay areas

Forage fish often hold in
eddies where drainages
meet, attracting hordes of
hungry blue catfish.

marsh

marsh

These corks work well with the current and displace lots of water when popped, which often draws strikes.

TIDES

We've already mentioned that tides are one of the most crucial factors when pursuing brackish-water blues. Unfortunately, though, tides are misunderstood by many anglers, especially those who aren't familiar with coastal fishing.

Like other bay dwellers such as red drum and flounder, catfish usually feed most aggressively during the first couple of hours of tidal movements. This most likely can be attributed to a greater influx of baitfish into key areas. But remember that all tidal movements are not created equal.

A common question is, "The high tide was going to be at 11:15 a.m., but the water was low at the boat dock. How could the water be so low during high tide?" Tides are the periodic rise and fall of ocean waters, caused by gravity of the moon, sun, and earth. To understand how these tidal movements work, compare them to a wave. In essence, a tide is a large, slow-moving wave that starts in the ocean, moves through a pass, and ends up in the back of a bay or river system. Most waves are influenced by wind, and tides are no different.

North winds, which are common during winter, push water out of a bay. That's why we get low tides during fall. "Blue northers" in conjunction with a strong tidal pull can drain an area and help cleanse coastal marshes. Also, tides at points away from the immediate coastline won't be as strong as those at a pass near the Gulf.

Like any wave, a tide weakens as it moves inland. So the strongest tide are near the Gulf, with the weakest far into the bay or river.

Another frequent question is: "The high tide was to occur at about 5:00 a.m., but the tide didn't move for hours. Was the tide table wrong?" Probably not. Tides given in papers and on television merely indicate lows and highs. They don't show the change between tides.

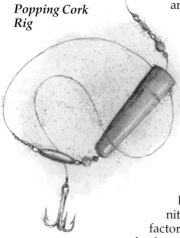

Popping Cork Rig

If a tide table predicts two high tides at 3:35 a.m. and 12:58 p.m., and low tides at 8:55 a.m. and 8:37 p.m., the National Weather Service charts may forecast a drop of only 8 inches between the 3:35 a.m. high and the 8:55 a.m. low. And it may rise only about 5 inches between that 8:55 a.m. low and the 12:50 p.m. high. But look farther, and you might learn that between that 12:50 p.m. high and the 8:37 p.m. low, the tide is forecast to drop more than 2½ feet, which is a strong tide for the Gulf Coast.

To plan a catfish trip around tidal movements, watch how much change occurs between tides. Blue cats are opportunists, and big tides provide the biggest feeding opportunity. Anglers who best understand tides and other factors related to catching brackish water blue cats make the most of their fishing opportunity.

Using Pole Lines

Many catfishermen use limblines in the coastal areas of Southeast Texas and Southwest Louisiana. Since trees are scarce in many of these areas, enterprising anglers use bamboo poles. They tie the line off at the limber top part of the pole and then run the line down to the middle and tie it off there.

This is done for two reasons:
(1) Alligator gar are common in these areas and are known to break flimsy limblines. Gar weighing as much as 150 pounds are caught on lines in the region, so all precautions need to be taken.
(2) Big blue cats also inhabit these areas. Michael Flaten of Sulphur, Louisiana,

set five lines one weekend in 1997 and caught five catfish totaling 150 pounds. Flaten says the secret to keeping a big fish on a limbline is to use a heavy circle hook. He uses 14/0 Eagle Claw Circle hooks on all his lines. "I've had J-style hooks flattened out many times, but I've never had that happen with a circle hook," he says.

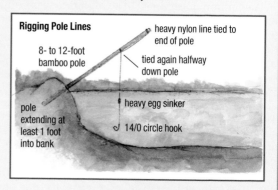

Rigging Pole Lines

8- to 12-foot bamboo pole

heavy nylon line tied to end of pole

tied again halfway down pole

pole extending at least 1 foot into bank

heavy egg sinker

14/0 circle hook